# DATE DUE

| | | | |
|---|---|---|---|
| ~~AP3 '09~~ | | | |
| ~~NO30'00~~ | | | |
| | | | |
| | | | |
| | | | |
| | | | |
| | | | |
| | | | |
| | | | |
| | | | |
| | | | |
| | | | |
| | | | |
| | | | |
| | | | |
| | | | |
| | | | |
| | | | |

DEMCO 38-296

# POLICING CHANGE, CHANGING POLICE

CURRENT ISSUES IN CRIMINAL JUSTICE
VOLUME 14
GARLAND REFERENCE LIBRARY OF SOCIAL SCIENCE
VOLUME 1025

# CURRENT ISSUES IN CRIMINAL JUSTICE

FRANK P. WILLIAMS III AND MARILYN D. MCSHANE

*General Editors*

# POLICING CHANGE, CHANGING POLICE
## INTERNATIONAL PERSPECTIVES

EDITED BY
OTWIN MARENIN

GARLAND PUBLISHING, INC.
NEW YORK AND LONDON
1996

**Library of Congress Cataloging-in-Publication Data**

Policing change, changing police : international perspectives / Otwin Marenin.
        p.    cm. — (Garland reference library of social science ;
  vol. 1025. Current issues in criminal justice ; vol. 14.)
    Includes bibliographical references and index.
    ISBN 0-8153-1995-9 (alk. paper)
    1. Police administration.    I. Title.  II. Series: Garland reference library
of social science ; v. 1025.   III. Series: Garland reference library of social
science. Current issues in criminal justice ; v. 14.
HV7935.M36   1996
363.2—dc20                              95-37407
                                                      CIP

Printed on acid-free, 250-year-life paper
Manufactured in the United States of America

To

Martha

for her support,

to C. and A. for their

help in typing,

and to D.R.S.O.S. and N. for

their unwavering

cheer

# CONTENTS

# FIGURES

# Series Editors' Preface

In keeping with the other volumes in the *Current Issues in Criminal Justice* series, this anthology is a prime example of joining readability and scholarship. Editor Otwin Marenin has thoughtfully commissioned and compiled an excellent group of essays on the role of police in changing societies by a very knowledgeable group of scholars. Moreover, Marenin has added substantially to the collection through his own insightful contributions.

The essays, taken collectively, focus on the synergistic effect of social change and police responsibility. Indeed, one can ask if the task is to explain how police change and adapt to a changing society or, perhaps, whether the police themselves serve to change society. Fortunately, the various authors here tend to seek answers to both questions. What, for instance, do the experiences of developing countries tell us about emerging forms of policing, what are the lessons of policing instability while police organizations undergo change, or under what circumstances do police themselves become pivotal instruments of social change? Such questions and evidence not only serve to provide a comparative basis for understanding police and policing, but also yield valuable information for U.S. cities (such as Los Angeles and Miami) attempting to chart a course in the emerging new cultures of diversity.

Those who teach comparative courses, and those who are simply curious about the functions of policing in other nations, will find much to think on here. The authors lend their cultural awareness, their insights, and their expertise to the reader throughout this work. Professor Marenin and his contributors seem to have provided us with relevant research and thoughts for policing the next decade.

Marilyn D. McShane
Frank P. Williams III

# FOREWORD

## David H. Bayley

This is a deceptive book. Fortunately. The clever title seems straightforward. It promises a book about reform in the police as well as about the adaptations police make in societies that are themselves changing. Both topics are hot. Police throughout the developed democracies, hard-pressed by rising crime, are caught up in an intense reappraisal of their basic strategies. The widespread discussion of community policing, for example, is evidence of this. At the same time, the collapse of Communism has brought agonizing change throughout the world, especially in eastern Europe and the former Soviet Union, and with it unprecedented problems for the police. So this book is important because it is topical. But it is more than that. Its essays address a topic that has been unaccountably neglected in police studies during the last half century--namely, the reasons why police institutions behave as they do. By laying the empirical groundwork for the development of a theory of police institutions, the book makes a larger contribution than one might think upon reading the title.

The modern era of police scholarship is generally considered to have begun with the publication of the report of the President's Commission on Law Enforcement and the Administration of Justice, *The Challenge of Crime in a Free Society* in 1967. This volume sparked an enormous outpouring of original research and commentary on the police throughout the developed democratic world. This scholarship has had two main focuses: (1) the behavior of individual police officers and (2) the effectiveness of the dominant strategies in policing. Both concerns reflected continuing policy preoccupations, namely, the issues of police discretion and strategic effectiveness.

The study of the behavior of individual officers began most notably with Jerome H. Skolnick's *Justice Without Trial* (1966). Since then a host of scholars have described and tried to explain the decisions police officers make in deciding, for example, whether to arrest or to employ deadly or non-deadly force. Excellent summaries of the quantitative research can be found in Sherman's "The Causes of Police Behavior: The Current State of Quantitative Research" (1980) and Riksheim and Cermak's "Causes of Police Behavior Revisited" (1993).

Studies of the effectiveness of police strategies have sought to determine whether activities such as preventive patrol, rapid response, and crime investigation have achieved the goals expected by the police and the public. Such studies are often referred to as evaluation research. In general, they have failed to show that the occurrence of crime is much affected by variations in the intensity of these activities (Kelling, 1988; Goldstein, 1990). Although patrol, rapid response, and criminal investigation may be useful in other terms, they have generally been disappointing in terms of preventing crime (Bayley, 1994).

The point is that modern scholarship on the police has been notably successful in developing a theory of individual police behavior and in evaluating the crime-preventive performance of the police, but it has not tried to explain why police institutions and the activities they undertake vary from place to place. This is ironic. One of the most famous books from the early years of police scholarship was James Q. Wilson's *Varieties of Police Behavior* (1968). It tried quite explicitly to explain why the style of policing varies from city to city within the United States, developing the well-known categories of watchman, legalistic, and service-oriented to describe them. The book is famous, in the sense that it is often cited, but it has not been influential in encouraging similar research. There has been no sustained interest subsequently in developing a theory of the institutional behavior of the police.

The neglect of institutional theory is ironic for another reason as well. Organizational context has often been flagged as an important variable in explaining the behavior of individual officers and the success of reforming efforts (Reiss, 1971; Sherman, 1980; Friedrich, 1980; Manning, 1977; Goldstein, 1990; Kelling, 1988; Brown, 1988; Bayley, 1994). While scholars have understood that police institutions are not all the same and that these differences matter, they have not been concerned to account for them.

To put the point in technical terms, police organizations have been recognized as important independent variables within existing research agendas, but differences in their activities have not been considered a worthwhile research agenda. The institutional activities of police agencies have generally not been studied as a dependent variable.

An important qualification needs to be made to this appraisal. Although mainline scholars of the police, that is people who belong to the American Society of Criminology and the Academy of Criminal Justice Sciences, have suffered from this blindspot, two other groups of scholars have been much quicker to recognize the importance of explaining variations in the institutional behavior of the police. These are historians and comparativists. One thinks of the excellent work done by Wilbur Miller (1977), Richardson (1970), Eric Monkonnen (1981), Allan Silver (1967), P.K. Reynolds (1926), Clive Emsley (1983 and Samuel Walker (1977). Among comparativists there are Raymond Fosdick (1915), Peter Manning (1988), R.I.Mawby (1990), P.J.Stead (1957) and David Bayley (1975, 1994). And the almost-forgotten Bruce Smith (1960), who was both historian and comparativist. Scholars of the law and legal institutions have also treated policing as problematic and made notable contributions to what may yet emerge as a theory of policing--Sally F. Moore (1972), Richard Abel (1973), or Steven Spitzer and Andrew Scull (1977). But all of this work, substantial though it is, occupies the fringe of police scholarship. It is considered "academic," unrelated to the pressing policy concerns of contemporary policing.

This book should help refocus the attention of scholars onto the neglected topic of varieties of institutional police behavior. It does so because its essays are comparative, treating a variety of foreign experience, and historical, treating the challenge and reality of change over time. This book should dramatize that policing is not the same from place to place in the modern world and that these differences matter. Moreover, it advances the search for a theory of the institutional development of policing, a theory which is urgently needed if reform is to be carried out anywhere in a deliberate and ultimately successful manner.

# SOURCES

Abel, Richard L. (1973), "A Comparative Theory of Dispute Institutions in Society," *Law and Society Review*, 217-347.

Bayley, David H. (1975), "The Police and Political Development in Europe," in C. Tilly (ed.), *The Formation of National States in Europe*, Princeton: Princeton University Press.

------ (1994), *Police for the Future*, New York: Oxford University Press.

Brown, Lee P. (1988), "Excellence in Policing: Models for High-Performance Police Organizations," *The Police Chief*, 55 (April), 68.

Emsley, Clive (1983), *Policing and Its Contexts, 1750-1870*, London: Macmillan.

Fosdick, Raymond B. (1915), *European Police Systems*, New York: Century Company.

Friedrich, Robert J. (1980), "Police Use of Force: Individuals, Situations, and Organizations," *The Annals of the American Academy of Political and Social Science* (Nov.), 82-97.

Goldstein, Herman (1990), *Problem-Oriented Policing*, Philadelphia: Temple University Press.

Kelling, George L. (1988), "Police and Communities. The Quiet Revolution," Washington, D.C.: National Institute of Justice.

Manning, Peter K. (1977), *Police Work*, Cambridge: M.I.T. Press.

------ (1988), *Symbolic Communication: Signifying Calls and the Police Response*, Cambridge: M.I.T. Press.

Mawby, R.I. (1990), *Comparative Policing Issues: The British and American Experience in International Perspective*, London: Unwin Hyman.

Miller, Wilbur, R. (1977), *Cops and Bobbies: Police Authority in New York and London*, Chicago: University of Chicago Press.

Monkonnen, Eric (1981), *Police in Urban America, 1860 to 1920*, Cambridge: Cambridge University Press.

Moore, Sally F. (1972), "Legal Liability and Evolutionary Interpretation: Some Aspects of Strict Liability, Self-Help and Collective Responsibility," in Max Gluckman (ed.), *The Allocation of Responsibility*, Manchester: Manchester University Press.

President's Commission on Law Enforcement and the Administration of Justice (1967), *The Challenge of Crime in a Free Society*, Washington, D.C.: U.S. Government Printing Office.

Reiss, Albert J., Jr. (1971), *The Police and the Public*, New Haven: Yale University Press.

Reynolds, P.K. Baillie (1926), *The Vigiles of Imperial Rome*, London: Oxford University Press.

Richardson, James F. (1970), *The New York Police: Colonial Time to 1901*, New York: Oxford University Press.

Riksheim, Eric C., and Steven M. Cermak (1993), "Causes of Police Behavior Revisited," *Journal of Criminal Justice*, 21, 353-382.

Sherman, Lawrence W. (1980), "The Causes of Police Behavior: The Current State of Quantitative Research," *Journal of Research in Crime and Delinquency*, January, 69-100.

Silver, Allan (1967), "The Demand for Order in Civil Society: A Review of Some Themes in the History of Urban Crime, Police, and Riot," in David J. Bordua (ed.), *The Police: Six Sociological Essays*, New York: John Wiley and Sons.

Skolnick, Jerome H. (1966), *Justice Without Trial: Law Enforcement in a Democratic Society*, New York: John Wiley and Sons.

Smith, Bruce (1960), *Police Systems in the United States*, New York: Harper and Row.

Spitzer, Steven, and Andrew T. Scull (1977), "Social Control in Historical Perspective: From Private to Public Responses to Crime," in David F. Greenberg (ed.), *Corrections and Punishment*, Beverly Hills: Sage Publications.

Stead, P.J. (1957), *The Police of Paris*, London: Staples Press.

Walker, Samuel (1977), *A Critical History of Police Reform: The Emergence of Professionalism*, Lexington: Lexington Books.

Wilson, James Q. (1968), *Varieties of Police Behavior*, Cambridge: Harvard University Press.

# PREFACE

Any book results from the efforts of many people. Many of the chapters in the book were originally presented at the 1993 annual meeting of the American Society for Criminology. The contributions to two panels at that meeting form the core of the book. Additional chapters were solicited from knowledgeable scholars. In the end, this is their book. My efforts have simply sought to arrange and present their arguments and ideas in publishable form.

In addition to the contributors, I wish to thank Martha Cottam who commented on many drafts and parts of my arguments, always with insight and forbearance and always to the book's improvement. To David Bayley go many thanks for agreeing to write the Foreword. The series editors, Marilyn McShane and Frank Williams III, encouraged this project and allowed me free rein (but within orderly limits), a rare discretion. Finally, I must thank many of my students, both graduate and undergraduate, who without knowing their part in developing my thinking, contributed by their willingness to put up with my speculations and by their direct reproaches when speculations turned to fancy.

# ACKNOWLEDGMENTS

Transaction Publishers has kindly given permission to reprint William Stanley's chapter which originally appeared in the *Journal of Studies in Comparative and International Development,* 30, 1, May 1995, but in a somewhat longer form.

# POLICING CHANGE, CHANGING POLICE

# POLICING CHANGE, CHANGING POLICE:
## SOME THEMATIC QUESTIONS

### Otwin Marenin

What happens to the roles, functions, and activities of the police during major societal changes, such as now occurring in the former USSR, Central America, South Africa, or the European Community? What role do the police play and what role can they play in periods of massive social change? How do they respond to the changes going on around them and how do they affect such changes? It is argued in this book that the police are at the core of changes in society and the state and that their roles in the reproduction of both change and order need to be addressed empirically and theoretically.

The collapse of the Soviet Union clearly presents the challenges and difficulties of creating a new order. Ethnic conflicts, political violence, a tremendous rise in normal and organized crime, widespread corruption, a widening and visible gap in social well being, and an inability to settle on even basic political, economic and social institutions cast into precise focus the question what policing can and cannot accomplish during such periods. The police are major actors in these changes: they continue to deal with crime; they protect some political incumbents and arrest others; they interact with the other uncertain coercive instrument of state building and rule, the military; they seem to have continued some of their old ways--in intelligence gathering, in arbitrary and corrupt decisions on the street, in their perception that they are a political agency or in how they conduct investigations, while other aspects of their old roles seem to have dissipated (Galeotti, 1993). The demise of the Communist Party freed the police from direct political control, yet they are still enmeshed in the reconstruction of new and diverse social orders.

Central American countries are seeking to create democratic polities and economic development. In El Salvador, the ceasefire agreement between the government and the rebels, signed under UN sponsorship, included provisions on restructuring the police forces of the country and the aid and assistance necessary to accomplish this goal. International advisors and police officers from many countries now instruct the new police in democratic and fair ways and procedures of policing (Holiday and Stanley, 1993; Stanley, 1993). In Panama, after the largest drug arrest conducted by the USA, the police were deNoriegaized in an effort to root out corrupt, brutal, and undemocratic elements and help stabilize the elected (and imposed) regime and state (US, GAO, 1992a). In Haiti, US military troops with no experience or preparation in policing now patrol the streets of Port-au-Prince dispensing candy bars and justice with even hands. An emergency "police" force, largely recruited from the least discredited and hated elements of the former police, were given a few days' training in new ways and attitudes and expected to form the core of what will be a new civilian police. Clearly, what happens to democratic aspirations and reforms will suffer or be helped by the actions of these new forces in all these countries. The police will help determine the ideological and political character of the new regimes and states.

In South Africa, the police have been enmeshed in the turmoil of political change, as brutal defenders of the decaying apartheid order, as objects of reform, as victims of mob violence, and as a hope that they can help stabilize the emerging non-racialist society (Cawthra, 1993). There has been little agreement among white political leaders (Weitzer, 1991), among leaders and followers of major black organizations, among social groups, many of which have formed private security forces and armies (Smaldone, 1992: 57-59), and, one would suspect, among the various publics about the organization, composition, or roles of the to-be-created police forces.

As the European Community moves, falteringly, toward political integration, questions of law and policing have come to the forefront. The police themselves are advocating specific policies, powers, and institutions to deal with such problems as immigration, drugs, terrorism, and fraud, cross-border pursuit, carrying of firearms, surveillance, information exchange, or the reconciliation of laws (Fijnaut and Hermans, 1987; Gregory, 1991; Phillips, 1993). In the process, emerging policing institutions and agreements will channel and constrain the emergence of new super-territorial political authority (den Boer and Walker, 1993; Walker, 1995).

Many other societies are in the throes of massive changes and the viability of the state hangs in precarious balance. Their police forces have been little studied (e.g., Croatia or Angola) or are just barely beginning to exist, often predating the state and society which are to be their master (e.g., Palestine). Other countries and political entities (e.g., Brazil, Italy, Hong Kong, China, Northern Ireland) may be less turbulent in the process of transition to a new order; still they face massive changes. The problems and dynamics of policing societies in change are there, though muted and overlaid by established practices and more or less routine political and social patterns and norms.

External pressures and advice flow freely towards changing societies. A vast number of international advisors and consultants, some sponsored by international agencies or by foreign governments as well as private entrepreneurs or representatives of professional interest groups, stand ready to offer goals, procedures, means, and methods for achieving a new and better society and the kind of policing appropriate to it (e.g., Nadelman, 1993; US, GAO, 1992b).[1]

Such developments merit attention and study.

## THE POLICE IN CHANGE

Massive societal changes, which are not unique to our era but have occurred before and will occur again, expose the role of the police in clear and precise light for they strip away the certainties and comforts of an established social order which cloaks policing as the routine defense and administration of order and justice, as "part of the administrative 'tidying-up' of the disorderly edges of society" (Brogden, 1987: 6).

Periods of massive change require a rethinking of preferred social order. What is to be reproduced in the place of vanquished institutions and powers and who will have the say? Forms of policing and the structure of police institutions are major prizes and objects in contests over the shape of the future, for coercive power lies at the heart of state reproduction and guarantees stability to the state, order to society and power to the police. The ability to stabilize the new conditions, whatever they are, and the continuing capacity to reproduce these new conditions will depend fundamentally on the levels of legitimacy and effectiveness achieved by the police.

To develop a theory of police in change requires that changes in the organization, structures, roles, responsibilities, and powers of the police be described first. Much will change, yet the police will also retain many of their former roles. Even in times of massive social upheavals, crime will still occur and people will still demand order, and the police will still have their own preferences for defining their job. What happens to the police during such times? Where do they go? What do they do? What roles do they continue to play and which do they withdraw from? This interconnection of policing and social change is rarely posed as a theoretical question.

The general question, then, is this: how is policing reconstituted as an aspect of the state and the new society? What role do the police play in reproducing preferred social change and the supporting legitimacy which will transform change into order? Do the police promote or hinder fundamental societal and political changes? What powers do they have as an institution and as individuals to influence the reproduction of themselves, of the state and of civil society, and to what degree are they influenced by forces outside their organizations? In short, how autonomous are they as actors in the reproduction of change and order?

Other questions reference practice. Description and theory ultimately assist policy. The reproduction of the police is a practical challenge to societies and a theoretical opportunity for scholars to develop more grounded and complex explanations of forms and habits of policing. Change is guided even in revolutionary periods. What are the goals enunciated for the police by international and internal experts and consultants (e.g., Mathews et al., 1993)? What do the police, what does the public, what do social leaders advocate as the preferred forms of policing which change should move toward? Do such preferences coalesce around "universal" standards of "good" policing? In short, what can we learn about moving the police toward "good" policing by studying the police during change?

## MODELS OF POLICING

To answer such questions presupposes conceptions of policing and theories of the relations of the police to society and to the state. Definitions of policing abound, each stressing particular aspects of functions, goals, or means. Policing will be defined broadly, in order to accommodate the varieties of historical policing efforts, as "social ordering structures" (Brogden, this book). As structure, policing is a persistent effort by (somewhat) specialized personnel to reconstruct order in preferred forms of social arrangements, often by coercive means. The four core elements in this conception of policing are structure (persistence and identity), specialization (at the time policing is done), coercion (applied or potential), and social goals.

Policing, to be studied and explained, requires identity (separateness as a social institution) and persistence (some continuity as a social practice). Policing is a specialized type of job with particular characteristics, most distinctly the delegated authority to use force. The specific structures and functions of policing are defined for and by each society and can appear, legitimately, in many forms--e.g., private actions, community based and informal order maintenance, or state police organizations. The identities and practices of legitimate coercion fluctuate with social norms and demands.

Policing seeks social goals--it is work done for stated, socially accepted ends and values. The goals can be many but their promotion is policing only when sanctioned by its relevant society. (The definition of who counts as relevant is itself an object of contention.)

These four core traits can be and have been structured in various patterns. The arrangement of these traits--or models of policing or ordering structures--will differ by the sources of legitimacy, complexities of organization, multiplicity of functions, and societal consequences or "outcomes" (Bayley, 1985) of policing. Policing has not developed and does not happen in the same way everywhere. Legitimacy "implies that the police are granted some degree of monopoly by those in society with the power to so authorize," which can be "the legal system, the community, the state, the police organization itself or the political elite" (Mawby, 1990: 3, 192). Organization implies some degree of specialization within and codes of conduct for the work to be done as well as the overall institutionalized structure within which the work occurs. Functions refers to the authorized and expected work of the police, that is, their jobs. Consequences refers to the impacts of policing on themselves and their societal contexts, e.g., whether the police serve to perpetuate or undermine a capitalist or socialist order or whether their work enhances perceptions of public safety or whether they become the criminal element in society (e.g., Callaghy, 1982).

Different scholars have developed distinct typologies of policing based on their general understanding of the functions of policing and the skills and traits essential to performing that role and job and the connections of policing to wider statist and societal forces.

Mawby (1990), for example, distinguishes between primitive and modern forms of policing and within modern policing initially discerns an Anglo-American, a continental and a colonial model (pp. 16-33). His analysis of policing in Cuba, Japan, and China leads him to a fourth, the pervasive or comprehensive model (pp. 199-200). The models differ by the bases for their legitimacy, their organizational characteristics, and the range of their functions.

Brogden (1987) examines explanations for the development of policing and finds these ethnocentric (an almost exclusive focus on Anglo-American patterns of policing) and insufficiently supported by historical evidence. Neither riots, increases in crime, urbanization, the growth of the administrative state, nor functionalist motives explain the development of the five basic forms of policing observed so far: the preventative and administrative models which developed in Europe; commercial and private police forces; occasional democratic, populist forms; and the colonial model, which is in structure and function characterized by its direct linkage to colonial state power and its proximity in location and work to the military and in goals and consequences seeks the delegitimization of "indigenous customs," the imposition of "centralized social control," and the incorporation of "local society as a branch of imperial society" (p. 10; also see Ahire, 1991; Jeffries, 1952).

Brodeur (1983) distinguishes low and high policing forms with high policing emerging, under the impetus of policing mandates and increasingly sophisticated technology, as the dominant form. The irreducible mandate and justification of the police, and that is how their work is judged, is "to produce suspects" (p. 511). High policing seeks to absorb all information, derives its mandate from the necessity for social order, perceives crime as an authorization and opportunity for state actions and expansion, and practices "open secrecy" in order to intimidate the potentially disorderly. The goal of high policing is general surveillance; information in society becomes divided into that which is public, that which is still private, and that which is "recorded for the benefit of some agency or some organization" (p. 517). The distinction between low policing (the stress on order maintenance and law enforcement and services) and high policing (the need to know in order to prevent and control) is more apparent than real. "Political policing and police work in general" overlap (p. 517).

Shearing and Stenning (1987: 13) distinguish two basic forms: public and private policing, one an expression of state power and the other the addition of private control efforts to state control or, more radically, a reflection of "the reemergence of private authorities who sometimes effectively challenge the state's claimed monopoly over the *definition* of order" (their emphasis). Private policing done by corporations--though legally private as corporations are individuals under a liberal conception of state-society relations--resembles state policing in all but its "public" authorization (p. 15).

Findlay and Zvekić (1993: 7) distinguish "policing styles" which reflect "unique structural adaptations of power relations" within any society. Styles range along a continuum from state centered policing to community-based policing, each situated "primarily in terms of [its] relationship with state bureaucracy" (p. 26): covert, sub-contracted, entrepreneurial, "blind eye," co-optive, compulsory, and confrontational policing. State and private/community interests and actors participate in the creation of preferred social orders. Such alternatives to state centered policing can appear in a vast variety of forms which often mix, and incorporate public, private and community control over the police (e.g. Marenin, 1992).

Bayley (1985: 7, 10) defines the police as "people authorized by a group to regulate interpersonal relations within the group through the application of physical force. This definition has three essential parts: physical force, internal use, and collective authorization....Without these elements, police do not exist." Modern police forces are public, specialized and professional in form. (p. 14) Early forms and some current "police" lack all three modern traits, but Bayley does not deal at length with other possible forms based on various combinations of the public-private, specialized-non-specialized, and professional-non-professional distinctions.

## THE EMERGENCE OF TYPES OF POLICING

How do various forms develop? Again, the answers vary. Explanations for the emergence of the police themselves and for shifts over time from one form of policing to another tend to fall into three categories. One set of explanations stresses societal and state changes and their impact on policing. Forms of policing are reflections of contextual historical processes. The police are objects in history.

A second set of explanations argues for dialectical or reciprocal networks of relations between the police and their state and societal contexts, all affecting the others. Lastly, the police may be seen as subjects of history who help shape not just their own work but also developments in the statist and societal contexts within which they ultimately work. Each viewpoint contains or accommodates different policing models. For example, the police in colonial and Marxist models are perceived as reflections of contextual forces.

## THE POLICE AS OBJECTS

The police as reflection approach is the dominant one. It is normally assumed that the police are not actors in the reproduction of themselves, the state or their societies; in fact, they are most often defined as the core characteristic of the state, inseparable, as the knife's edge is from the knife, in practice and thinking from the state. Their actor status (and potential autonomy) is confined to small scale discretion in their work routines. Societal and state contexts determine the functions and structures of policing in which such discretionary work is done.[2]

For example, to Mawby (1990: 23), forms of policing are simply one aspect of general modernization and rationalization processes in society which, though, once established, continue to develop by their own initiatives and inertia, by, in Gurr's (1976: 118) nice phrase, the "internal, system maintaining dynamics of bureaucratic organizations." Changes in policing are driven by the same political, cultural, social-structural and external-international factors which shape developments in other governmental policy areas. The creation of policing parallels the development of the modern territorial state (Liang, 1992: 4-7).

In Tilly's words (1975: 59, 60), "the manner and form of policing register with extraordinary clarity the history of the interaction between state makers and the people they seek to control....Like the routinization of taxation, the regularization of policing imprinted the state's mark on the everyday life of its citizens." The police emerge as part of the state's apparatus for social control and the protection of favored groups, preferred values, and dominant ideologies. They cannot be distinguished from the roles and functions of the state (in fact they embody the core functions of coercion and make possible taxation and conscription), and they are controlled by the state or those who stand behind the throne.

## THE POLICE IN THE WEB OF DIALECTICAL MUTUALITY

The dialectical approach is exemplified in the writings of Bayley and Reiner.

Bayley has studied the police and change in a variety of settings and times but usually as the dependent variable for changes occurring in their societal environments. Yet he also emphasizes the persistence and impermeability of the police, their capacity to "filter back, like water rising through sand, both in terms of the forms of administration and the very personnel themselves" (1975: 372) after societal upheavals.[3] The police know what their interests are and how to protect themselves.

Generally, Bayley sees the police as influenced in their tasks, structure, accountability, image, and internal organization by societal developments. State practices, violent public resistance to state demands, socioeconomic changes, geopolitical position, religion, and political participation are the dominant causal forces (1975: 375). Specific patterns of policing reflect patterned changes in the "transformation in the organization of political power, prolonged violent popular resistance to government, and the creation of new law and order tasks as well as the erosion of social bases upon which community authority relations were established" (p. 378). In sum, the "police are intimately part of the political system" and how it developed (p. 368) and are influenced in their development by the same forces which shaped the development of societies.

In his later comparative study, Bayley (1985) focusses on the determinants of policing forms (their auspices, focus, rationalization, structure, strength, function, and political position) and situations or encounters (the work that the police actually do rather than their formal assignments or the outcomes of their work). Included in causative factors are police-controlled variables (organizational priorities, capacity, selection decisions, and (for outcomes) enforcement proclivities (Tables 6:2, 6:3). The determination of the nature and impact of police work includes the actions of the police themselves, working within the context of societal forces and demands.

Bayley discusses six ways in which the police impinge on political life directly: "by determining the players, regulating competitive processes, defending or not defending regimes from violent attack, covertly monitoring and manipulating political groups, advocating policy inside and outside government, and providing material aid" (p. 197). Police also affect politics indirectly, through their participation in processes of socialization, legitimization, symbolic representation, and social development.[4]

Despite the impressive list of ways in which the police affect other state agencies and social groups, Bayley tends to see them as acted on rather than actors. Many of the direct ways of police impingement on politics are, in turn, the outcomes of societal factors. The police merely carry out their tasks when they have political impact; e.g., they determine the players when they arrest challengers to the political elite because the political elite tells them so.[5] Bayley concludes that countries have historically developed patterns of such political involvement by the police. The task and goal of comparative analysis, then, is "to explain them in terms of contextual factors" (p. 203).

Yet, in his final discussion of likely developments and strategies for the future of policing, Bayley uses phrases which imply both contextual and police agency ("strategies that countries adopt," "police forces will choose" p. 228, 227). But the interactions of contextual causes and police agency in the creation of new forms of policing or state and civil society are only suggested in broad strokes.

Reiner (1986) argues that the police in recent English history were legitimized by conscious policy decisions and tactical choices made by police administrators as well as by wider social processes of social pacification and class reconciliation. Seven policies--bureaucratic organization, submission to the rule of law, minimal force, non-partisanship, service role, preventive policing, and effectiveness--helped legitimize the power of the police and overcome suspicions and resistance by all classes, mostly the working class. All these policies have been challenged or have changed recently, by the initiative of the police as well as in reaction to societal developments and have led, in an "uncanny return" (p. 189) to the beginnings of modern policing in Britain, to the desubordination of classes to political authority and the delegitimation of the police in the eyes of many. The pacification of class conflict and the incorporation of the working class into the social system collapsed in strikes and riots during the 1970s and 1980s. The changing fate of police legitimacy has been determined by wider social forces and by the efforts of the police themselves, e.g., the "bobby lobby" which sought to rewrite the legal authority for the exercise of force.

## THE POLICE AS SUBJECTS

Whether the police can be autonomous actors in the reconstruction of the state and society is a question rarely raised, though hints are abundant.

The police have many state and society reproduction powers. They can protect the emerging state structure during periods of change; they can help set the agenda for societal changes; they can constrain unwanted changes which contravene the agenda; they can shape the policies for implementing desired change; and they can help in the reproduction of the state, of society, and of their linkages. This last is their most autonomous power and its elucidation requires more than a theory of police--it requires a theory of state change and reproduction which can incorporate the police as actors in that reproduction.[6]

Brogden (1982) comes close to granting the police in Britain substantial autonomy. He critiques five models of state-police relations: managerialist, pluralist, instrumentalist, structuralist, and *Polizeistaat* and develops a model of the police as managers who can negotiate control over substantial space between citizens and the state though their efforts are constrained ultimately by ecological, political, and economic forces.

## THE ORGANIZATION OF THE BOOK

The issue of autonomy or actor status distinguishes the three approaches to explaining forms of policing most clearly. The police are perceived as having autonomy in all approaches but in very different arenas and processes. In the "police as object" approach (which includes most police histories as well as Marxist views of the police as the tools of ruling classes, e.g., Harrington, 1983), the police have discretion and can affect their surroundings by the small-scale exercise of judgments and choices in how, when, against whom, and for what reasons to use their force.

In the "police as web" approach, the police do participate in the development of their own organizational roles, priorities, or tasks; they can develop "organizational self consciousness" (Walker, 1977: 35) and seek to promote and protect their status as a professional organization through interest group activities (Steedman, 1984).[7] They can purposefully structure their behavior to shape public opinion about themselves.[8] They can influence the nature of political life from which they receive guidance (e.g., Dutton, 1992). As Bayley pointed out (1985: 190-201), the police impinge on politics in significant ways but within the general structures and guidelines set by community and state authorization. In sum, the political, that is the democratic or authoritarian nature of a polity is heavily influenced by the choices made and foregone by the police, no matter what their formal authorization (Goldstein, 1993).

In the "police as actors" approach, the question whether the police have autonomous powers is, at the very least, not foreclosed by the conceptualization of policing, of the state, and of social reproduction employed. Whether and under what conditions the police become autonomous actors is an open question. Where the police fit on the range of autonomies is an empirical question, but data will be looked for only when theory opens a space for them to have meaning.

The chapters in this book are an attempt to both describe the changing patterns of policing as they are being developed in the societies studied and to evaluate what such changes contribute to our understanding of the natures and forms of policing in general.

Chevigny shows how political and cultural traditions in Brazil led to the legitimation of police violence and torture as a form of delegated vigilantism, the police being expected to deal with crime and disorder effectively rather than be constrained by legal and human rights standards. He also shows the difficulty as well as the possibilities of changing the relations between the police, the state, and the public toward more democratic and accountable forms of policing.

Stanley examines, in concrete details (and that is where change matters), efforts by political factions and international agencies to construct a new democratic police force in war-torn El Salvador. The struggle to construct a new form of policing is at the same time a struggle to overturn established forms of coercion and political and economic power. That task is not easy and the outcome of this experiment is still uncertain.

Ross describes the legal and police systems of three Arab countries and shows how a major international intrusion into the area-- the war between Iraq and the United Nations which brought about 200,000 foreign soldiers to the region as well as their disruptive western customs--has sown potential seeds for political instability in

Yemen, Kuwait, and Saudi Arabia. Domestic consequences of the Gulf Conflict--the return of workers, social unrest, internal security threats-- have imposed new demands on the state and on the police. Such demands challenge traditional social practices, legal precepts, and distributions of political power.

One problem all police forces face is that of legitimating their uses of coercion and control. Vagg's discussion of Hong Kong shows the complexities of the concept "police legitimation," its relations to policies, to public consent and to changes in state structures. There is often a disjuncture between the official justifications or legitimating accounts for policing and public consent which may be to police policies which are corrupt or illegal but are effective as crime control and order maintenance.

Den Boer shows how the police have been restructured to deal more effectively with three threats to order and political stability in Italy: illegal immigration, terrorism, and organized crime. At the same time, the political order is beset by scandal and corruption, vast public resentment at elite malfeasance, and general incivility.

Ellison and Smyth detail the efforts by British security forces and constabulary to suppress threats to the political order and British and Protestant control over Northern Ireland. In the process, the police have become almost a power onto themselves, willingly abetted by political and social leaders who argue the legitimacy of state survival, and have engaged in systematic and unchecked repression and extra-legal executions.

Brogden describes the three forms of policing--state, private (mostly in white areas and for corporations), and civil (mostly in black townships)--which have emerged in South Africa. He argues that all three forms must be acknowledged as legitimate expressions of community preferences as long as these are constrained by general legal and political accountability mechanisms. Dual or triple policing systems will need to be negotiated as part of the transition toward a post-apartheid state.

Shelley delineates the decline of the militia during and after *glasnost*. It fractured into decentralized, often ethnically conscious forces and private alternatives for social control have emerged as well. Yet the militia's functions have stayed largely intact even as the state changed and even as the police themselves sought to help shape the emerging political and legal order toward their own interests.

Walker discusses the processes of police cooperation as Europe has moved toward union and how European integration has affected the domestic and (formerly) international activities of the police. As the sovereignty of the nation state is challenged and a new supranational political state may emerge, the roles and functions of the police may be losing a statist and societal anchor they took (as did most scholars) for granted. If the state disappears, where do the police go and to whom are they accountable?

Shearing argues that the current, global push toward privatization and market based allocation rationales and systems for societal and state resources will affect the institutions of governance, including the police, in profound ways. Policing, as a set of security providing activities and services, will move toward and be controlled by subnational centers of authority and power. Such private centers may become unequally capable of protecting themselves and their clients, unless conscious policies are set into motion to distribute power more broadly. He describes the efforts by himself, his colleagues, and local people to establish such new policing powers centers in the new South Africa.

In the last chapter, Marenin sketches general themes about policing and change. He suggests that the development of policing, of the state, and of society are parallel and intertwined yet distinct processes and that the police have the capacity, under certain conditions, to shape the production of themselves and their societal and statist environments.

## NOTES

1. International policing (for example, English bobbies to help supervise elections in the *Saargebiet* in 1935 or international health police to help safeguard Alexandria after the opening of the Suez canal) has a long history (Liang, 1992) and so have imitation, borrowing and teaching.

The United States seeks to teach but has also imitated developments in other countries. Fosdick's (1972) and Glueck's (1974) descriptions of European police systems influenced the development of professional policing models in the United States. More recently, the notion of community policing clearly reflects observed efficiencies in policing in East Asian countries. Japan's policing systems, in turn, have been heavily influenced by borrowings from Europe (Westney, 1987) and, even though only temporarily, by the Allied occupation (Shannon, 1961).

2. Sykes (1977: 255) elaborates this view in a functionalist model of system maintenance. Policing is a form of regulation of systemic disturbances which "are relatively brief," their occurrence "have low predictability and are not well understood, [and] the unit of regulation is the individual." Policing is "a basic and permanent regulatory activity of every human group."

3. He does attribute this ability to inertia and habit as much as conscious awareness. "The fact is that people seem to become habituated to certain procedures and organizational patters; they do not know what else to do even when given the chance" (1975: 370).

4. In an earlier work, Bayley (1977: 234-35) concluded that "the police themselves are formative elements in society....It would be extremely short-sighted to ignore the effect that the police have on public attitudes toward law, government, force, arms, corruption, and civic responsibility."

5. The political outputs of the police cannot be explained by the characteristics of police themselves but require another variable. "This critical variable is the determination made by a political elite about the use to which it is to be put. Thus, while attributes of police systems do affect their political output, they are not a sufficient cause for the nature of political impingement by the police establishment" (Bayley, 1975: 379).

6. I have outlined such a theory in Marenin (1987; 1988; 1990). The argument is heavily indebted to Therborn (1978) and Thompson (1975; 1978).

7. For example, the South African police have met with leading representatives of the ANC "to discuss the implications for the security forces of the negotiations to end apartheid" (Cawthra, 1993: 167).

8. A colleague once described to me her experiences riding with the Dutch police. They were dispatched to intercept a car driven by armed bank robbers. The police parked their car, stood beside it, and waited for the bank robbers to arrive, but they did not draw their guns nor assume protective positions. She asked them later why they had not prepared themselves differently knowing that the robbers had used guns when they robbed the bank and were now in flight. They explained to her that the Dutch police wish to maintain the theory that the public and criminals will not attack the police with guns. They do not wish to undermine that theory by being the first to initiate armed behavior.

## SOURCES

Ahire, Philip Terdoo (1991), *Imperial Policing*, Philadelphia: Open Universities Press.

Bayley, David H. (1969), *The Police and Political Development in India*, Princeton: Princeton University Press.

------ (1975), "The Police and Political Development in Europe," in Charles Tilly (ed.), *The Formation of National States in Western Europe*, Princeton: Princeton University Press, 328-379.

------ (1977), "The Limits of Police Reform," in David H. Bayley, ed., *Police and Society*, Beverly Hills: Sage Publications, 219-236.

------ (1985), *Patterns of Policing*, New Brunswick: Rutgers University Press.

Brodeur, J. (1983), "High Policing and Low Policing: Remarks about the Policing of Political Activities," *Social Problems*, 30, 5, 507-520.

Brogden, Michael (1982), *The Police. Autonomy and Consent*, New York: Academic Press.

------ (1987), "The Emergence of the Police--The Colonial Dimension," *British Journal of Criminology*, 27, 1, 4-14.

Callaghy, Thomas (1982), "Police in Early Modern States: the Uses of Coercion in Zaire in Comparative Perspective," paper, American Political Science Association, Denver.

Cawthra, Gavin (1993), *Policing South Africa. The South African Police and the Transition from Apartheid*, London: Zed Books.

den Boer, Monica, and Neil Walker (1993), "European Policing After 1992," *Journal of Common Market Studies*, 31, 1, 3-28.

Dutton, Michael (1992), "*Dreaming of Better Times*. Traditions, Utopias and the Chinese Public Security Bureau," paper, American Society of Criminology Conference, New Orleans.

Fijnaut, C.J.C.F. and R.H. Hermans (eds.) (1987), *Police Cooperation in Europe*, Lochem: Van den Brink.

Findlay, Mark and Uglješa Zvekić (eds.) (1993), *Alternative Policing Styles. Cross-Cultural Perspectives*, Boston: Kluwer Law and Taxation Publishers.

Fosdick, Raymond (1972; 1915), *European Police Systems*, Montclair: Patterson Smith.

Galeotti, Mark (1993), "Perestroika, Perestrelka, Pereborka: Policing Russia in a Time of Change," *Europe-Asia Studies*, 45, 5, 769-786.

Glueck, Sheldon (1974; 1926), *Continental Police Practice in the Formative Years*, Springfield: Charles C. Thomas.

Goldstein, Herman (1993), "The New Policing: Confronting the Challenges of Complexity," Washington, D.C.: U.S. Department of Justice, National Institute of Justice, Research in Brief.

Gregory, F.E.C. (1991), "Police Cooperation and Integration in the European Community: Proposals, Problems, and Prospects," *Terrorism*, 14, 145-155.

Gurr, Ted Robert (1976), *Rogues, Rebels, and Reformers*, Beverly Hills: Sage Publications, Inc..

Harring, Sidney L. (1983), *Policing a Class Society*, New Brunswick: Rutgers University Press.

Holiday, David and William Stanley (1993), "Building the Peace: Preliminary Lessons from El Salvador," *Journal of International Affairs*, 46, 2, 415-438.

Jeffries, Sir Charles (1952), *The Colonial Police*, London: Max Parrish.

Liang, Hsi-huey (1970), *The Berlin Police Force in the Weimar Republic*, Berkeley: University of California Press.

------ (1992), *The Rise of Modern Police and the European State System from Metternich to the Second World War*, New York: Cambridge University Press.

Marenin, Otwin (1987), "The Managerial State in Africa: A Conflict Coalition Perspective," in Zaki Ergas (ed.), *The African State in Transition*, New York: St Martin's Press, 61-85.

------ (1988), "The Nigerian State as Process and Manager. A Conceptualization," *Comparative Politics*, 20, 2, 215-232.

------ (1990), "The Police and the Coercive Nature of the State," in Edward S. Greenberg and Thomas F. Mayer, eds., *Changes in the State. Causes and Consequences*, Newbury Park: Sage, 115-130.

------ (1992), "Policing the Last Frontier: Visions of Social Order the Development of the Village Public Safety Officer Program in Alaska," *Policing and Society*, 2, 273-291.

Mathews, M.L, Philip B. Heymann, and A.S.Mathews (eds.) (1993), *Policing the Conflict in South Africa*, Gainesville: University Press of Florida.

Mawby, R. I. (1990), *Comparative Policing Issues*, London: Unwin Hyman.

Nadelman, Ethan A. (1993), *Cops across Borders. The Internationalization of U.S. Criminal Law Enforcement*, University Park: University of Pennsylvania Press.

Phillips, Derek (1993), "Frontiers and Firearms: The Drafting of a European Directive," *CJ Europe. A Criminal Justice Newsletter*, January-February, 3, 1, 7-14.

Reiner, Robert (1986), "Policing, Order and Legitimacy in Britain," in *Research in Law, Deviance and Social Control*, Vol. 8, 173-194.

Shannon, James O. (1961), "An Evaluation of the Influence of the Allied Powers' Occupation upon the Police System of Japan," Pullman, Washington State University, Department of Police Science and Administration, M.A. Thesis.

Shearing, Clifford D., and Philip C. Stenning (1987), "Reframing Policing," in Clifford D. Shearing and Philip C. Stenning (eds.), *Private Policing*, Newbury Park: Sage Publications, Inc., 9-18.

Smaldone, Joseph P. (1992), "The Security Crisis in South Africa: Crime, Violence, and the Security Establishment," paper, African Studies Association Conference, Seattle.

Stanley, William (1993), "From Vigilante to Public Safety: Demilitarizing Internal Security in El Salvador," paper, International Studies Association, Acapulco.

Steedman, Carolyn (1984), *Policing the Victorian Community: the Formation of English Provincial Forces, 1856-80*, London: Routledge and Kegan Paul.

Sykes, Richard E. (1977), "A Regulatory Theory of Policing--A Preliminary Statement," in David H. Bayley (ed.), *Police and Society*, Beverly Hills: Sage Publications, Inc., 237-256.

Therborn, Goran (1978), *What Does the Ruling Class Do When It Rules? State Apparatuses and State Power under Feudalism, Capitalism and Socialism*, London: NLB.

Thompson, E.P. (1975), *Whigs and Hunters. The Origin of the Black Act*, New York: Pantheon Books.

------ (1978), "An Orrery of Errors," in E.P.Thompson, *The Poverty of Theory and Other Essays*, New York: Monthly Review Press, 1-210.

Tilly, Charles (1975), "Reflections on the History of State Making," in Charles Tilly, ed., *The Formation of National States in Western Europe*, Princeton: Princeton University Press.

United States, General Accounting Office (1992a), "Aid To Panama. Improving the Criminal Justice System," Washington, D.C.: General Accounting Office (GAO/NSIAD-92-147).

------ (1992b), "Foreign Aid. Police Training and Assistance," Washington, D.C.: General Accounting Office (GAO/NSIAD-92-118).

Walker, Neil (1995), "European Integration and European Policing: A Complex Relationship," in N. Anderson and M. Den Boer (eds.), *Policing across Transnational Boundaries*, Pinter Publishers, forthcoming.

Walker, Samuel (1977), *A Critical History of Police Reform*, Lexington: Lexington Books.

Westney, D. Eleanor (1987), *Imitation and Innovation. The Transfer of Western Organizational Patterns to Meiji Japan*, Cambridge: Harvard University Press.

Weitzer, Ronald (1991), "Elite Conflicts over Policing in South Africa," *Policing and Society*, 1, 257-268

# CHANGING CONTROL OF POLICE VIOLENCE IN RIO DE JANEIRO AND SÃO PAULO, BRAZIL

Paul Chevigny

## BACKGROUND

To understand police violence and its control in Brazil requires some understanding of the contexts in which both occur. Brazil is thought to have the most pronounced income inequality in South America (Denslow & Tyler, 1988). Until the mid-eighties, it had one of the most durable military dictatorships in the hemisphere, lasting almost twenty years, although with a gradual easing (*abertura*) from the late seventies. The national government now is a democratic federal system, in which the states actually have more autonomy than the states in the US.

The state of São Paulo is the industrial giant of Brazil, producing some fifty percent of the nation's manufactured goods as well as much of the agricultural product. Its stage of economic and social development is estimated to be like that of Mexico (*Forum Nacional*, 1991: 39). The state has some thirty million people, of which nearly half are in the city's metropolitan area. Rio de Janeiro, both the state and the city, is much smaller.

The political flavor of the governments of the two states is extremely different. Rio's governor until 1994, Leonel Brizola, a populist liberal, was driven from politics by the dictatorship but has returned to popularity since its demise. Those in charge of criminal justice under Brizola are people who protested the repression of the dictatorship; they proudly refer to themselves as "human rights militants." Of course, they would at the same time like to make the city less crime ridden. In contrast, the governor of São Paulo at the time of this writing, Luiz Antonio Fleury, is a tough law-and-order prosecutor who was earlier trained as an officer in the police. He has tried to use the police as an instrument for the direct repression of crime.

The police are organized on a statewide rather than municipal basis. (A small federal police fills a function analogous to that of the Federal Bureau of Investigation, the FBI.) The investigative/judicial police are called civil police; they are organized separately and stationed in different offices from the military police (PM), who do the patrol work. The latter are organized hierarchically, with a specially trained officer staff. They are not part of the military forces, although they were absorbed into them during the dictatorship.

In 1987, 1991 and 1992, in the course of writing extended reports for Americas Watch (a non-governmental human rights organization) concerning police violence in the two states (Americas Watch, 1987; 1993), I visited both cities collecting data, and I had an opportunity to observe changes during the intervening five years. At the time I started, the only relevant piece in English, I think, was Deborah Jakubs' in David Bayley's book (Jakubs, 1977). Although it was a fine piece, it was handicapped by the difficulty of fact-finding during the dictatorship. That difficulty has disappeared--the São Paulo military police now seem to me less secretive than, say, the New York police--but it suggests the aim of the present project. My principal problem is to understand how massive police abuses can prevail in a democratic society; a subsidiary problem is to understand the transition to democracy in the police--to see the aftereffects of dictatorship on police in a democracy. The abuses I concentrate on are the classic worst--coerced confessions and the misuse of deadly force.

## COERCED CONFESSIONS

The torture of suspects in Brazil was traditionally out of control--thought to be so entrenched that it was doubtful it could be improved. Before the dictatorship in 1964, coercion to confess was general, so routine that it was not really a scandal (Pinheiro, 1979). Brazilian liberals say bitterly that torture became an issue in the years after 1964 only because it was for the first time being used against upper- and middle-class people.

After the fading of the dictatorship in the eighties, coercion of suspects continued, using methods such as electric shock that were probably a little more technical than had been generally used before 1964. But of course they were no longer used against middle-class political suspects; as before the dictatorship, they were virtually never used against anyone but the poor or suspects who were at least accustomed to the system. The disciplinary officer of the civil police in São Paulo opened more than forty investigations of torture every year from 1983 through 1987. In Rio, a special prosecutor for human rights was on call during those years, jumping into her car and driving out to police stations to try to put a stop to tortures (Americas Watch, 1987).

Virtually all the cases occurred in the civil police because it is they who do the investigative work. The sociologist Guaracy Mingardi, an agent of the civil police during the years 1983-85, tells in his book (Mingardi, 1992) how the system worked after the dictatorship had ended. When a suspect was arrested for a property crime, for example, he would be hung up on the parrot's perch[1] until he was ready to talk. The confession, moreover, was often an instrument of corruption. The police would work out a deal with the suspect's lawyer in which the accused might pay them for a lesser charge or even to be released; at the same time, the police would get the proceeds of a property crime from the accused and would extract a fee from the victim for the return of the property.

The difference from the days before 1964 was that torture was an increasing scandal because of the revulsion against the dictatorship. The disciplinary officer in São Paulo convicted dozens of officers. The new Constitution of 1988 (Art 5, secs. III and XLIII) made torture a non-bailable crime for which the perpetrator cannot be pardoned. Brazil also ratified the UN Convention against Torture. The cultural attitude to torture was changing.

By 1992, the change in law enforcement was dramatic. Controls of judicial police functions in São Paulo are largely administered through the administrative judges, who require that any suspect being held for questioning be examined medically before and at the end of his police detention. Of course, there can be secret detentions, and there sometimes are. But the judges have their own staff of lawyer-investigators who look into allegations of abuse by the civil police. Everyone, even Guaracy Mingardi, who is hard to convince, agrees that most civil police are simply afraid to use the old ways.

The controls in Rio are quite different for interesting reasons. There is not the activist judiciary which is found in São Paulo, but there is an activist executive. The attorney general established an Advisor for Human Rights and Collective Interests (similar to the earlier human rights prosecutor), who takes and investigates complaints, passing them on if he can authenticate them to the office of the prosecutor.

Both in Rio and in São Paulo, the incidence of torture has clearly declined since 1987. It is chiefly due to the fact that the executive and the judiciary have a lot of control over the police in connection with the trial process; they can stop the abuse if they really try. But it is also due to a cultural change; although a lot of people still accept the belief that torture is necessary to solve crimes, most have now rejected it.

## DEADLY FORCE

If coerced confessions are a problem of the civil police, then correspondingly the abuse of deadly force in the streets is a problem of the military police. It has been a notorious and increasing problem with the PM in Sao Paulo in the years since the end of the dictatorship. The official figures are impressive (see Table 1):

Table 1

Civilian Deaths in Military Police Actions,
State of São Paulo

| | |
|------|-------|
| 1987 | 305 |
| 1988 | 294 |
| 1989 | 532 |
| 1990 | 585 |
| 1991 | 1,074 |
| 1992 | 1,470 |

Source: São Paulo Military Police.

When challenged, the state administration always claims for journalistic purposes that all of these deaths are the result of shootouts, of bullets for bullets. Other related figures raise some doubt about that; the police account for about 20 percent of all the homicides in the state, and the chief in metropolitan São Paulo allowed that in his area the proportion was expected to rise to almost half of all the homicides in 1992. According to the police themselves, about four times as many people are killed as are wounded in these confrontations (Americas Watch, 1993: 4-5; figures drawn from the PM in São Paulo).

A great deal of evidence about specific cases confirms that the claim of self-defense is not true in many cases. For example, on the evening of May 21, 1991, in Bela Vista, a neighborhood near the center of the city, two military policemen approached three teen-age boys. One stood still for them, but the other two ran away. The policemen chased the two boys, who were unarmed, one of the policemen firing at them. He wounded one but the other got away. The policemen took the wounded boy and the one who had not run to battalion headquarters, where a group discussed the problem and apparently concluded that the two officers were likely to be in a lot of trouble. The two policemen took the boys to an open field and simply shot them. Fortunately, one survived to tell the tale. Independent witnesses to the original stop were found in Bela Vista, and the policemen were ultimately convicted of homicide (Americas Watch, 1993: 7).[2]

Dozens of other examples appear in the newspapers. Most of them do not result in convictions, but prosecutors in the police tribunal told me that they believe that such stops and shootings are not uncommon. Caco Barcellos, a well-known TV journalist, studied all the police killings since the early seventies in which he could identify the victims and get some history of the incidents. In a best-selling book, *Rota 66*, he persuasively describes a pattern in which the police, especially those in a tough special squad called the Rota, shoot those who defy their orders. They then take the dead to the hospital as if they were alive, which tends to destroy the forensic evidence at the scene and suggests that the police at least hoped that the victims would live; the police sometimes plant weapons at the scene. Such shootings are particularly common after automobile chases (Barcellos, 1992).[3]

In reality the police do not press the shoot-out scenario very consistently or as if they expected the public to take it quite seriously. In October 1992, men from the special squads of the PM stormed the House of Detention in São Paulo to put down a rebellion. Many of them were armed with automatic weapons; they killed 111 inmates in a short time. Although the police said they believed at the time that the prisoners were armed, no one seriously claimed that the prisoners had firearms (Americas Watch, 1992). As a former prosecutor in the military tribunal put it to me, "The PM [military policeman] believes he is allowed to kill when the person is poor, black, and a thief." Superior officers appear to believe it as well; the prosecutors all agree

that it is very difficult to obtain discipline in a case where the police
have killed a person with a criminal record and even more difficult
when the person is shot running away from the police.

There is a lot more evidence that could be offered. But the
interesting question is: why does this happen in a democratic society?
The simplest reason is that the policy is popular; a great many people
agree with the sentiment that thieves deserve nothing better than
shooting. In a public opinion poll, 41 percent of São Paulo residents
expressed approval of the killings in the House of Detention in October
1992 (Brooke, Aug. 31, 1993). But that simplest reason pushes us back
to another question: why is the policy popular?

There is massive economic inequality in Sao Paulo, as there is
everywhere in Brazil. Many hard-working people are poor and
becoming poorer with the growing burden of external and internal debt
and the constant inflation. Their resentment of those who break the
law, when they themselves resist the temptation to do so, even under
infuriating economic stress, is enormous. Many poor working people
want to see criminals punished, and they do not trust the formal
criminal justice system to do it, even minimally.

There is very little respect for the rule of law. There is a
widespread perception that the law is a mass of technicalities that can
be manipulated infinitely by the rich and skilled. The impression is
strengthened for example by the legal fact that the educated, if they
should by chance happen to be convicted of crime, are by statute
incarcerated in special prisons. Thus the sense that something called
"rights" are a bulwark against the state, pushing in the direction of
equal treatment, is very weak. "Rights" are likely to be perceived as a
set of scams for escaping justice; thus the recent spate of talk about
"human rights" creates an especially emotional conflict between liberals
and those who are suspicious of the formal legal system, because for
the latter, human rights are just going to be more technicalities that will
allow the guilty to go free (Pierucci, 1987; Caldeira, 1994). At the Bar
Association human rights office in São Paulo, I read a statement by a
group of black youths who had been pulled off a bus by the police after
an argument in which someone had pulled a gun. The precinct (civil)
police could not find the weapon, and they beat the boys to make them
tell where it was. According to their account, the club with which they
were whacked had the words "human rights" written along its length.
No one seemed to think that the story was untrue.

Part of the problem with public attitudes is a sense that the justice system does not work to punish criminals. The penal system has been greatly liberalized to afford shorter sentences and increasingly lower security for prisoners as they serve their sentences. These changes have been greeted with a suspicion that is only increased by the special treatment that is afforded the educated under the system and by the belief that those who have money are, by one means or another, virtually never incarcerated at all (Brooke, Aug. 29, 1993). The military police add to this perception an argument that the civil police, to whom by law they are supposed to take prisoners they arrest on the streets, are corrupt and are likely to let the prisoners go before they ever make it to the prosecutor and the courts. The PM literally give this as a justification for their policy of violence; they said to me in August 1991, that they cannot get the confidence of the public except by reducing crime, and they cannot reduce crime except directly, by acting against criminals in the streets. In 1992, they proudly pointed out that the crime rate was falling while the number of dead suspects was rising in Sao Paulo.

The police are part of a culture in which a person is expected to solve problems through personal and informal, rather than formal, legal means. Politics even on the national level has traditionally been "clientelistic," with petitioners seeking patronage and special help from leaders instead of through the creation and assertion of rights (Roett, 1984). On a local level, even more is done through personal relations and what we call networking. In that society, given the massive lack of confidence in the criminal justice system, people frequently try to avenge wrongs privately. They hire a gang, called a "grupo de exterminio" in Rio, to kill thieves; sometimes they bypass the grupo and outright lynch the suspect. In this situation, the violence of the the police against "criminals" is "delegated vigilantism," to use a phrase coined by Allan Silver in a somewhat different context (Miller, 1977: 20).

The cultural situation I have just described might serve to explain why the public would accept police killings of those who are rapists and robbers, or anyway are supposed to be. It does not go very far to illuminate the reasons why the police kill many who seem not dangerous, if not outright innocent, and why the public does not seem more upset by those killings. Barcellos found that in more than half of the cases he was able to identify, the victim had no previous contact with the law (Barcellos, 1992: 258); and the crimes for which the police purported to stop the victims were not usually violent crimes in any case, but more usually involved such areas as drugs or stolen cars. Sometimes the police shoot people who are little more than mischievous, like children who are accused of petty thievery.

The aftereffects of the dictatorship help to explain this casual attitude toward violence. During those years, the military's actions were justified by the ideology that they were fighting a subversive "enemy within." A war on crime was simply assimilated to that aim. Heavily armed squads like the Rota were organized specifically to shoot it out with common criminals as well as with radicals. Thus the shootings became like shootings by soldiers; the policeman was admired because he was willing to shoot those were thought of, in however vague a way, as "enemies of society." Superiors encouraged men to be violent in just that way and they still do; in 1992, a group of troops from the 25th battalion wrote a letter to the state bar association complaining that the commanding officer was offering special rewards for any policeman who killed a suspect (Americas Watch, 1993). Those who have been violent are indeed rewarded; they are promoted, and the tribunals are likely to clear the accused perpetrator in any killing who at least acted in the line of duty and for "law enforcement" motives.

It is not very satisfactory to explain the violence as a hangover from the dictatorship, however, because most of the hangovers of the dictatorship have been vigorously rejected; the question remains why these police practices have continued to be accepted and even sometimes popular. For many Brazilians, class differences really do separate people radically. A person who may not be a dangerous criminal but is "marginal," a word used constantly by the police, or a "*vagabundo*," hence is of little account, different from a solid citizen, including a worker. Furthermore, there is a long tradition of dealing with problem people, whether criminals, radicals, or merely "vagabonds," by violent and informal means. For years, the authorities in Sao Paulo used to ship the denizens of the jails, including anarchists and bums, as they saw them, to ports in the northeast where they were unceremoniously left to shift for themselves (Pinheiro, 1979). Now the authorities cannot do that anymore, but the longing for simple solutions to the problem of "vagabonds" has not passed away.

Thus, as DaMatta (1992) has said, Brazil must be seen as a very hierarchical society, in which people are friendly to one another, even willing to help one another, at least on a personal basis, as long as the hierarchy is maintained. But those who fall outside it or cease to have a place in it through having become separated from their families, as in the case of the homeless children, are likely to suffer brutally. To this hierarchical society has come a democratic government, very fragile to be sure, which as yet has not been able to change the traditional relations.

This is not to say that there cannot be change, and perhaps very radical change, in the violent practices. In Rio, led by the human rights militants in office, the chief of the PM, Nazareth Cerqueira, has been trying to institute community policing, with special citizen service centers in the neighborhoods, and citizen councils to help to advise the police, and even to assist with complaints against the police. He has been trying to cut the violence of the Rio PM by individually disciplining officers, with some success. The level of deadly violence on duty is much lower than it is in São Paulo. On the other hand, the level of vigilante violence by the *"grupos de exterminio"* is higher.

In São Paulo as well, following the international scandal after the massacre in the House of Detention, combined with the public reception of Caco Barcellos' book *Rota 66*, the level of police killing in 1993 is said to be much lower. I am not sure how trustworthy such figures are, but it is possible that the state actually is trying at last to get control of the PM.

## VIOLENCE AND THE STATE

Brazil is in a situation where its component states, not to speak of the national government, have not pacified the country in the way similar to Europe and to a lesser extent in North America (Giddens, 1987). The state does not have a monopoly of legitimate force; it does not seem to be strong enough to take and enforce that monopoly if it wanted it. People continue routinely to deal by private means with matters that in Europe are given to the government, particularly to the criminal justice process.

The pacification process in modern societies is mediated, made acceptable, by a system of criminal law enforcement and civil justice that is perceived to be minimally effective and equitable. In a democratic society, a system of rights that protects citizens from the worst intrusions by others, as well by the government, and that is applied in a way that makes an effort to be neutral, is essential to that perception.

That system has been perceived as largely missing in Brazil. People go on settling things as they always have done, through channels that are personal and sometimes communal, because they believe that the government cannot settle the matters in a way that will be helpful to them. And the government alternative never takes hold because the perception is probably largely correct.

At the same time that the central government in a modern society is seen to take power away from private government and to centralize control of violence, in a parallel process, citizens begin to lose their appetite for public violence. Manifest, public punishment is abandoned for less violent means such as oversight and prison in a process made famous by Foucault (1977) and elaborated by, for example, Garland (1990: Chapt. 10) and Giddens (1987). The use of manifest punishment, of forthright violence, has to a large extent not been extinguished in Brazil by the government. It continues to be expressed in vigilantism and also in police violence.

In this connection, the contrast between the control of the use of torture by the civil police and the use of deadly force by the PM is illuminating. In the case of torture, governance by law and public revulsion against summary punishment seems to have begun to take hold, through the agency of the judiciary and the executive; because confessions are used in trial proceedings, elements in the criminal justice system other than the police have some control over them. In the case of deadly force, the PM is still insulated from these influences by institutions such as military justice that were inherited from the past.

When I was in São Paulo, I interviewed the chief of the metropolitan division, a very nice man who loves to lecture. He gave me one of his talks, showing slides as he went along. One of them illustrates, as he sees it, the difference between violence in a place like Brazil and in the First World. It is a drawing of the mushroom cloud of an atomic explosion, with an angry, "tough" face sketched into the lines of the cloud like a ghost. The talk that goes with it tells us that in the First World, violence has become distant, technological, clinical. The face of the killer is concealed. But in Brazil, that face of the killer is right before you, contorted with violence. And you have to deal with it the same way. I sat there, stunned by the profundity with which he perceives his place in the world. He is telling us that violence must be dealt with directly by society, just as society experiences the violence.

The reasons for the conditions in which Brazil finds itself are not far to seek. It is clear that the prevalence of slavery in Brazil until almost the end of the nineteenth century, followed by a semi-Colonial relation to the developed world, has distorted the nature of government. Poor people did not develop a sense that the government and society was theirs, that they were citizens with a right to be treated as such by the state. At the same time, the middle and upper classes had no sense that they were in any respect on an equal footing with the have-nots. This situation was not helped by the dictatorship; quite the contrary. The appearance of arbitrariness was reinforced by the dictatorship, which in fact acted in concert with secret and informal private gangs.

During the present period of transition to democracy, the forces of civil government and law are trying, hesitantly and intermittently, to gain control over the violence of the police. They have begun the process strongly with the civil police, but the work of the military police still tends to track private vengeance instead of replacing it with a system of law.

## NOTES

1. The parrot's perch is a simple device. A rod is placed in back of the knees of the suspect, who is suspended over the rod by the knees, with the head hanging down and the hands tied to the ankles.

2. São Paulo Military Tribunal Case #44639/91.

3. The same pattern was found in the suburb Guarulhos in 1991 in a more limited investigation by the state legislator Eloi Pieta, *"Notícias de Crimes na Polícia Militar,"* Aug. 29, 1991, quoted in Americas Watch, 1993: 8.

# SOURCES

Americas Watch (1987), *Police Abuses in Brazil*, New York: Americas Watch.

------ (1992), *Brazil: Prison Massacre in São Paulo*, New York: Americas Watch.

------ (1993), *Urban Police Violence in Brazil: Torture and Police Killings in São Paulo and Rio de Janeiro after Five Years*, New York: Americas Watch.

Barcellos, Caco (1992), *Rota 66: a História da Polícia que Mata*, São Paulo: O Globo.

Brooke, James (1993), "Brazilian Justice and the Culture of Impunity," *New York Times*, August 29, E6.

------ (1993), "21 Shot Dead in Rio Slum; Policemen Are Suspected," *New York Times*, August 31, A3.

Caldeira, Teresa (1994), *City of Walls: Crime, Segregation and Citizenship in São Paulo*, Berkeley: University of California Press.

DaMatta, Roberto (1992), *Carnivals, Rogues and Heroes: An Interpretation of the Brazilian Dilemma*, South Bend: Notre Dame University Press.

Denslow, David and William Tyler (1988), "Perspectives on Poverty and Income Inequality in Brazil," *World Development*, 12, 1019-1028.

*Forum Nacional* (1991), *A Questao Social o Brasil*, São Paulo: Nobel.

Foucault, Michel (1977), *Discipline and Punish*, New York: Pantheon.

Garland, David (1990), *Punishment and Modern Society*, Chicago: University of Chicago Press.

Giddens, Anthony (1987), *The Nation-State and Violence*, Berkeley: University of California Press.

Jakubs, Deborah (1977), "Police Violence in Times of Political Tension: the Case of Brazil, 1968-71," in David H. Bayley (ed.), *Police and Society*, Beverly Hills: Sage Publications, Inc.

Miller, Wilbur (1977), *Cops and Bobbies: Police Authority in New York and London, 1830-1870*, Chicago: University of Chicago Press.

Mingardi, Guaracy (1992), *Tiras. Gansos e Trutas: Cotidiano e Reforma na Policia Civil,* São Paulo: Scritta.

Pierucci, Antonio (1987), *"As Bases da Nova Direita,"* Novos Estudos, 19, 26-45.

Pinheiro, Paulo Sergio (1979), *"Violencia do Estado e Classes Populares,"* *Dados,* 22, 5-24.

Roett, Riordan (1984), *Brazil: Politics in a Patrimonial Society,* New York: Praeger.

# INTERNATIONAL TUTELAGE AND DOMESTIC POLITICAL WILL: BUILDING A NEW CIVILIAN POLICE FORCE IN EL SALVADOR

## William Stanley

## THE POLITICAL SIGNIFICANCE OF CIVILIAN POLICING

### *INTERNAL SECURITY V. NATIONAL DEFENSE*

As unprecedented numbers of Latin American countries have undergone transitions from military to civilian rule, scholars have begun to focus on how countries can move beyond mere elected civilian rule to establish more broadly participatory, genuinely competitive electoral systems, impartial judiciaries, and accountability for those in office to the publics they represent and serve. One of the potential barriers to deepening democracy in Latin America is the entrenched presence of militaries in internal security and domestic intelligence roles (Bayley, 1993). Military involvement in internal security in Latin America dates back to the late nineteenth and early twentieth centuries, during which military forces began to undertake broad modernization functions (Nunn, 1993). Military control of domestic order expanded markedly in the 1960s and 1970s, as militaries adopted variants of a "national security doctrine" which presumed internal subversion as the primary mode of geostrategic aggression by the Communist world against the Western Hemisphere.

José Manuel Ugarte (1990) argues that these militarized internal security institutions and the practices and philosophy which they embody represent a fundamental impediment to more profound democratization. While the reins of government have passed from military officers to civilian politicians, the institutions and doctrine for internal security have generally remained unreformed, that is to say, the national security state has remained intact. According to Ugarte, the defining characteristic of national security institutions and doctrine is that they do not distinguish between the realm of *national defense*, which involves the organization and maintenance of force and intelligence to defeat potential enemies, and *internal security*, which is the task of protecting the rights of citizens as defined under the norms of liberal democracy. National security doctrine places a priority on protecting the nation as an organic whole: applied to internal security, this approach negates the importance of individual rights and defines entire classes of people and currents of political opinion as threats to the security of the nation (Lopez, 1986). The tendency to define citizens as enemies leads to the practice of waging of war against them, usually through the illegal detention, torture, and murder of citizens. The forces that "fight" such "dirty wars" expect, and usually enjoy, impunity for their actions even after transitions to civilian rule.

Unless civilian governments carry out a fundamental transformation of internal security institutions, separating them completely from national defense institutions, policing remains in the hands of untouchable forces who view much of the free political expression and organization that underlie democratic politics as a threat to the state. In such a context repression is likely and the capacity of a new democracy to channel discontent into the political system is jeopardized.

A related concern is how the role of the military in internal security affects patterns of civil military relations and the life expectancy of civilian governments. Alfred Stepan (1988: 128) argues that "the capacity of the military as a complex institution to develop a consensus for intervention is greatly aided to the extent that civil society 'knocks on the doors' of the barracks." To the extent that the military retains an active role as protector of domestic order, it is more likely that civilian elites will turn to the military in moments of political or social tension. I have argued elsewhere that the relationship between the Salvadoran military and civilian elites after 1932 amounted to a "protection racket" in which the military claimed privileges in exchange for guaranteeing domestic order (Stanley, 1991).[1] The military there has at times manipulated civilian elites by using conspicuous violence to create the appearance of a greater internal threat than actually existed, much as the Brazilian intelligence apparatus did between 1974 and 1975 (Stepan, 1988: 28) Removal of the military from internal security functions, at least as a part of its normal duties, reduces its capacity to manipulate perceptions of domestic threat or to provoke conflicts which then serve to increase elite and middle class demands for military protection.

There is a growing current of scholarly opinion which argues that civil-military relations can improve if militaries refocus their efforts on less politically-contentious national defense issues (Norden, 1990; Stepan, 1988; Zagorski, 1992; NDI, 1990a). Separating internal security and national defense functions is thus arguably a prerequisite for civil-military cooperation. Once militaries get out of the role of political police, civilian legislators and executives are likely to find them less threatening and are likely to be more receptive to militaries' professional concerns and needs, while militaries are less likely to perceive and treat civilians as subversive enemies. This can lead, at least in theory, toward mutually respectful dialogue and increased civilian participation in the management of national defense, leading eventually toward effective civilian supremacy along the lines of western democracies.

In practice, civilian regimes have found it relatively difficult to wrest control of internal security from the military. The handful of cases in which it has happened are ones where the military was especially weak politically at the time civilians took office. In Argentina, for instance, the military was deeply discredited by its brutality during the "dirty war" of the 1970s, its general mismanagement of the economy, and its defeat at the hands of the British in the War of the South Atlantic. As a result, the civilian government of Raúl Alfonsin was able to civilianize police functions and circumscribe the military's involvement in domestic intelligence (Ugarte, 1990; Anderson, 1993; Di Renzo, 1990; Miguens, 1990). In Bolivia, the military was similarly vulnerable politically because of its mismanagement and corruption while in government, with the result that the succeeding civilian government felt empowered to shift resources from the military to the civilian-controlled police and to pass new legislation which greatly limited the role of the armed forces in internal security (Gamarra and Morón, 1993). In Panamá, of course, the military was defeated and dismantled by the U.S. invasion of December 1989, and a civilian police force (the Panamanian Public Force or PPF) was created with U.S. assistance to replace the military Panama Defense Force (PDF) in internal security functions (NDI, 1990b). Despite early signs of political restiveness by PPF officers, it is generally subordinate to civilian authority and plays a more limited role in society than did the omnipresent PDF (Ropp, 1992).

In cases where the military was in a position to manage its own withdrawal from power, transitions to civilian rule have not been accompanied by full civilianization of internal security. With the end of the Pinochet dictatorship, the *Carabineros de Chile* returned to Interior Ministry control, but the Investigations Police remained under Defense and the *Carabineros* retained the greater military influence and ideological outlook they developed under military rule. Civilian governments have proven unwilling or unable to push farther against military resistance (Varas, Cancino and Fuentes, 1993). In Guatemala, after initially promising efforts by President De León Carpio to civilianize the police, the military acted to regain control and at this writing there seems little likelihood that a major police reform will result from peace negotiations with the Guatemalan guerrillas (Aguilera Peralta, 1993). In Honduras, despite a growing current of opinion among civilian political parties in Honduras that internal security functions should be civilianized, a promising initiative to civilianize a notorious special investigations unit has proven difficult to carry out in practice as the unit has retained organic links to the military. Meanwhile, civilians who have spoken publicly for civilianization of internal security have suffered bomb attacks and death threats. Though civilians have worked to build political support for civilianization of police, the military has consolidated its control over the security forces, transferring senior Army officers to key commands (Salomón, 1993). In Nicaragua, the formal separation of police and military institutions hasn't meant much, as the two forces share political loyalties to the opposition FSLN party, enjoy impunity from civilian prosecution, and have tended to blur any separation between military and police roles as they jointly combat various illegal armed groups (Millett, 1993).

The police civilianization project in El Salvador, part of the January 1992 Chapultepec peace accords which ended the civil war between the Government of El Salvador and the Farabundo Martí National Liberation Front (FMLN), constituted the most radical attempt to date to put internal security firmly under civilian control. In contrast to efforts elsewhere, the Salvadoran project provided for a completely new National Civilian Police (PNC) force which incorporated relatively few personnel from the military-controlled security forces it replaced. The peace agreements greatly reduced the constitutional powers of the armed forces, called for the complete elimination of the existing public security forces, and provided a very specific institutional and legal framework for the new police force and a timetable for its development and deployment. The international community provided unprecedented levels of technical assistance, training, on-the-job supervision, and material assistance to the new police force. The development of the PNC in El Salvador therefore represented a critical test of how rapidly and effectively civilian policing could be established and of how the international community could contribute to such a process of institutional development.

From promising beginnings, the El Salvador police project developed into a cautionary tale about the crucial importance of political will for developing new police institutions, the difficulty civilian governments have in enforcing their independence from militaries, and the limited weight of international pressures relative to domestic political considerations. This article will explore the achievements and failures of the PNC project in El Salvador and consider what lessons it may carry for civilianization of internal security in other contexts.

## INTERNAL SECURITY IN EL SALVADOR

Internal security in El Salvador was historically based on vigilance by militarized security forces and paramilitary organizations under the direct control of the military. For most of the twentieth century, in fact, the military's primary mission was internal security and control of the population.[2] The Chapultepec peace accords changed all of this. Under the accords the government agreed to eliminate the old public security forces--the National Guard, Treasury Police, and National Police--and disarm and abolish the paramilitary patrol structure in the countryside.[3] Constitutional reforms included in the peace accords prohibited the armed forces from participating in internal security, except under emergency conditions and with approval of the Legislative Assembly. In place of the military and its auxiliary forces, the accords provided for creation of the PNC, a completely new, civilian-controlled institution with a new training academy, a new doctrine emphasizing the protection of individual rights and minimal use of force, and a majority of personnel who took no part in the armed conflict from either side.

PNC agents, inspectors, and commissioners were to be better educated than personnel of the previous security forces, with higher levels of professional police training. After an initial transition period, PNC personnel would live in their own homes as part of the civilian community, rather than in barracks as a society apart. The law and doctrine regulating the new police, and the curriculum of the new academy, conform to modern standards for police conduct, accountability, and democratic civilian control and were specifically designed to uphold the spirit and letter of the peace accords. These were developed with extensive participation of an international technical advisory team made up of Spanish and U.S. civilian police.[4] The implementation of the accords was monitored by a Salvadoran agency, the Commission for the Consolidation of Peace (COPAZ), created by the Accords and made up of representatives of political parties, and by an observer mission of the United Nations called ONUSAL.

The replacement of the old security forces is a vital part of El Salvador's transition to a more fully democratic society. The old forces were explicitly political and ideological institutions: they were an integral part of the armed forces, and until the late 1980s their officers were trained in the military academy with an emphasis on anti-communism and counterinsurgency. Even after distinct training programs were developed for the security forces, officers continued to move freely between security forces and regular army assignments. Because the military as an institution governed the country between 1932 and 1979 in alliance with civilian social elites, an important role of the military's security forces was political repression and exclusion. This politicized role continued, under the rubric of counterinsurgency, despite the transition to civilian rule in 1982.

Security forces at the local level were very closely associated with powerful landowners, functioning virtually as private security forces, with barracks sometimes actually located on large private farms. As political opposition and labor unrest grew in the 1960s and 1970s, the security forces became the primary instruments of political surveillance and repression. From the late 1970s through the early 1980s, units of the security forces tortured, killed, and "disappeared" thousands of regime opponents and activists of popular organizations in what can only be characterized as a campaign of state terrorism.

Besides being politicized, the old security forces were not very good at policing, and their approach to their work was fundamentally hostile to the rights of individuals in a democratic society. The essence of the old system was to maintain order through vigilance and intimidation. The security forces had poor investigative skills and lacked the most basic skills for protecting, recording, and using evidence. Activities focused on counterinsurgency: suspects of political infractions were arrested, detained without trial, and subject to torture and abuse, largely to obtain information. The old security forces seldom obtained convictions and gave little attention to crime.[5] Their use of plainclothes agents and unmarked cars for political surveillance intentionally blurred the lines between state agents and civilian vigilantism. Their reputation for brutality and arbitrariness created very poor community relations, and they seldom obtained information about criminal activity from cooperative citizens, further hampering their ability to investigate crimes.[6]

### PROMISE AND PROBLEMS OF THE NEW POLICE

The creation of the PNC potentially represented a thorough break from this past. Because the accords provided for a completely new institution, it was more likely that a new organizational culture and adequate guarantees for civilian rights can take hold. Yet the very features of the PNC project that made it so promising also created serious obstacles to success. Creating a wholly new institution required time and a massive initial investment, which both the government and the international community found difficult--or chose not--to finance. Meanwhile, the elimination of the National Guard, Treasury Police, rural paramilitary patrols, the army's own internal security functions (as required by the accords), and the armed structure of the FMLN effectively removed much of the old system of vigilance before a new professional law enforcement system was in place.

The reduction in security forces, combined with the unemployment, social dislocation, and ready availability of heavy armaments that are common to most post-civil war situations, created a dramatic increase in the frequency and boldness of crime, particularly armed robbery and murder. The government responded to this by expanding the old National Police (PN) through transfers of military personnel and ongoing training of new PN agents. Later it deployed military units in a quasi-public security role, undermining the spirit and letter of the accords. The government also for a time postponed the demobilization of the PN in what appeared to be an effort to retain the old force indefinitely. These actions raised fears in some sectors of a remilitarization of the country and were thought to have intimidated some voters in the elections of March and April 1994 (Vickers and Spence, 1994).

The government also took a number of actions that threatened to militarize the new PNC even as it was being developed. Some military personnel who transferred into the National Police were able to gain admission to the new PNC; two special units with origins in the military--criminal and narcotics investigations units--were transferred wholesale into the PNC with virtually no training to reorient them to norms of the civilian force; several military officers were allowed to join the new force in command positions; and a former military officer was placed in operational command of the PNC, contributing to a marked deterioration in respect for human rights by the new force.

During the peace negotiations the Salvadoran government received international assurances that it would receive significant international support for creation of a new civilian police force and academy. In practice, international donations to support new public safety institutions were markedly less generous than those to other provisions of the Accords, despite the pivotal role of police reforms to the whole peace process. In part this reflected the general absence of international police assistance programs; in part it reflected dissatisfaction on the part of potential donors with the Salvadoran government's own budgetary and political commitment to the project. The choice faced by the international community was whether to aid the project, despite the government's half-heartedness, in hopes of strengthening the project and gaining influence over how it is implemented, or to withhold support during the critical formative period of the new institution, the period during which its organizational culture will be formed, for better or for worse.

## NEGOTIATING POLICE REFORMS

The idea of creating a wholly new civilian police force had its origins in the concerns of the FMLN for the safety of its members as they reentered the political and social life of the country. Given the ideological and repressive background of the existing internal security regime, broadening the democratic political spectrum clearly required some sort of profound reform. Initial proposals by the FMLN sought to abolish the military, but the unacceptability of this proposal to the government led to a scheme under which the armed forces would be retained but confined to national defense duties, with a new civilian police force taking over internal security functions.

The basic framework for this solution was put in place by the Mexico accords of April 1991, which included constitutional reforms excluding the military from internal security functions, subjecting the armed forces more clearly to civilian control, and reforming the judiciary to reduce partisan political control of the courts.[7] The FMLN continued for several more months to insist on either abolition of the armed forces or integration of FMLN units into the armed forces, but in the September 1991 round of negotiations in New York the FMLN accepted that the safety of its members would be adequately protected by having presence in the new police force so long as additional measures were taken to ensure that the military would function within the bounds of its new, more restrictive constitutional mandate. This concession by the FMLN, combined with pressure on the government from the United States, which was unwilling to continue financing the war, and from United Nations Secretary General Javier Pérez de Cuellar, who had taken a personal interest in the negotiations, pushed the Cristiani government (and the Salvadoran military) into agreeing.

The New York accords provided for a purge of the armed forces, a new armed forces doctrine, reforms in military education, major reductions of the armed forces, the formation of COPAZ to verify compliance with the peace accords, and an agreement that former FMLN members could participate in the PNC without discrimination so long as they met the admissions standards.[8] A secret agreement accompanying the New York accords provided that a majority of PNC members would be civilians with no role in the armed conflict, while equal percentages of the remaining agents could be former FMLN and former National Police.[9]

The final accords signed in Mexico City (Chapultepec) on January 16, 1992 filled in the details of the general framework approved in New York in September, providing detailed specifications for reforms to the armed forces that would help ensure that they remain excluded from internal security activities: the accords required that the paramilitary patrol system be disarmed and legally abolished and that the intelligence system of the armed forces be abolished and a new civilian-controlled intelligence entity be created under the direct control of the president. The army was required to cut its forces by approximately one half, including the demobilization of the special counterinsurgency batallions that had conducted the majority of offensive operations against the FMLN during the war. Other institutional reforms provided by the accords include the creation of a Human Rights Ombudsman's office with broad powers to investigate rights violations, to inspect police and military facilities without advance notice, and to refer cases to the courts. The judicial system was also to be reformed, with an increased budget, measures to require broader political consensus for the appointment of judges, and new minimum standards of professional qualification.

The final accords provided a detailed discussion of the doctrine, structure, functions, personnel, and training of the PNC, including drafts of secondary legislation (*leyes organicas*) for the PNC and the National Public Security Academy (ANSP), which were annexed to the final accords. These laws, which had been developed with extensive technical assistance from the UN, were subsequently approved by the Legislative Assembly with minor changes.[10] The doctrine of the PNC gives highest priority to the protection of individual rights, to minimum use of force by the police, and to absolute adherence to professional, apolitical conduct by the police. The PNC is composed of nine divisions, including public safety, criminal investigations, immigration and border control, finance, arms and explosives, protection of important persons, environmental protection, anti-narcotics, and regulation of ground transportation. It is the only armed police institution with national jurisdiction, replacing all existing organizations with responsibilities in the above areas. The PNC is a decentralized organization, commanded at the departmental level by commissioners who are required to have university degrees (though some exceptions have been made to educational requirements, see below). Sub-delegations are commanded by inspectors who are supposed to have at least three years of university education (again, exceptions have been made), and sergeants with at least a high school education command smaller posts. All commissioners and inspectors were to receive at least ten months of training at the ANSP or abroad, though in practice some former anti-narcotics officers without such training held command positions in 1993 and 1994.[11]

The PNC was to be deployed over a two-year period, dating from the opening of the ANSP. During that transition period, the public safety division gradually deployed throughout the national territory, then other divisions were formed and took over functions previously carried out by the National Police (PN) and other entities. During the transition, the old PN would continue to function, but under the supervision of the 277-member police division of ONUSAL. The PN was to be demobilized progressively as the PNC took over its functions, though in practice its demobilization was considerably delayed. The PNC was to be considered fully deployed when it reached 5,700 agents and 240 inspectors and commissioners, though it will continue to increase personnel until it reaches 10,000, a target scheduled for 1999.

## DEVELOPING THE NEW FORCE[12]

### SELECTION AND TRAINING

The importance of the police reform to the overall peace process and the urgency of completing the transition from the old force to the new during the brief tenure of the UN observer mission led to an extremely ambitious timetable--three and a half months--for development of the new ANSP. Delays set in almost from the outset. Devising a curriculum took longer than anticipated, and the government initially failed to provide funds for recruitment, testing, students' uniforms, food, stipends, and other operating costs. International donors, nonplussed by the government's own lack of commitment, held back, and a kind of stalemate ensued.[13] The military contributed to delays and resource shortfalls by refusing to hand over the existing public security academy which the military instead appropriated as a new facility for its own academy.[14] The military even went so far as to strip one smaller facility that it did turn over, removing doors, lockers, window frames, and even the lightbulbs (GAO, 1992a).

The ANSP opened in a small facility in Santa Tecla that was inadequate even for the first contingent of trainees. Thereafter, most training was shifted to a sweltering, ill-equipped temporary facility at Comalapa on the coastal plain, which the government spent a million dollars on during 1992, and an additional $3.5 million during 1993, to refurbish.[15]

The recruitment and testing processes were predictably fraught with organizational problems. Some of the initial tests were not well adapted to Salvadoran conditions, and early testing placed priority on physical fitness rather than intellectual skills, leading to entering classes of cadets whose aptitudes were not optimized for the new institution's emphasis on knowledge of the law, intelligence, and interpersonal skills rather than force. Also, there were some lapses in psychological testing that may have admitted some candidates whose mental health was suspect. Following criticism from ONUSAL and COPAZ, the exams were changed.[16] Throughout the first two years of recruiting, the number of applicants was lower than had been hoped. At the outset this resulted from a lack of publicity; thereafter, low police salaries and public perceptions of other, more attractive economic opportunities (especially in the eastern part of the country) seemed to be the main obstacles.[17]

Admissions to the ANSP are governed by an Academic Council which included representatives of a broad political cross section. In contrast to COPAZ and its sub-commissions, where the political balance built into the commission's makeup led to fairly consistent adherence to the peace accords, the Academic Council was essentially controlled by the government. The Academy Director had a tie-breaking vote; the FMLN was not represented on the council; and one of the opposition party members on the council did not attend. The government took advantage of this situation to admit a number of former Army and Treasury Police officers, as well as National Police officers who lacked the requisite educational background, all of whom were legally ineligible.

A contributing factor in these decisions was that fact that until early 1993 ONUSAL was not allowed to have a representative present at Academic Council meetings (representation it did have with COPAZ and its sub-commissions). After ONUSAL began sitting in, the Council's decisions began to conform more closely to the requirements of the accords and related laws.[18]

The quality of training at the ANSP has been somewhat mixed. While enormous credit is due to all involved for training a completely new national force in little over two years, some aspects of training have been shortchanged. The first PNC delegations to deploy quickly showed that they did not know how to deal with common policing situations. Moreover, there were numerous vehicle and firearm accidents, including some involving fatalities. Partly this was a startup problem: the early classes had been trained without access to such basics as handcuffs, batons, fingerprinting sets, basic crime lab equipment, a photography lab, vehicles, a driving instruction track, adequate firearms, and a shooting range. The U.S. Justice Department's International Criminal Investigative Training Assistance Program (ICITAP) responded to some of these problems, but firearms handling and knowledge regarding the use of force remained serious problems as of October 1994.[19] Legal training proved overly theoretical and lacking in practical guidance for how police agents may conduct themselves in dealing with suspects, witnesses, and citizens in general. ANSP graduates remained badly trained in the specifics of criminal procedure and legal norms, and ONUSAL officials believe this contributed to the number of lapses in due process protections as well as to the more serious human rights violations that began to emerge in late 1993.[20]

Another area of concern about the ANSP was a tendency toward militarization. In early 1994, ONUSAL noted that almost all "monitors" responsible for internal discipline were former National Policemen (this was later corrected), and even ANSP faculty were subject to "barracks discipline," suffering indignities such as having their telephone calls monitored (United Nations, 1994b: 6).

Some of the best training received by the new PNC has actually been outside the country, particularly at an academy in Puerto Rico, where 60 officers received an accelerated training course to serve as transitional commanders during the initial deployment of the first PNC contingents. Officers who attended this program were uniformly positive about the experience.[21] Some of the future commissioners received additional training in Spain.

With the pressures to quickly prepare a basic public security force, the ANSP had little time or resources to develop the capacity to provide specialized training for the regulation of ground transportation, immigration and border control, customs, drug enforcement, control and arms and explosives, criminal investigations, fiscal investigations, environmental protection, and protection of VIPs, all of which are legally mandated divisions of the PNC (United Nations, 1994b: 7). These gaps were gradually overcome by bringing in foreign instructors and sending some PNC personnel abroad for specialized training, enabling them to return as ANSP instructors.

## DEPLOYMENT AND DEVELOPMENT OF THE PNC

As with the ANSP, the PNC was initially plagued by serious resource shortfalls. Just before the first class graduated from the ANSP, PNC Director José María Monterrey announced that salaries would be only 75 percent of what had previously been discussed. ANSP cadets protested and 19 were expelled for organizing demonstrations.[22]

When the PNC first deployed to the rural department of Chalatenango, the provisional commanders in charge felt they had been sent there to fail. Virtually no organizational work had been done prior to their return from Puerto Rico, so they found that they had to take it upon themselves to design the force they would command. Working night and day, they accomplished more in the few days before the actual deployment than the PNC administration had accomplished in months.[23] The PNC began its work with severe shortages in uniforms, radios, sidearms, vehicles and fuel. Living conditions at many of the posts were extremely austere.[24] There were also some instances of PNC agents receiving their pay months late, causing particular hardships for those with dependents.

The most severe problems were gradually resolved as funds began to flow, but by late 1993, ONUSAL still characterized the government's support for the PNC as "blatantly insufficient" (United Nations, 1993c: 9). U.S. embassy officials correctly pointed out that PNC posts are already better equipped than those of the old PN; however, the PNC has taken on the duties of three former public security forces bolstered by the Army and various paramilitary structures.[25] For a force of 5,940 police to maintain security in a country of over five million, it needs mobility, communications, and the ability to conduct investigations rather than have to depend on catching criminals in the act. From this point of view, the PNC was still severely short of equipment as of late 1994.[26]

In its first year, the PNC lacked the most basic investigatory tools, such as fingerprinting equipment, making it very difficult for them to gather sufficient evidence to obtain arrest warrants. Many posts lacked handcuffs, which forced them to restrain individuals they arrested by tying their thumbs together with the prisoner's shoelace, a practice historically associated with the security forces and death squads. Moreover, since many PNC posts lacked jails, prisoners had to be watched constantly, increasing the strain on personnel.

The overall effect of these material shortages was to strain the morale of the new force. While members of the PNC began their work with great enthusiasm and voluntarism, the poor working and living conditions and lack of sufficient material support compromised the new force's ability to perform its job effectively and establish a positive reputation for itself (United Nations, 1993c: 9).

The resource problems for the PNC stemmed in part from the fact that El Salvador had not in the past had a genuine police force.[27] The old National Police, for example, had little equipment that would be appropriate to the needs of the PNC, despite very high levels of aid from the U.S. to the Salvadoran military during the war. The National

Police had a minimal motor pool, consisting of a few aging radio patrol cars and heavy pickup trucks. Most of the weaponry of the National Police consisted of long arms, many of them on loan from the military. Other items of equipment common to police forces, such as handcuffs, batons, and basic investigation tools like cameras and fingerprint kits, were virtually unknown (GAO, 1992b).[28]

One of the PNC's most urgent tasks was to secure the trust of the population in order to build political support for the institution and to enable the PNC to operate effectively on the basis of information provided by the public. One of the greatest weaknesses of the military's security forces was that they were more feared than trusted and therefore received little information and assistance from the population. The PNC initially made signficant strides towards earning popular confidence, aided in part by the fact that the first communities to which it was deployed were ones that had received little or no service from the police in the past.

This led to helpful cooperation from citizens, such as lending horses to enable PNC agents to reach remote communities. It also increased denunciation of crimes. In Cabañas, the PNC acted on tips from citizens to capture members of two notorious gangs who had been robbing, killing, and raping in the department with impunity since the mid-1980s.[29] This willingness to take on some of the most dangerous and heavily armed criminals in the department helped instill confidence that the police would act on information from the population and that informants would be protected. Whether the PNC will achieve comparable success in urban areas remains to be seen.

As it deployed to new areas, the PNC found it needed to orient the population to its different way of operating. PNC personnel held meetings with organized sectors of the population to inform them of the new community-service approach of the PNC. At the same time, people were warned that customary practices of the past, such as operating vehicles without proper licenses and documents, dealing with infractions by bribing police agents, and paying the police to mediate and resolve minor legal disputes, would be discontinued. Citizens were given a one-month grace period to get their legal affairs in order, after which laws would be enforced to the letter.

The PNC's novel insistence on actually enforcing the nation's laws generated friction between the police and the not-yet-reformed judicial system. The PNC's higher activity level, and its greater propensity to investigate crimes and seek arrest warrants, increased the work load on local justices of the peace, many of whom had held office for years despite not being lawyers. In some cases, local judges failed to respond to PNC requests for arrest or search warrants, despite carefully prepared documentation. In other situations, the shortage of public defenders forced judges to release suspects without trial. PNC commissioners and inspectors attempted to work with the courts to explain their needs, but the PNC ultimately deferred to the courts. PNC officials interviewed for this study expressed the hope that by doing their own work efficiently, they might eventually pressure the judiciary into greater activity and professionalism but saw a growing risk that the influence would flow the other way.

## *LEADERSHIP, INTERNATIONAL TUTELAGE, AND HUMAN RIGHTS*

The government dealt a serious blow to the civilian nature of the police in September 1993 when it appointed former Army Major Oscar Peña Durán as Sub-Director of the PNC. Peña acted quickly to consolidate operational control of the new force, reducing PNC Director Monterrey to a more or less decorative role. Peña brought to the PNC an unreconstructed militarist attitude about policing. He told PNC officers in internal meetings to forget about the "compassion" they were taught at the ANSP. He regularly asked former National Police officers in the PNC about the activities of former FMLN personnel within the PNC, a practice clearly out of step with the intent of the peace accords which threatened to politicize and create divisions within the PNC (Call, 1994: 3).

ONUSAL and the FMLN challenged Peña's appointment from the beginning, arguing that he could not be considered a civilian simply by resigning from the Armed Forces. The FMLN's main concern was that the government was opening the door to an ongoing pattern of assigning recently-resigned military officers to operational command of the PNC, thus threatening its status as a *de facto* as well as *de jure* civilian-controlled agency.[30] ONUSAL officials voiced these same concerns, viewing the appointment of a former Army officer as inconsistent with the spirit of the peace accords.[31] However, the FMLN found it lacked the leverage to block Peña's appointment and ultimately agreed to it as a one time exception.

Perhaps in retaliation for ONUSAL's opposition to his appointment, Peña severed relations between the PNC and ONUSAL. For the first six months of PNC deployment, the ONUSAL police division had played a crucial role in helping to compensate for the new force's lack of equipment, experience and practical training and in reinforcing the human rights orientation provided at the ANSP. ONUSAL officials provided between 70 percent and 80 percent of the vehicular transportation for the first PNC delegations deployed, and PNC agents in the field depended heavily on ONUSAL's radio communications network to pass on messages and request instructions from superiors.[32] ONUSAL police observers accompanied PNC agents in their duties, tutoring them in both practical and legal aspects of policing, helping to fill gaps in their training and compensate for their lack of experience. ONUSAL police observers also served as the main mechanism for identifying gaps in the training being provided by the ANSP and informing the Academy administration about them. Though ONUSAL's training role was not well coordinated, the sheer number of people at ONUSAL's disposal (277 officers in the police division, plus dozens of human rights officials), meant that ONUSAL's technical assistance role was the most substantial contribution by the international community to the PNC project.

In some of the departments where there was already a strong working relationship, some contact continued through ONUSAL's human rights division, but where the PNC was newly deployed after September 1993, ONUSAL had very little access to the PNC. In a number of departments where ONUSAL had worked for months to develop basic manuals to assist police in following due process or to improve coordination between the PNC and the judiciary, all relations were severed and ONUSAL's efforts discarded. The break with ONUSAL raised serious questions about why the international community should provide further material assistance to the PNC project while the PNC itself was rejecting a very significant free gift from U.N. members in the form of advising and on-the-job training. Eventually, international criticism led to Peña's resignation and replacement with a civilian.[33]

In April 1994, Peña resigned under international pressure and was replaced by former Sub-Director for Management Rodrigo Avila, a civilian. During Peña's brief tenure, however, human rights performance by the PNC deteriorated dramatically. In early 1994, ONUSAL reported an alarming increase in complaints against the PNC, including such actions as mass arrests of youths on the grounds of vagrancy and "indocumentation," attempted arrests by plain clothes agents who failed to identify themselves as police, and, in one well-documented case, the use of torture (near-drowning) to extract a confession from two suspects, followed by a coverup (United Nations, 1994a). Abuses increased ten-fold in October 1993, as compared with previous months. While the human rights record of the PNC remained far better than that of the PN--the PNC committed only 3 percent of reported abuses between January and October 1993, while violations by the PN were "systematic"--the trend toward greater abuse by the PNC threatened to undermine the PNC's positive image in the eyes of the public. Damage to its image, in turn, could undercut the public's willingness to cooperate with the new force. Should the PNC come to be seen as essentially the same as the PN, it would likely suffer the same fate as the new Panamanian Public Force, which has enjoyed little public support.

The problems associated with Peña point to an important lesson for police civilianization in general. Ex-PN, ex-FMLN, and civilian personnel in the PNC showed remarkable capacity to work effectively and cooperatively as professionals alongside one another, giving the PNC in its first six months the reputation of being one of the most important and effective venues of national reconciliation. This positive early experience suggested to many observers that individuals' openness to learning and the nature of their new institutional environment were more important than their personal background in shaping how they conducted themselves as civilian police. This observation led to early optimism that Peña, despite his military background, might provide leadership consistent with the civilian standards of the new institution. However, most PNC officers and agents had been through a socialization process at the ANSP and abroad which gave them a shared set of reference points. Peña, by virtue of training and experience, did not share that set of reference points. To place him in a key position of authority was to invite an infusion of old, militarist values into the new institution. One of the difficult choices facing the government in selecting Peña was the fact that no true civilians with law enforcement experience were available. The reversals that occurred during Peña's brief tenure suggest that an inexperienced civilian might well have been less harmful to the development of the new institution.

### INCORPORATION OF FORMER MILITARY UNITS INTO THE PNC

A contributing factor to the reversals of late 1993 and early 1994 was the transfer into the PNC of two special law-enforcement units made up of former military personnel. One of the units was the Commission to Investigate Criminal Acts (CIHD). The CIHD was originally established, with extensive U.S. assistance, to investigate sensitive human rights cases. Despite the fact that its members had received advanced training in investigative and forensic techniques, the CIHD often failed to adequately investigate human rights cases. In fact, the unit repeatedly participated in cover-ups of prominent human rights abuses. The other special unit was the Executive Anti-Narcotics Unit (UEA) formed in 1990 to respond to increased cocaine transhipment through El Salvador. Made up of former military or security forces personnel, the UEA had established a reputation for effectiveness, personal loyalty to Major Peña Durán and to President Cristiani, and willingness to arrest military officers involved in organized criminal activity. It also had an organizational culture prone to secrecy and disregard for civil liberties (Call, 1994: 3).

There was no provision for including these units in the PNC under the original *Ley Organica*, but the government had a strong interest in preserving them. Despite strong criticism from opposition parties, the United Nations, and the San Salvador daily *La Prensa Grafica*, the government and the FMLN signed a private agreement on December 22, 1992, which provided that the personnel and resources of the CIHD and the UEA would be transferred to the PNC, pending investigation and review of the individual's records and administration of a special course of studies in the ANSP on human rights and PNC doctrine (Popkin, 1993: 33).

In practice, UEA personnel were transferred into the PNC in October 1993 with effectively no screening or transition training and immediately began to play a prominent role within the new police force. Former UEA officers were soon promoted to commissioner positions and took over responsibilities outside the realm of anti-narcotics investigations, outranking and eclipsing officers who had graduated from the ANSP. This preferential treatment quickly undercut the civilian character of the PNC[34] (United Nations, 1994b). International instructors at the ANSP concluded in early 1994 that "The PNC is adapting itself to the reality of the UEA, rather than the reverse." Another remarked that "I think we now run the risk of returning to the old ways--corruption and abuses--in two years" (Call, 1994: 4).

Only after the April 1994 elections and the removal of Peña as Sub-Director did the government agree to properly screen CIDH and UEA officers and to remove them from positions outside their areas of specialization. An agreement was later reached with ONUSAL in which the government committed itself to properly screen all former CIDH and UEA agents and to send them to an extended retraining program at the ANSP (U.N., 1994d: 5).[35]

A final issue regarding the PNC was internal discipline. An Inspector General was not appointed until after the Calderón Sol government took office in June 1994--18 months after the PNC was first deployed. The lack of a working Office for Internal Affairs and Discipline probably contributed to very lax standards of conduct evident during the formative months of the new force. Early cases of human rights abuses were not dealt with adequately within the PNC, raising concerns that the institutionalized impunity for rights abusers which characterized the Salvadoran armed forces could be taking hold in the PNC (Call, 1994: 7). In one case, a PNC inspector from Cabañas (an ex-PN member) was charged with mistreating individuals detained under his authority. Instead of disciplining or dismissing the officer, however, the PNC directorate merely transferred him to another post.[36]

## HAZARDS OF THE TRANSITION

### *THE TRANSITIONAL REGIME*

As noted earlier, the old National Police remained on duty as the PNC was developed, operating under the Presidency and supervised by ONUSAL. Special arrangements were made for areas of the country in which the FMLN had significant military presence during the war. Both the PN and military patrols were excluded from these zones. At the beginning of the cease-fire period, policing of these areas was handled on an ad-hoc basis by patrols of the FMLN, in violation of the accords. Shortly after the ANSP opened, however, newly recruited cadets from the academy were rotated through short-term assignments as Auxiliary Transitory Police (PAT) under close supervision and tutelage of ONUSAL police division personnel.

The transitional regime dramatically reduced the felt presence of government authority and vigilance throughout the country. The suppression of the National Guard and Treasury Police abruptly cut the available personnel for public security from 14,000 to roughly 6,000. During the war, as many as half of the regular Army forces (over 20,000 troops) were deployed protecting fixed installations and were therefore also serving a kind of vigilance function. In rural areas, civil defense and village patrols added roughly 30,000 additional part-time representatives of government authority, and in areas where the FMLN predominated, its combatants and local officials constituted a system of authority and sometimes ruthless *de facto* law enforcement. In effect, forces of vigilance abruptly dropped from roughly 75,000 during wartime to around 6,000.[37] The impact of these cuts was compounded by the fact that the Defense Ministry retained the majority of the vehicles belonging to the former public security forces, rather than transferring them to the PN or the PNC. As a result, PN agents patrolled on foot, without radios and with little ability to respond to reports of crime. PN agents suffered from low morale, expecting that their institution was going to be dismantled.[38]

## CRIME AND GOVERNMENT POLICY

There are few valid crime statistics on El Salvador, for the simple reason that most crimes go unreported because most citizens see nothing to be gained by reporting them (IUDOP, 1993). Even official figures showed a marked increase during the transition. ONUSAL statistics based on complaints filed with the National Police showed a 300 percent increase in violent crime from January to September 1993 (United Nations, 1994a: 24). Popular perceptions of crime centered on armed robbery and murders, both astonishingly frequent and often carried out with weapons of war, including fully-automatic assault rifles, submachine guns, and grenades. In a February 1993 survey by the University of Central America, 34 percent of respondents from urban areas said either they or an immediate family member had been robbed in the past four months, clearly an extraordinarily high rate.[39] While the poor are the most heavily affected, social elites are also extremely concerned about crime, including armed robberies, organized thefts of the coffee crop during the harvest season, and, in mid-1994, frequent kidnappings.

Not surprisingly, the problem of crime created considerable political pressures on the government to take strong measures to protect citizens. While full deployment of the PNC represented the best strategy in the long run, in the early months of the transition the government had no choice but to depend upon the PN. Rather than dealing with the PN's lack of material resources, however, which would have required a confrontation with the military over the vehicles and other equipment appropriated by the Defense Ministry, the government responded by increasing the PN's manpower, initially by transferring over 1,000 Treasury Police and 111 National Guard effectives into the National Police, in clear violation of the Peace Accords. The United Nations challenged this practice and the government agreed in May of 1992 to stop it (United Nations, 1993b). Despite the government's promises, however, ONUSAL subsequently discovered that several self-contained Army units from a demobilized counterinsurgency battalion, complete with officers, had been transferred into the National Police in what the U.N. characterized as "a redeployment of army personnel" (United Nations, 1993a: 9-10).[40] Another concern, from the U.N.'s point of view, was that the National Police training school continued to operate until December 1993, graduating between 60 and 100 new police agents every month. The Secretary-General's report commented that the collective effect of these measures was to "give rise to concern in so far as they reflect a certain reluctance, in some quarters, to accept fully the spirit and the thrust of the peace accords as regards public security matters" (U.N., 1993b: 9-10).

Concerns about the remilitarization of internal security were compounded when the government began proposing in late 1992 to deploy the military in a "dissuasive," quasi-internal security role. The U.N. consistently questioned the necessity of such deployments, proposing various measures such as accelerated deployment of the PNC as highway patrol and temporarily transferring vehicles and radio communication equipment from the military to the National Police. In July of 1993, however, the government deployed troops, mainly along the nation's highways and in areas where the PNC hadn't been deployed. These forces lacked the authority to arrest (except individuals caught in the act), stop vehicles, or search residences; they were excluded from the formerly conflictive zones; and patrols in rural areas were monitored by ONUSAL. With these restrictions, the government claimed the deployment was not a public security operation and therefore declined to inform the Legislative Assembly as required by the constitution that "ordinary means of maintaining internal peace have been exhausted," justifying military deployment to restore order. Instead, the government called the deployments "training exercises," an assertion which clearly undermined the intent of the accords to separate police and national defense functions. It also left wide open the duration of the military deployment, since unlike the emergency procedures provided for under the constitution, the approach taken by the Cristiani administration could not be challenged by the Legislature and involved no time limit or reporting requirements.[41]

Another problem stemmed from the fact that nothing in the accords specified exactly when or how the PN would be demobilized. The government didn't issue a plan until late 1993, and the plan it finally produced called for demobilizing only 300 PN agents per month through April 1994 (after the national elections), and for demobilizing almost the entire National Police--almost 7,000 agents--from May through September 1994 (Holiday, 1994: 6-7). The government went on in early 1994 to suspend the demobilization of the PN altogether, proposing to prolong the transition period until March of 1995 (Call, 1994: 5). It also sought, and obtained, an agreement from the FMLN allowing it to introduce an additional 1,000 ex-PN members into the PNC. The government further sought to retain some 1,100 members of the so-called *Batallon Fiscal* of the PN, which included the former Customs Police which were notorious for corruption and, historically, for involvement in political intelligence and violence.[42] These moves, along with the delays in demobilizing the PN and the fact that there was no constitutional basis for the PN during the transition, raised doubts in some circles as to whether the government would ever really demobilize the PN.

## POLITICS OF THE TRANSITION

Ultimately, the completion of the transition from the old regime of armed vigilance to a modern system of professional law enforcement depended on the ability of the PNC to prove its capacity and develop a political constituency, a constituency stronger than that of the Armed Forces and the PN. Interviews with leaders of business associations suggest that the PNC was viewed with considerable hope and anticipation by members of the private sector, who felt their safety and that of their businesses had been ill-served by the PN and the armed forces. The PNC directorate began cultivating private sector support through seminars during which PNC officers explained the nature and goals of the new institution. The main concern of business leaders was that the PNC not be politicized, but most were optimistic that it would become a professional, apolitical force.[43] Popular confidence in the old PN was extremely low, and 56 percent of respondents in a recent survey of the urban population expect the crime situation to improve once the new PNC is deployed (IUDOP, 1992: 1993).

In view of this degree of public support for the PNC, it is striking that the PN's lease on life (and its command over budgetary resources) was so prolonged and that the government didn't respond to the crime problem by devoting resources more quickly to the PNC. It is also striking that significant improvements in the outlook for the PNC finally emerged after the election of Calderón Sol, who was generally viewed as more conservative in his politics than was Cristiani. On May 19, 1994, before Calderón's June inauguration, an agreement was reached between ONUSAL, the FMLN, and the government regarding procedures for verifying that PN and former anti-narcotics unit officers would not be given preferential treatment and for addressing concerns about the possible infiltration of military personnel into the PNC under guise of civilians. The incoming administration was said to have influenced the terms of the agreement. The Cristiani administration nonetheless held to its plan to retain the PN until March of 1995.[44]

The political tide finally turned against the PN, however, when the second-in-command of the PN Criminal Investigations Division, Lt. José Rafael Coreas Orellana, was videotaped along with a group of other PN and former National Guard personnel carrying out an armored car robbery in which three guards were killed and several bystanders wounded. The spectacular and widely televised tape of the robbery prompted an investigation that uncovered a web of complicity of PN and ex-military personnel in organized crime (*Fundación Flor de Izote*, 1994). Newly inaugurated President Armando Calderón Sol summarily dismissed the entire 700 member Criminal Investigations Division of the PN and advanced the date for final PN demobilization to December 1994. These decisions, along with the appointments of widely respected civilians--Hugo Barrera as Vice-Minister of Interior for Public Security and Rodrigo Avila as PNC Director--raised hopes that the new administration would act decisively to complete the transition and avoid further militarization of the PNC. This turnaround reveals the importance of internal political factors in shaping the political will of government to implement genuine police civilianization. Calderón, as a relative hardliner within the ARENA party, could afford politically to act against the interests of the old military security forces. Unlike Cristiani, Calderón had not been responsible for signing the peace accords which stripped so much power from the military, purged its officer corps, and exposed it to highly public human rights criticisms. At the same time, Calderón lacked Cristiani's caché with the international community and therefore had incentives to yield to U.N. and U.S. concerns about the PNC in order to build greater credibility.[45]

It is significant and disturbing that the opposition parties, including the FMLN, the Democratic Convergence, and the PDC, were extremely cautious in criticizing the preservation of the PN and the deployment of the military, perhaps because the intensity and political saliency of public concerns about crime made it politically dangerous to oppose *any* measure that appeared to offer some promise of relief from crime. Representatives of the opposition Christian Democrats went so far as to call for expansion of the deployment of the military, asking only that the President act through proper constitutional channels (CENITEC, 1993).

The difficulties in the transition process demonstrate a central dilemma in the consolidation of a civilian-controlled law enforcement regime: to build public support for its deployment and budget, for the definitive exclusion of the military from internal security roles, and for the timely demobilization of the old militarized police, a new civilian police force must demonstrate its effectiveness, thereby establishing a political counterweight to the claims of the military and old police forces to be necessary for public order. Yet to be effective, a small, inexperienced new force needs more equipment and better salaries, as well as ongoing access to international training and advising. In the Salvadoran case, neither the government nor the international community (see below) had the needed resources. The members of the PNC themselves compensated through exceptional dedication and voluntarism during the first months of deployment, but it remained in doubt whether this would prove to be sufficient, and sufficiently durable, to realize a full transition to civilian policing.

### INTERNATIONAL COOPERATION

The Salvadoran government has consistently claimed that U.N. and U.S. officials gave assurances during the peace negotiations that the international community would pick up the tab for the predictably expensive process of creating a new police force from scratch. In practice, such support was not forthcoming, in part because donors were leery of contributing to a project that the government itself seems reluctant to support. As noted, the government's early commitments to both the ANSP and PNC were lackluster at best.

The meager support from the international community is especially noteworthy in view of the fact that support for the public safety components of the peace process were markedly lower than those for other aspects, such as land transfers. Using the government's estimates of needs and international commitments for 1993 as an example, international donors committed 26 percent of the $491.7 million needed for reconstruction activities in 1993. For reconstruction activities related to public security, however, international donors promised to provide only 12 percent of the costs. Overall, the international community promised to support only about 9 percent of the costs of public security reforms for 1993 and 1994.[46] Repeated appeals by the United Nations Secretary General, the United Nations Development Program (UNDP), and the United States went largely unanswered. The ability of the United States to provide additional funds in 1995 and 1996 will be greatly hampered by its heavy commitment to the new civilian police development project in Haiti.

The lack of international support for these programs was extremely unfortunate in light of the importance of the transformation of public security institutions to the overall democratization goals of the peace accords. Unlike many elements of the reconstruction program which benefitted only particular groups such as ex-combatants or residents of formerly conflicted areas, the reform of internal security institutions affected all Salvadorans and clearly had a major impact on the political environment of the country, despite flawed and underfunded implementation.

One possible explanation for the inaction of the international donor community is that relatively few countries have legal mechanisms in place to provide assistance to foreign police forces. Negative past experiences with police aid that merely fed into corrupt and politicized police forces have made many countries leery of establishing such programs (Anderson, 1993). As United Nations officials Alvaro de Soto and Graciana del Castillo have written, financing for the ANSP and the PNC

> not only suffers from being outside the mainstream of the international donor community's pet projects; it falls into the category of projects which this community normally does not *want* to assist; indeed, taxpayers oppose them almost as a reflex action. This is precisely because the police tends to be bunched together in the mind with the military, and is associated not with what is commonly understood as "development" but rather with the idea of "violent repression"...(de Soto and del Castillo, 1993).

Yet ironically the high cost of the Salvadoran police development project stemmed precisely from the fact that it was designed to overcome problems of earlier police development projects by creating a completely new force. Material and technical assistance to the ANSP and PNC had the potential to reinforce the formation of a new institutional culture rather than be coopted and misused by an old one.

One international aid observer commented that "In the end, it's their police force, and they have to find a way to fund it." A sober analysis of the Salvadoran national budget, however, reveals that there was very little room for savings in any spending categories other than the military, given the urgent post-war need to maintain spending in health, education, and poverty alleviation.

Indeed the only two obvious sources for budget resources transferable to the PNC were the PN and the military. The PN's budget for 1994 amounted to over $20 million, for a force with declining responsibilities. Defense spending fell by only 6.4 percent between 1992 and 1993, despite the military's reports of an approximate 45 percent cut in military manpower, and remained constant in nominal terms between 1993 and 1994 at $100 million, or roughly 9 percent of the 1994 national budget, compared with the 3 percent allocated for the PNC.

Nonetheless, it may not have been realistic for international donors to hope for cuts in defense to finance the PNC. The civilianization of internal security, and all of the reforms embodied in the peace accords, were *coerced* by the armed force of the FMLN.[47] The creation of the PNC represented a radical reduction in the prerogatives and political powers of the armed forces. There continued to be extreme distrust both within the military and in many sectors of political society regarding the intentions of the FMLN, and the military retained considerable capacity to manipulate this distrust for its own political--and budgetary--advantage.

## CONCLUSIONS

There is a growing consensus in the international community that prospects for both development and political democracy can be enhanced by reducing the resources and prerogatives of militaries. In countries where militaries have played a prominent role in internal security based on broad, heavily ideological national security doctrines, police civilianization has the potential to substantially change the relationship between citizen and state. El Salvador's police project is a test of whether one of the more visible elements of the authority of the state, the police force, can be converted from oppressor to public servant.

Many of the features of the Salvadoran experiment seemed especially conducive to success. The plan to create a wholly new institution made it more likely that old patterns of abuse and impunity would be broken and that the PNC would remain genuinely independent of the military. The accords created an environment in which significant international attention and resources were devoted to carrying out, advising, and observing the project, in which the international community had an important stake in the outcome and in which the government was at least somewhat accountable to the United Nations for carrying out the project as designed.

Even in this unique situation, international support was less than needed. The failure of international donors to more actively support the Salvadoran reform process, despite its visible successes, points to the need to establish new international mechanisms for assisting genuine civilian police development programs. The need for international assistance is made all the more urgent by the fact that any police civilianization project worth its salt is, by definition, taking away from the military one of its established roles and, in many cases, one of its main bases of political power. It is unrealistic for the international community to expect governments with tenuous authority over military institutions to civilianize policing without encountering some effective resistance by the military, whether in the form of impeding the transfer of facilities or resisting budget cuts. International assistance can play a crucial role in temporarily easing zero-sum budget conflicts, at least until new civilian forces can prove themselves and gain domestic political support sufficient to offset the more established constituency of the military. Such assistance may be a necessary cost of demilitarization.

That said, it is important to note that for police civilianization to be successful, a government must have the will to actually implement the project, even if its initial ability to provide material support to the project is limited by overall budgetary constraints and/or military resistance. Some of the greatest failings of the Salvadoran process resulted from initial government sabotage of the substance of civilianization, including efforts to smuggle military personnel into the new force, to preserve the old PN, to suppress contacts between the civilian police and international police observers and advisors, and to retain a substantial *de facto* role for the armed forces in internal security. The government's posture on these issues was to some extent predictable in view of the historical ties of the ruling party to the military and the still extreme polarization of Salvadoran politics; nonetheless, the remarkable capacity of the government to undercut the civilian nature of the PNC within months of its creation, despite intense international involvement and scrutiny, is a very sobering lesson. The El Salvador police project clearly shows that international donors should not contemplate assisting police projects in other countries unless the government demonstrates unequivocal political will to carry out the project in good faith, especially since almost nowhere (with the possible exception of Haiti) will a police development project enjoy the degree of international supervision seen in El Salvador.

Another lesson from the Salvadoran experience is that considerable attention must be given to how the state will deal with the problem of crime during the transition from one internal security regime to another. While El Salvador's situation was particularly difficult in this regard, given the massive demobilization of security forces combined with post-war unemployment and super-armament, any police civilianization process would likely involve risks that crime will increase, undercutting political support for the new force and reinforcing elements who favor a return to the old ways of maintaining order.

Finally, one of the central lessons of the 1980s for the United States in assisting the Salvadoran military was that it was easier to teach techniques than to change attitudes and institutional norms. The same problem applies to civilianization of police. There is an inherent tension between preserving and taking advantage of the existing knowledge and experience of available personnel from the old force on one hand and creating an institution that breaks from past practices on the other. The negative impact of Sub-Director Peña and the Executive Anti-Narcotics Unit on the PNC project in El Salvador suggest that such conflicts are best resolved in favor of newness and good will, at the expense of experience and technique, even if this results in initial errors. The likelihood of creating a new and distinct organizational ethos is greater without representatives of the old order in charge.

## NOTES

1. The notion of governments as protection rackets is from Charles Tilly (1984).

2. One illustration of this is that most military barracks are located in densely populated areas near the center of towns.

3. The National Guard and the Treasury Police were absorbed into the army as Special Brigade for Military Security, which combines Military Police functions and readiness to perform border security functions in the event of a cross-border military conflict. The Security Forces had an extensive network of informants regarding political activities, and these connections no doubt occasionally served to call police attention to crimes, but general community relations were poor.

4. The initial plan for the police, embodied in an annex to the peace accords, was largely the work of Jesús Rodés, as Spanish Police Academy director on assignment to the U.N. Subsequent work was elaborated by the Spanish and U.S. technical teams, which included five members each. The U.S. technical team belongs to the Justice Department's International Criminal Investigative Training Assistance Program (ICITAP). Two Salvadoran military officers represented the government. As a result of an oversight by the UNDP, which coordinated the police project, the FMLN was not included in the process at the outset. Following FMLN protests, it was included in regular meetings from April 1992 onward.

5. National Police, Treasury Police, and National Guard intelligence units were highly effective at counterinsurgency work during the war but functioned more as death squads, particularly early in the war, than as legal investigatory agencies. For an illustrative case of the use of extrajudicial confessions, see Popkin (1993: 90)

6. According to a January 1992 national opinion survey conducted by the University of Central America, 50.1 percent of respondents had "little" or "no" confidence in the existing security forces and 64 percent favored dissolution of the Civil Defense structure. See IUDOP (1992). In a February 1993 survey of the urban population, IUDOP found that 76.4 percent of crime victims did not report incidents to the police. See IUDOP (1993).

7. See "*Acuerdos de México*," in United Nations (1992: 13-19).

8. COPAZ was made up of two representatives each from the government and the FMLN and one each from the political parties represented in the Legislative Assembly at the time, including the National Republican Alliance (ARENA), the National Conciliation Party (PCN), the Authentic Christian Movement (MAC), the Christian Democrats (PDC), the Democratic Convergence (CD), and the National Democratic Union (UDN). This makeup usually created a deadlock, since ARENA, PCN and MAC generally sided with the government, while the PDC, CD, and UDN generally opposed. The composition of the COPAZ sub-commission on the National Civilian Police was similar.

9. The parties subsequently agreed that 60 percent would be noncombatants, while 20 percent each could be ex-FMLN and ex-National Police. In practice, the FMLN had difficulty fully utilizing these quotas, as too few of their personnel met the admissions standards for the PNC. According to FMLN officials, the height restrictions were a barrier to many otherwise qualified ex-FMLN candidates.

10. Interview, Jesús Rodés, Director, *Escola de Policia de Catalunya*, November 1994.

11. Confidential U.N. source, October 1994.

12. For a more detailed account of the early development of the ANSP and PNC, see Stanley, 1993.

13. The initial budget estimate developed by the joint technical team for the first two years of operation of the ANSP came to $42 million. Of this, the Salvadoran government committed $13 million, the United States pledged $10 million, Spain pledged almost $3 million, and Norway offered $300,000. This left an anticipated budget shortfall of over $15 million. In practice the government was very slow to actually disburse the amounts it had committed. Moreover, the first year of operation of the ANSP revealed the initial estimates to have been conservative, leading the government to increase its estimates for the cost of the ANSP for 1993 and 1994 to $69 million. The government committed $28 million for this period and received pledges for an additional $12 million committed by the United States, Spain, and Norway. This left a balance of $29 million for which support was not yet available. See *Presidencia de la Republica de El Salvador* (1993a: 2)

14. The Military School had little need for the old 114-acre public security academy, since entering classes had fallen to their pre-war level of around 110, attrition would reduce graduating classes to about 35, and the total student population was unlikely to exceed 300, in contrast to the peak enrollment of over 2,200 at the ANSP (U.N. 1994b, 6).

15. The facility, owned by Treasury Ministry, had served as a military base for the Ramón Belloso Battalion during the war but seemed to be equipped to house only half of the 800 soldiers who were supposedly based there. Significant additional housing, water supply, and sewerage had to be constructed.

16. Interviews, ONUSAL officials and members of the COPAZ sub-commission on the ANSP/PNC, September/October 1992. It was recognized from the beginning that many ex-combatants would not meet the formal educational requirements for the "basic" level, so special remedial courses were set up with the cooperation of the Ministry of Education to bring former combatants up to the ninth grade level. The government did not finance the program, however, which mainly

benefitted members of the FMLN. After some delay, a European donor provided the necessary funds for the first several months of operation. Funding for these mini-courses was soon exhausted, complicating the task for the FMLN of preparing enough qualified candidates to fill their 20 percent quota. Interviews, Miguel Eduardo Mira, September and October 1992, Claudio Armíjo, August 1993. Both are members of the FMLN committee that monitors development of the PNC.

17. Interviews, U.N. officials, October 1994.

18. Interviews, United Nations officials, November 1992, January, July and August 1993.

19. Interviews, U.N. officials, October, 1994.

20. Personal communication, ONUSAL officials, January 1994.

21. Significantly, both ex-National Police and ex-FMLN members of the PNC command made extremely favorable comments about the Puerto Rico program. Interviews PNC commissioners and inspectors, Chalatenango and Cabañas, March and July, 1993.

22. Interview, José María Ramirez of the Salvadoran Center for Juridical Studies (IEJES), which has filed a legal appeal on behalf of the expelled students. July 1993, San Salvador.

23. Interviews by David Holiday and Tommie Sue Montgomery with PNC officials in Chalatenango, March 1993 and August of 1993, respectively.

24. For the duration of the transitional period, PNC personnel lived in their delegations or posts, moving into their own residences only after the PNC was fully deployed and longer-term assignments become possible. They spent nine days on duty, three days off. After the transitional period, they will work 8-hour shifts. All PNC officers interviewed reported that 12- to 14-hour days were the norm.

25. Interviews, U.S. ICITAP officials, San Salvador, August and September 1993.

26. Interviews, United Nations officials, September 1993 and October 1994.

27. The government's initial budget estimate for the PNC, presented several months late in December 1992, was $84.5 million. Later, more realistic, analysis of the PNC's equipment needs increased this projection to $127.7 million for the first two years, of which the Salvadoran government pledged to provide $62.2 million. (GAO, 1992b; *Presidencia*, 1993b) Delivering on these commitments was complicated by the fact that the PNC, though constitutionally mandated, did not appear in the 1993 budget, and the government's actual budget allocations for the PNC for 1993 and 1994 combined amount to $56.7 million. The United States committed $6 million in technical assistance via ICITAP, plus $5.75 million for vehicles, computers, and other non-lethal equipment for the PNC, but few other countries contributed major funding to the PNC itself.

28. The demobilization of the National Guard, Treasury Police, and National Police should have made large numbers of buildings around the country available for use by the PNC. In practice, the Defense Ministry has retained some of these properties, while the rest turn out to have been rented and have simply reverted to their owners. Only in the few cases where municipalities owned them have former security forces posts been available to the PNC. Many PNC officers view this as a blessing in disguise, since they hope to distinguish the PNC as much as possible from the old forces and therefore prefer to operate out of different locales.

29. A special operation by the PNC in Usulután arrested two gang leaders, one ex-FMLN and one ex-military, using tips from the population. *Fundación Flór de Izote* (1993).

30. Similar practices have been used to maintain military domination of formally civilian police forces in countries such as Guatemala and (in the past) Argentina. This has had catastrophic effects on morale in police forces in those countries, since the most talented police commissioners can never aspire to top leadership posts and military officers--accustomed to impunity and an entirely different organizational culture--can undermine efforts to establish lawful and

democratic policing practices. The precedent of treating a former Army officer as a civilian could also influence whether former National Police would be able to apply to the PNC as "civilians" after the end of the transition period in September 1994. Interviews, Claudio Armíjo, Eduardo Solorzano, and Miguel Saenz of the FMLN, San Salvador, July 1993.

31. Interviews, July and September 1993.

32. Interviews, United Nations officials, San Salvador, July 1993. The PNC obtained its own vehicles in April 1993 and had its own radios from July 1993 onward.

33. Confidential interview, January 1994, Washington, D.C.

34. Interview, Chuck Call, Washington Office on Latin America. Mr. Call conducted field research on the PNC in January 1994.

35. Interviews, U.N. officials, October 1994.

36. Interview, Claudio Armíjo, FMLN commission on the ANSP/PNC, San Salvador, July 1993. This information was confirmed by Professor Tommie Sue Montgomery of the Southern Center for International Studies, in interviews with PNC officials in Chalatenango and Cabañas. Personal communication, September 1993. According to Robert Loosle, director of the United States' ICITAP program in El Salvador, a panel of three PNC officers including one ex-PN, one ex-FMLN, and one civilian, investigated this case and made a recommendation based on the provisional disciplinary code of the PNC. Personal communication, September 1993.

37. Subsequent transfers of military and security personnel into the PN raised its numbers to around 8,000, though only about 6,800 of these were regular patrolmen, the balance performing administrative and investigative functions.

38. Because of an oversight in setting up the social programs for demobilizing combatants, PN agents were left in limbo for about a year as to whether they would enjoy the same economic benefits and training as other demobilizing combatants. The U.S. embassy clarified that

U.S. funding would be available for this, but the GOES delayed putting programs in place.

39. The Ministry of Justice's (1993) figures show that crime increased by 83 percent between 1990 and 1991, prior to the signing of the final accords. In the IUDOP poll on crime, only 22.4 percent of those who claimed to have been victims of crime reported the incident to authorities. Of those who did not report crimes, over 60 percent reported that they were either afraid to do so or felt it would accomplish nothing. See IUDOP (1993).

40. As noted above, it has proven difficult for ONUSAL to track the transfers of military personnel into the National Police because of lack of access to records. One U.N. official interviewed estimated that half of the new recruits of the National Police are from the Army.

41. Article 168, section 12 of the 1983 Constitution, as reformed under the peace accords, states that: "Exceptionally, when the ordinary means of maintaining internal peace, tranquility, and public security have been exhausted, the President of the Republic may make use of the Armed Forces for this purpose. The actions of the Armed Forces shall be limited to the time and magnitude strictly necessary for the restoration of order and will cases as soon as this goal has been achieved. The President of the Republic will keep the Legislative Assembly informed of these measures and the Assembly may, at any time, effect the termination of these exceptional measures. In all cases, the President of the Republic will present a report to the Legislative Assembly regarding the actions of the Armed Forces within fifteen days of the termination of these measures." (Author's translation.) See *Corte Suprema de Justicia* (1992).

42. According to journalist Tom Gibb, who has conducted extensive interviews with former rebels and security forces personnel, the Customs Police were used as institutional cover for the notorious Salvadoran National Security Agency (ANSESAL) in the 1970s to gather political intelligence and operate death squads. Interview, February 1994.

43. Interviews with representatives of the National Association of Private Enterprise (ANEP), the Salvadoran Foundation for Economic and Social Development (FUSADES), the Chamber of Commerce, the Center for Democratic Studies (CEDEM), and the Cotton Growers' Cooperative, July and August 1993.

44. Personal communication, David Holiday, July 1994.

45. This analysis from David Holiday, personal communication, July 1994.

46. The ANSP received commitments of $13.3 million from the United States, Spain, and Norway for its first years of operation. The PNC initially received little support: during 1993, only $650,000 from the Swedish government and 10 vehicles from the United States were delivered to the PNC. The United States subsequently obligated $11.75 million for the PNC, part of which was delivered during 1994 (Call, 1994: 9). Besides the United States, donors to the ANSP and PNC include Spain ($3 million), Sweden ($1.3 million), Germany (<$1million), and Norway (<$1million). See Call (1994) and *Presidencia* (1993a and 1993b).

47. The international community, including the United Nations and the "four plus one" countries--the United States, Mexico, Venezuela, Spain, and Colombia--played an important role in pushing for these reforms as well, but in the final analysis there is no reason to think that the Salvadoran government would have undertaken such profound changes had it not been coerced by the FMLN.

## SOURCES

Aguilera Peralta, G. (1993), *"Función policíaca y transción a la democracia: el caso de Guatemala,"* Typescript.

Anderson, M. A. (1993), "International Administration of Justice: the New American Security Frontier," *Sais Review*, Winter/Spring, 13, 1, 89-104.

Bayley, D. H. (1993), "What's in a Uniform? A Comparative View of Police-Military Relations in Latin America," Typescript.

Brewer, J. D. (1993), "Re-educating the South African Police: Comparative Lessons," in M.L. Mathews, Philip B. Heymann, and A.S. Mathews (eds.), *Policing the Conflict in South Africa*, Gainesville: University Press of Florida.

Call, C. (1994), "Recent Setbacks in the Police Transition; El Salvador Peace Plan Update #3," Washington D.C.: Washington Office on Latin America.

Call, C., and L.Wirspa (1993), "The Colombian National Police, Human Rights, and U.S. Drug Policy," Washington, D.C.: Washington Office on Latin America.

*Centro de Investigaciónes Tecnologicas y Cientificas* (CENITEC) (1993), *"Los Patrullajes de la Fuerza Armada,"* Paid advertisement published in *La Prensa Grafica* (*Martes, 3 Agosto*) p. 27.

*Corte Suprema de Justicia* (1992), *Constitucion de la Republica 1993; Reformas de 1991/1992*, San Salvador: Marzo.

Costa, Gino (1994), "Police Reform in El Salvador," Paper presented at the conference The International Community and Police Reform in Central America and Haiti, Washington, D.C., November 3-4.

de Soto, A. and G. del Castillo (1993), "Post-Conflict Peace-Building in El Salvador: Strains on the United Nations System," Typescript, May.

Di Renzo, O. (1990), *"La seguridad interna en la Argentina actual,"* In NDI 1990a.

*Estado Mayor Conjunto 9* (1992), *"Ausencia de la Fuerza Armada y auge de la criminalidad,"* Revista Militar, Fuerza Armada de el Salvador (*Julio*) i-ii.

*Fundación Flor de Izote* (1993), *Cronologia de El Salvador*, 84, Sept. 6. Electronic publication.

------ (1994), *Weekly Report*, 5, 25, June 27. Electronic publication.

Gamarra, E. and R.B. Morón (1993), *"Seguridad ciudadana y seguridad nacional: relaciones policía-militares en Bolivia,"* Typescript.

General Accounting Office (1992a), "Aid to El Salvador: Slow Progress in Developing a National Civilian Police," Washington D.C.: Congressional Record, S14801, September 23.

------ (1992b), "El Salvador: Efforts to Satisfy National Civilian Police Equipment Needs," Washington, D.C.: GAO/NSIAD-93-100BR, December.

Holiday, D. (1994), "Police Issues," Typescript.

*Informe de la Sub-Comisión de COPAZ para la PNC* (1993), San Salvador, *17 de febrero.*

*Instituto Universitario de Opinión Publica* (IUDOP) (1992), *"Los Salvadoreños ante los acuerdos finales de paz,"* San Salvador: Universidad Centroamericana José Simeón Cañas, *30 Abril.*

------ (1993), *"La delincuencia urbana," Estudios Centroamericanos*, 534-535, *Abril/Mayo*, 471-9.

Lopez, G. A. (1986), "National Security Ideology as an Impetus to State Violence and Terror," in M. Stohl and G.A. Lopez (eds.), *Government Violence and Repression*, Westport, CT: Greenwood Press.

Miguens, J. E. (1990), *"Orden social e inteligencia interior,"* in NDI 1990a.

Millett, R. (1993), "Policing Nicaragua: An Ongoing Dilemma," Typescript.

*Ministerio de Justicia* (1993), *El Sector Justicia de El Salvador en Numeros*, San Salvador.

Nathan, L. (1993), "From a Police Force to a Police Service: The New Namibian Police," in M.L. Mathews, Philip B. Heymann, and A.S. Mathews (eds.), *Policing the Conflict in South Africa*, Gainesville: University Press of Florida.

National Democratic Institute (NDI) (1990a), *Hacia Una Nueve Relacion: el Papel de las Fuerzas Armadas en Un Gobierno Democratico,* Washington, D.C. and Buenos Aires: National Democratic Institute and *Fundación Arturo Illia.*

------ (1990b), *Panama: Hacia Un Modelo Policial. El Informe de Un Mision Internacional*, Washington, D.C.: National Democratic Institute.

Norden, D. (1990), "Democratic Consolidation and Military Professionalism: Argentina in the 1980s," *Journal of Interamerican Studies and World Affairs*, 32, 3, Fall.

Nunn, F. (1993), "Professionals, Praetorians, and Police: On Internal Role Potential of Armies in Twentieth-Century Latin America," Typescript.

*Partido Demócrata Cristiano* (1992), "*PNC: 10,000 ¡Ya!*," San Salvador, 25 *de marzo*.

Popkin, M. (1993), "El Salvador's Negotiated Revolution: Prospects for Legal Reform," New York: Lawyers Committee for Human Rights.

*Presidencia de la Republica de El Salvador* (1993a), "*Requerimientos de cooperación internacional para el funcionamiento de la Academica Nacional de Seguridad Publica*," San Salvador, *junio*.

------- (1993b), "*Requerimientos de cooperación internacional para el funcionamiento de la Policía Nacional Civil*," San Salvador, *junio*.

*Presupuesto General de la Nación* (1993), *Report from el Salvador*, 4, 35, October 4.

Ropp, S. (1992), "Explaining the Long-Term Maintenance of a Military Regime: Panama before the U.S. Invasion," *World Politics*, 44, 2, January.

Salomón, L. (1993), "*Fuerza policial y fuerzas militares in Honduras*," Typescript.

Stanley, W. (1991), *The Elite Politics of State Terrorism in El Salvador*, Doctoral Dissertation, Massachusetts Institute of Technology.

------ (1993), "Risking Failure: Neglect of the Promising New Civilian Police in El Salvador," Washington, D.C., and Cambridge, MA: Washington Office on Latin America and Hemisphere Initiatives, Fall.

Stepan, A. (1988), *Rethinking Military Politics*, Princeton, N.J.: Princeton University Press.

Tilly, C. (1984), "War Making and State Making as Organized Crime," in P.B. Evans, D. Rueschemayer, and T. Skocpol (eds.), *Bringing the State Back In*, Cambridge: Cambridge University Press, 169-191.

Ugarte, J. (1990), *Seguridad Interior*, Buenos Aires: *Fundación Arturo Illia*.

United Nations (1992), *Acuerdos de El Salvador: en el Camino de la Paz*, United Nations Document Number DPI/208-92615. New York: Department of Public Information, United Nations, June.

------- (1993a), "Report of the Director of the Human Rights Division of the United Nations Observer Mission in El Salvador up to 31 January 1993," U.N. Document A/47/912 and S/25521, New York: 5 April.

------ (1993b), "Report of the Secretary-General on the United Nations Observer Mission in El Salvador," U.N. Documents S/25812 and S/23999, New York: 26 May.

------ (1993c), "Further Report to the Secretary-General on the United Nations Observer Mission in El Salvador," United Nations Document S/26790, New York: 23 November.

------ (1994a), "Ninth Report of the Director of the Human Rights Division of the United Nations Observer Mission in El Salvador (ONUSAL), 1 August-31 October 1993," United Nations Document A/49/59 S/1994/47, New York: 18 January.

------ (1994b), "Report of the Secretary-General on the United Nations Observer Mission in El Salvador," U.N. Document S/1994/5-61, New York: 11 May.

------ (1994c), "*Calendario para la ecjecución de los acuerdos pendientes más importantes*," U.N. Document S/1994/612, New York: 24 May.

------ (1994d), "Report of the Secretary-General on the United Nations Observer Mission in El Salvador," U.N. Document S/1994/1-000, New York: 26 August.

Varas, A., J.Cancino and C. Fuentes (1993), "*Carabineros de Chile: la función policial y la seguridad ciudadana*," Typescript.

Vickers, G and J. Spence (1994), "Elections: The Right Consolidates Power," *NACLA Report on the Americas*, 28, 1, July/August.

Zagorski, P. (1992), *Democracy vs. National Security: Civil Military Relations in Latin America*, Boulder: Lynne Rienner.

# POLICING CHANGE IN THE GULF STATES:
# THE EFFECT OF THE GULF CONFLICT[1]

### Jeffrey Ian Ross

## INTRODUCTION

The Gulf States are what many comparativists call traditional societies and as such have a number of unique features (Lerner, 1964). Yet these countries experience the forces of modernization, including economic growth, increases in population, a rise in crime and educational attainment, technology, and the presence of foreigners. In fact, according to Norton (1993: 216), "the best opportunity to create a vibrant civil society may come in those states widely viewed as 'traditional' or 'backward.' In cases where the state has not erected elaborate mechanisms for control and intimidation, nor fostered an enormous bureaucracy or a big state elite, political development may follow different paths." The Gulf crisis and war of 1990, hereafter referred to as the Gulf Conflict, left in its wake the potential for major western style democratic reforms, many of which can affect policing.

Although a number of books (e.g., Graz, 1992) and articles (e.g., Khalidi, 1991) have examined, in whole or in part, the general impact of the Conflict, this chapter specifically explores how the municipal police in three dominant Gulf countries--namely, the former Republic of Yemen, Kuwait, and Saudi Arabia[2]--were affected by the Conflict.[3] In particular, it analyzes the change process itself and how the police responded to calls for reform. In order to achieve this objective, the chapter briefly reviews the legal structures, history, organization, challenges, and changes that have been implemented in the municipal police forces of the three countries before, during, and since the Conflict.

The analysis depends on a review of English language, academic and popular, open-source literature. A thorough library search was conducted. Organizations with a vested interest in the Gulf States, such as Amnesty International, Middle East Research Institute, and Middle East Watch were contacted. The project also benefitted from a series of interviews with individuals and experts currently living in North America who have some information or knowledge concerning the police or political processes in the three countries.[4]

To begin with, the forces for change in these countries did not start with the Gulf Conflict. For example, the movement for democratization can be traced back at least two-and-a-half decades (e.g., Ibrahim, 1993: 292). In general,

> there is growing evidence of widening dissatisfaction with the reigning regimes. Governments, strapped by limited resources, massive and unwieldy bureaucracies, and burgeoning demands of fast-growing populations, frequently are failing to meet the needs and demands of their citizens....[This coupled with] repression at the hands of the state....and [vocal] human rights activists,... [has placed these states into] a persistent crisis of legitimacy... The 1991 Persian Gulf War did not create or unleash the discontent and the disdain that widely characterizes observers' and citizens' perspectives on government, but the war certainly accelerated the crisis of legitimacy by highlighting the inefficacy and the weakness of many of the regimes (Norton, 1993: 205-206).

In order to understand this "acceleration," the demands for reform should be placed in context. Consequently, the author will briefly review the legal and policing structures in these countries.

## LITERATURE REVIEW

To understand the municipal police in the Gulf states, one needs to appreciate the legal systems that support them. In general, most of the legal systems of Arabic countries are built on the platform of Islamic law referred to as the *Shari'a*. *Shari'a* are Koranic edicts developed during the fourteenth century that permit and restrict particular forms of behavior. Constraints are derived from interpretations of this Islamic code handed down by *ulemas* (i.e., senior religious figures). The *Shari'a* makes a number of practices westerners take for granted as our inherent and fundamental civil and human rights (e.g., consumption of alcohol or the socialization of men and women who are not related by blood or marriage) illegal. Also "[i]n Islamic law no office of public prosecutions is known" (Schacht, 1964: 189). Regardless of the seriousness of the offence (e.g., physical injury or homicide), litigation before a Shari'a judge or court requires the initiation of an action by a private claimant (e.g., the victim or relatives of the victim).[5] If Islamic law is not used, depending on the local customs and jurisdictions, citizens may resort to tribal and customary law. In some countries, the legal system is a blend of these two influences, plus the colonial laws that were implemented before independence (e.g., British statutory law), and socialist/communist ones that are/were experimented with (e.g., Southern Yemen).

Although a substantial literature has accumulated on Islamic law, little attention has been devoted to enforcement, and even less to policing in the Gulf States. After a comprehensive bibliographic search of English language sources, this writer uncovered six English language doctoral dissertations, three masters' theses, and two academic articles. With respect to the dissertations, one addressed changes in the Riyadh police department during the 1980s (Rajehi, 1981), another examined the history of the police in Kuwait with special attention to inter- and intra-organizational conflict (Al-Fahed, 1989), two conducted surveys of attitudes towards the police in Kuwait (Salem Ali, 1991; Al-Enezi, 1991), and two reviewed education and training programs in the Kuwait police department (Qatash, 1988; Saud, 1987). All the Masters' theses focus on Saudi Arabia, including the results of a survey of attitudes towards the police in Riyadh (Rajehi, 1977), the effect of Islamic law on police administration (Batal, 1973), and the consequences of modernization on law enforcement education (Al-Shunaber, 1984). With respect to the two academic articles, one details the use of night and shiftwork among police in Kuwait (Attia et al., 1985), and another summarizes the organizational structure of the Saudi Arabian police (Alobied, 1987). Thus, this author depends on research that was somewhat tangential to the police but offered clues to the changes that the police forces are undergoing.

Even though the Gulf Conflict had an impact on many countries throughout the world, the Middle Eastern states, because of their proximity, were most affected. In this region, three countries, from least to most affected were the former Republic of Yemen, Saudi Arabia, and Kuwait.

## YEMEN

### *INTRODUCTION*
After a stormy civil war during the 1980s, the two Yemens, the communist People's Democratic Republic (PDR) in the south and the moderate Yemen Arab Republic (YAR) in the north, formally united as the Republic of Yemen on May 2, 1990. This unification was met with considerable optimism as well as pessimism. According to Norton (1993: 216),

> on the one hand, elements in civil society...have shown real vitality and assertiveness. On the other hand, the tribal organization of Yemeni society is so marked that for Yemen's democratic experiment to succeed, there will have to be considerable tribal support for the effort.

### *THE HISTORY OF THE YEMEN POLICE*
The history of Yemen has been marked by considerable instability (Amin, 1987). Northern Yemen achieved independence from the Ottoman Empire in 1918, while Southern Yemen attained independence from Great Britain in 1968. The first Yemeni police system was started by His Majesty The Imam Yahya during the First World War (1914-1918). Police forces, composed of recruits "chosen from the Army," were created in the large cities including San'a, the capital (Cramer, 1964: 436). In an attempt to professionalize the police, "the Government established special colleges for the training of policemen and sent students to Egyptian and other foreign colleges and schools to study the tasks and duties of police. When they returned they were entrusted with the training of their own" recruits (Cramer, 1964: 436).[6] In general, however, the current policing system "is one of the un-uniformed quasi-personal retainers called 'soldiers' ... [working for] governors, district officers, and the judges" (Messick, 1983: 512).

Regardless, generalizations about police and organizational change in Yemen are difficult to make because of the differing roles of the urban and rural police officers and the existence of separate states before the short lived reunification experiment. Nevertheless, some broad statements can be made. First, police are more powerful in the cities than they are in the countryside. In the latter, the central government does not have as much control over affairs as do tribal chieftains "whose power in some provinces rivals that of the central government." Additionally, "Yemen enjoys a sense of frontier justice in which guns are the great equalizer" (Hundley, 1992: F8). Hence, in these contexts, sophisticated arms are readily available and loosely regulated.

Before unification, in North Yemen "public security was carried out by three organizations: the police, the tribes, and the Central Security Forces (CSF)."[7] The region

> remained essentially tribal,... and the central government, lacking the resources to assume close and direct police control of the tribal areas, had no alternative but to place the responsibility for internal order and security on the tribes themselves. Traditionally, the police were not welcome in the tribal region of the north (Krieger, et al. 1985a: 211).[8]

The police were a "national organization also directly under the Ministry of Interior. Control was centralized at the national level with provision for dual operational control and administration at the governmental level" (Krieger et al., 1985a: 211).

In order to become a police officer, applicants needed to be literate. "Officers and senior enlisted personnel were sent to police schools in Saudi Arabia, Kuwait, and Egypt. The police academy for officers, located in Sana, and other training units for enlisted personnel in the capital and in Hodeida and Taizz have gradually been strengthened and improved. The advice of police officials in Egypt, Britain, and Jordan [was] sought and followed in an effort to develop a more professional police force....With the exception of those who are in charge of traffic or social services," the North Yemenis saw police as a simple extension of the security forces "that in turn were linked with the military. In the mid-1980s, the government attempted to improve the image of the police. For example, they had been given the tasks of responding to medical emergencies and providing other social services" (Krieger et al. 1985a: 212). The most recent statistics available (1976) indicated that "police strength was 13,000, a figure that included not only uniformed police but also non-uniformed civilians in the Ministry of Interior." Police costs accounted for "approximately 16 percent of government expenditures for that year" (Krieger et al. 1985a: 211).

If information about policing in North Yemen is sparse, the situation is worse for the former South Yemen. Part of the reason for this is that until unification the South was Communist controlled, considered by "various human rights reports" to be one of "the worst police states in the Arab world," and "details of organization and operation of the Public Security Force (police) were not publicly available" (Krieger et al. 1985b: 317). What is known, however, is that "after the Marxist takeover of the country, all traces of British influence were purged from this force, and a new Public Security Force was set up in its place....As in other Communist countries, all police agencies are under the firm control of the National Front" (Kurian, 1989: 478). The police "cooperated closely with... the army, and with local tribal forces" (Krieger et al. 1985a: 211) and "were reorganized in the 1970s with East German assistance" and, consequently, reflect the advisors' "operational patterns and philosophy" (Kurian, 1989: 478). "The main police force [was] the paramilitary Public Security Force, with an estimated personnel strength of 15,000.... A separately administered Revolutionary Security Organization,... [was] in charge of intelligence gathering and the suppression of political offenders" (Andrade, 1985: 235).

In 1985, the Ministry of State Security "was one of three divisions of the security force, the other two being the Armed (or Civil) Police and the Rural Police. The total strength of the force was not known but was believed to rival that of the militia or the army." Furthermore, these forces were supplemented by the Popular Defense Committees. Approximately "one-quarter of its population" apparently perform "some kind of security work" (Krieger et al., 1985b: 317).

On May 2, 1990, after protracted negotiations, North and South Yemen finally reunited. The country "inherited two ruling parties that shared power in a delicate, often tense balance during the transitional period, each retaining control of its former military and security apparatuses" (Carapico, 1993a: 3).

## THE EFFECT OF THE GULF CONFLICT

Since unification and the Conflict, a number of challenges arose for the Yemeni municipal police, who responded in different ways. In general, these exigencies can be placed into six categories: the process of unifying the police forces of the formally separate countries, repatriating guest workers, dealing with increasing corruption, protests, internal security threats, and a supposed decrease in the power of the national security police.

To begin with, government organizations, such as the municipal police, had to be integrated. In general, most bureaucracies did not accomplish this task very well (Halliday, 1992: 26). The Ministry of Internal Security, which oversaw policing functions throughout the country, was overstaffed and there was duplication of efforts by employees. In addition, there were considerable differences in the philosophy and education of police officers and bureaucrats and in the enforcement of laws. The northern and southern police had different organizational cultures, stemming from their respective previously held ideological positions, which needed to be accommodated. Units maintained their old uniforms for a considerable length of time. Southern police officers, for example, vigorously enforced traffic laws, while the northerners seemed more relaxed. The Minister of Internal Security was a northerner and his subordinates at different levels were from the north and south. Moreover, there was great distrust of senior level-people in the bureaucracy who were former communists from the south.[9]

Two months after unification, Yemen successfully angered Saudi Arabia "by sympathizing with Iraq during" the Gulf Conflict (Hundley, 1992: F8). In October 1990, the Saudis expelled hundreds of thousands of Yemenis (*The New York Times*, October 30, 1990, p. A1). Additionally, "some 2,000 Yemenis were forced to leave Qatar, Bahrain, and the United Arab Emirates" (Stevenson, 1993: 15).[10] This situation worsened the already fragile Republic. For example, within a couple of months, there was a substantial growth in the resident population, thereby increasing the citizen-to-police ratio. This situation meant greater demands on the already limited police resources.

The repatriation of the guest workers also increased inflation "to record levels" as many "brought with them their savings or money received as a result of hurriedly selling their businesses in Saudi

Arabia" (Sultan, 1993: 390). Although many of them returned to the villages where they came from with considerable cash, others came back with vehicles which they quickly converted into taxicabs and became taxi drivers, particularly in San'a. This increased the already congested traffic problems for police. Inflation also led to an increase in corruption amongst poorly paid civil servants, including the police.

Moreover, primarily generated by economic problems such as inflation, unemployment, and increasing poverty,[11] demonstrations erupted throughout the country. Starting in October 1991, middle-class individuals protested in San'a. In mid-December 1992, thousands reportedly looted and burnt buildings in Ta'izz. The riots spread to San'a, where they lasted four days. In the latter episode, "[m]ore than 60 people were killed, hundreds injured, and thousands arrested. The government reportedly brought 8,000 armed tribesmen into the capital to maintain power" (Stevenson, 1993: 18). Later, from November 15 to January 1993, there were a series of protests and riots by public sector workers, soldiers, and noncommissioned officers. As before, many of the protesters were injured, and some were killed. In one riot, which took place December 10 in San'a, "the police fired on the crowd," and "four casualties were reported." In another, on the following day, "the police arrested 250 protesters on charges of fomenting riots" (*Middle East Journal*, Vol. X: 334). This last police use of force situation, it is argued, was prompted by lack of sufficient manpower.

Occasionally, bombs exploded throughout the country. It is speculated that people close to the leadership were responsible for or at least complicitous in those actions (Halliday, 1992: 26). Additionally, "[m]ounting incidents of violence, especially against leading figures of the Yemeni Socialist Party, one of the partners in the ruling alliance," occurred (Ibrahim, 1993: 297). Moreover, Yemen has an overabundance of arms, "many coming in on boats on the short sea journey from Somalia, Ethiopia, and Eritrea," leading to an increase in violence, lawlessness, fear, and perceptions of instability amongst the population and police. Consequently, there is an increase of armed guards surrounding politicians, protecting government offices, and present on the streets (Halliday, 1992: 26). In sum, many Yemenis believe that the police are incapable of deterring or controlling crimes.

Furthermore, "the grip of the *mukhabarat* [security police] has loosened." Intellectuals in San'a, of most ideological persuasions, reported an end to internal spying and harassment. The country improved its poor "human rights performance, freed scores of political prisoners and shrunk [its] once-pervasive state security apparatus" (Hundley, 1992: F8). Nevertheless, there was a feeling that the country needed "a governmental body to monitor human rights conditions" (Hudson, 1991: 421). The decrease in *mukhabarat* activities created a gap that needed to be filled by the local police. However, the police had to be vigilant that their members did not violate human rights as their predecessors once did.

Finally, there is considerable ethnic diversity that might lead to civil disturbances which the police will have to monitor. For example, "the population of North Yemen has often been considered a source of political weakness or potential divisiveness [because]... although nearly 100 per cent Muslim, [it] is divided into different Sunni and Shi'a sects, between which there exists a certain amount of competition, friction, and differential access to the levers of power and influence" (Werner, 1993: 173-174). In the North, "the Zaydi Shi'as, although probably a minority of the total, have determined the political as well as the socio-cultural patterns of the state since the ninth century AD. In the southern areas of North Yemen, as well as in all of South Yemen, the Sunni Shafi'is are the majority. Hence, in the new state, they are now an uncontested overall majority" (Werner, 1993: 174). The police also struggled with the representation of different ethnic and religious groups in their ranks in order to create and maintain legitimacy with some sectors of the population.

## SUMMARY

For all intents and purposes, the Republic of Yemen was quite unstable, and it came as no surprise that in May 1994 the delicate peace that had been forged completely broke down and the civil war resumed when the north invaded the south. One indication of the effect of the instability in Yemen was the postponement of the scheduled elections from November 1992 to the spring of 1993. After the unification, "the regime...announced its intention to introduce a multiparty system in a full-fledged democracy. An interim period not exceeding 30 months was to culminate in parliamentary elections" (Ibrahim, 1993: 297). Thus, the police until the election in 1993, were without stable leadership. The eventual breakup could have been predicted. Indeed, the whole unification process motivated one expert to suggest that "the

possibilities for derailment [of the unification process] are so numerous
that some analysts are still amazed that the recent steps could have been
taken" (Hudson, 1991: 424).

# KUWAIT

## *INTRODUCTION*
It is difficult to trace the beginning of Kuwaiti history.  It was
once under the control of the Ottoman Empire; in 1899 it became a
British protectorate, and in 1961 it achieved independence. The unique
structure and organizational culture of many of Kuwait's public
institutions are the result of this colonial, historical legacy.

## *HISTORY OF THE KUWAITI POLICE*
Until 1938, various small security-related forces, including a
night guard, the king's palace bodyguard, and tribal armies, had
policing functions (Crystal, 1990: 59). During the 1930s, as a result of
the *Majlis* ("Committee of Counsellors") Movement and the influx of
foreign workers due to the oil boom, the modern police of Kuwait took
shape. Consequently, "the government began to draw more formal
distinctions between internal and external security" motivating "the
ruler to take internal security more seriously" by establishing the Police
Department and the Public Security Department, the former
"responsible for policing the capital (Kuwait)" and the latter, charged
with policing "the country districts and national borders" (Al-Fahed,
1989: 127). The Police Department was created in 1938 by splitting the
Sheik's Guards into the Kuwait Police Force  and the Kuwait Army
(Cramer, 1964: 342; Andrade, 1985: 117; Al-Fahed, 1989: Chapter 3).
The police force at that time was under the command of the Sheiks,
consisted of only twelve men, and "was established to guard the peace
and fight crime" (Cramer, 1964: 342). In that same year, a police
training center was established and new technologies were introduced
into the forces. After 1938, "the security needs of the oil companies
accelerated" the growth of police forces (Crystal, 1990: 59). Despite
this progress, police were generally unprofessional as most of them
received their positions not because they had any special skills or
training, but because they were relatives of the ruling family (Crystal,
1990: 60).

In general, the police served their masters. "They were one part political police and one part the protectors of privilege and patronage" (Crystal, 1990: 93). Because of the country's colonial connections, the British pressured the Kuwaitis to make changes in their public institutions. During the 1950s, in an effort to achieve these objectives, many of the higher ranking police officers and administrators studied policing in England. Largely as a result of the British, the Kuwait Police Force "emerged into a small national armed force in the mid-1950's. A 600 man constabulary existed in 1954 and was expanded with the aid of British training and equipment until it reached a capacity of 2,500 men" (Al-Fahed, 1989: 89). In 1958, the two police forces were combined to form the present General Department of Police (Al-Fahed, 1989: 127). "The Force is financed by the Central Government and is under the control of the Minister of the Interior" (Cramer, 1964: 343).

Massive oil revenues and a desire to stave off discontent resulted in an increase in the number of individuals working for the Kuwaiti public bureaucracy. This situation continued during the 1960s to such an extent that a British doctor living in Kuwait commented that "jobs are invented for overstaffed... municipal policemen... and the town is liberally sprinkled with such individuals who really do nothing but walk around in their uniforms and lean against the buildings" (Klien, 1963: 766-767).

Generally, the Kuwaiti police are responsible for "patrol and crime investigation" (Becker and Becker, 1986: 291). In the 1970s, the police were kept active dispersing and arresting crowds of Islamic fundamentalists, particularly those who protested in front of the U.S. Embassy (Crystal, 1990: 102). They also became increasingly involved in intelligence collection and counterinsurgency as a result of a number of actual and potential oppositional political crimes which occurred or were launched in Kuwait (Becker and Becker, 1986: 291). Towards the end of the 1970s, "the government reorganized the internal police force as a result of its new security concerns. Twenty-six high ranking police officers went into early retirement in...1979, and the regime gradually demoted or eliminated the Shiites from sensitive security and military positions. Henceforth, the upper echelon of the security forces was to be composed entirely of reliable loyalist elements" (Assiri, 1990: 68).

As a result of "security concerns, excessive division, and the need for unity in the face of the Iran-Iraq war," the Kuwaiti National Assembly (their parliament) was closed in July 1986 (Crystal, 1990:

105). The government changed its focus "from representation to repression; it began relying more heavily on the police and the military, which had been increasing their coercive capacities over the last few decades" (Crystal, 1990: 106).

## THE EFFECT OF THE GULF CONFLICT

During the Conflict, many police either fled, joined the resistance, were recruited by the invading Iraqi forces, or were tortured or killed. After the Conflict, Kuwaiti police, among other organizations (i.e., military, vigilantes, etc.), carried out a series of illegal searches, lootings, arbitrary arrests, detentions, rapes, tortures, summary executions, and murders of foreigners, particularly Palestinians, who actually had or were suspected of collaborating with the Iraqis (Lawyers Committee for Human Rights, 1992; Middle East Watch, 1991; Warren, 1991). It has been reported that "up to 400 young Palestinians were kidnapped from their homes or off the streets in the first three days of liberation. A U.S. official also estimated that 200-600 disappeared in the first two weeks..." (Lesch, 1991:47-48). Moreover, shortly after the liberation, "more than 100 Filipino women, Sri Lankans and other foreigners have reported being raped or badly beaten in Kuwait city by Kuwaiti soldiers, police and citizens of the emirate" (Kelly, 1991).

According to Middle East Watch (1991: 1-2),

> although the Kuwaiti government has attempted to blame individuals beyond its control for these killings, most were committed by official security forces or by irregular armed groups working closely with official forces, including many returning exiles intent on revenge.... The most notorious source of abuse has been the State Security Secret Police...which reportedly recruited hundreds of youths, often of unscrupulous bent, who were granted wide discretion to arrest, beat and hold prisoners incommunicado for long periods.

Additionally, the government is screening *bidun*--an Arabic word meaning "without officiality," or foreigners--and expelling those that they believe are security threats. In particular, "almost 400,000

Palestinians who worked in the emirate before the invasion" were [expelled]... The move was in reprisal for PLO chairman Yasser Arafat's... support of Saddam Hussein [and because] a small minority of Palestinians in Kuwait collaborated with the Iraqi invaders" (Hepburn, 1991: H2). In addition to Palestinians, "tens of thousands of Egyptians and Syrians [were]...expelled (the diplomatic term is their work visas are not renewed)" (Hepburn, 1991: H2). It is highly likely that the municipal police were involved in the expulsion process.

After the Conflict, there was an abundance of arms in the country. The government placed an amnesty on their return, then made possession punishable by fine and imprisonment. The police were responsible for collecting the weapons (*Law and Order*, 1991a; 1992). Also ironic in post-war Kuwait is the fact that apparently more people were being killed as a result of traffic fatalities then by the invading Iraqis. This state of affairs is attributed to the fact that many of the traffic lights and signs were destroyed or torn down and the number of traffic police officers was limited (*Law and Order*, 1991b).

Even though the government gave assurances that the civil liberties of the *bidun* and suspected collaborators would be protected, according to the Lawyers Committee for Human Rights (1992: 13), the Kuwaiti government did not immediately uphold this commitment. However, in May 26, 1991,

> the Crown Prince (who was also the Martial Law governor) delivered a stern rebuke in a meeting with senior officials of the Interior Ministry. He emphasized that even if sons of the ruling family or high officials were implicated, they must be arrested, because 'nobody is above the law'.... While all the prison guards and officers in police stations were immediately aware of the speech, the short-term impact on their behavior was questionable.... Nonetheless, a shake-up in the upper echelons of the Interior Ministry took place in early June, which appeared to indicate an effort to discipline the vindictive impulse of the soldiers who serve as police and prison guards (Lesch, 1991: 50).

Complicating matters is the fact that "at least a third of Kuwait's soldiers and police officers are *bidun*." This means that the size of the police forces decreased, placing additional manpower strains on the remaining officers. Currently, "Kuwait police are rebuilding with the help of the US Army." Part of this process involves the recruitment of Kuwaitis (Greene, 1991: A, 5).

*SUMMARY*

Since the liberation of the country, in February 1991, there have been repeated calls for liberalization and democratization (Ibrahim, 1993: 229; Tétreault, 1993: 276-277). Consequently, "parliamentary life was resumed with a heated and spirited campaign during the summer and fall of 1992. In October of that year, elections were held with few or no complaints about irregularities. Several new faces won seats in the National Assembly, where the opposition forces won a clear majority and Sunni and Shi'i Islamist forces won at least one-third of the 50 seats" (Ibrahim, 1993: 299). While the movements for liberalization and democratization are bound to have an effect on the way policing is conducted, their effects, at present time, are unknown.

## SAUDI ARABIA

*INTRODUCTION*

Saudi Arabia is a "traditional personal authoritarian regime... where the ruler seeks to maintain a balance of power between two paramilitary units and the national military establishment in order to strengthen his regime" (Janowitz, 1977: 30). Policing in Saudi Arabia has developed within this context.

*HISTORY OF THE SAUDI POLICE*

The earliest recognized police force was established by Abdul al-Aziz Ibn Saud who in 1927 consolidated the Saudi state (Lipsky, 1959: 124). Even though the police operate both in the municipalities and frontier, in the latter tribal solutions to moral/legal violations still prevail giving "regional emirs... considerable autonomy in matters pertaining to public security. In addition to supervisory authority over the police of local emirates, regional emirs have command over their own personal guards, which supplement the regular police as needed"

(Lipsky, 1959: 124-125). Thus, the Saudi police system "has remained partly entrenched in the tribal social order under which the sheiks remain the primary guarantors of public order within their bailiwicks. Only when local efforts fail is the National Guard brought in. In this sense, the law enforcement agencies complement but do not intrude on tribal authority" (Kurian, 1989: 328).

Since the oil boom began, "a civil police system gradually has been put in place that, on occasion, can create some semblance of order out of chaos. Always cognizant of the divisiveness within its kingdom, the House of Saud from the beginning centralized control of the police. Consequently, municipalities neither hire nor command their own police forces. Every policeman who patrols the street works directly for and is answerable to the Ministry of the Interior Security Forces" (Mackey, 1987: 278).

The number of Saudi police had increased so much that in 1937 there were 33 police officers in the ranks of 2nd lieutenant and higher. By 1980, this rank was occupied by 3,800 individuals (Rajehi, 1981: 141, 147). In 1960, because the police were beginning to play a larger role in the country, the government created a Police College at Mecca and later one in Riyadh (Kurian, 1989: 328; Rajehi, 1981: 147). All that is needed for entrance is "a secondary-school certificate. Training is provided at the college in the use of sophisticated equipment such as radar and helicopters" (Kurian, 1989: 328). Nevertheless, police officers "are recruited mainly from nomadic tribes" (Lipsky, 1959: 125). Teachers "at the Saudi police school have often been Egyptian police officers and many policemen have been trained in Egypt" (Lipsky, 1959: 125).

The police force is now called the Department of Public Security and is accountable to the Ministry of the Interior (Andrade, 1985: 173). Despite the changes and modernization of the police force, there has been considerable continuity in the organization of the police. "The mechanisms now in force in Saudi Arabia for maintaining order remain essentially those devised by Ibn Saud. The present king, Saud, while retaining many features of his father's system, has, however, relied increasingly on police organized along modern lines and on military forces equipped with modern arms and transport" (Lipsky, 1959: 124).

In times of actual and potential internal disorder (e.g., the *Hajj*), the police are often assisted by other paramilitary and military forces. For instance, during the 1953 and 1956 strikes and demonstrations of ARAMCO employees, the personal guards of the emirs were used to restore order. Army units "regularly patrol port areas and usually assist the police and the White Army in the control of crowds during Ramadan and pilgrimage seasons" (Lipsky, 1959: 124-125).

The methods of the Saudi police seem cruel and unfair when compared with Western standards. The forces have routinely been accused of abusing the human rights of citizens and visitors and engaging in excessive force. Periodically, the police make arbitrary arrests, detain suspects without trial, punish dissenters, torture suspects, and break up public protests (Mackey, 1987; Ceasar, 1990; 1992). "The whole law enforcement system terrifies Westerners, who constantly live with the possibility of landing in jail. An expatriate faces the threat of jail for anything from driving without a license to the possession of alcohol" (Mackey, 1987: 278). What makes the situation worse is that "friends or relatives often use police ... to settle personal disagreements, especially with Westerners...." In late 1983, this problem "finally led the government to issue a set of detention laws that would apply to Saudis and foreigners alike" (Mackey, 1987: 279). The new rules

> forbid arrest or detention of any one unless there is ample evidence calling for his arrest and stipulates that investigation should be completed within three days of detention.... This procedure gives the governor authority to dispense quickly with cases of wayward expatriates, primarily Westerners, thus saving the government the embarrassment of formal protests about unjust detentions from foreign governments. Although they do not always work very well, the statutes are at least an attempt to get those accused out of jail, where they often languish for weeks without charges, and into other courts (Mackey, 1987: 279-280).

Police use of excessive violence can be traced back to 1956, in the aforementioned strike. Instead of negotiating with strikers, ARAMCO appealed to the Saudi government for help. Saudi police forces responded by attacking the strikers and torturing and executing the strike leaders (Abir, 1988). Striking workers have not been the only victims of Saudi police abuse. In 1984, for instance, American businessman Scott J. Nelson claimed that he was beaten, tortured and unlawfully imprisoned by Saudi police for 39 days (*The New York Times*, March 24, 1993: 19).

Besides the government-run civil police, approximately 50,000 zealous and fanatical *Mutawa*--missionaries or religious police--enforce the *Shari'a* laws (Al-Yassini, 1985; Mackey, 1987). Formally known as the Committee for the Protection of Virtue and Prevention of Vice, they "are drawn from older salaried men and young fanatical volunteers whom the Government wants to monitor" (Miller, 1991: 30). In general, the majority are older, self-appointed, uneducated, ignorant, often poor (Mackey, 1987: 70). A number of recent recruits, however, are "foreign-educated younger men, perhaps disillusioned with what they see as the decadence of the West, [who] return to Saudi Arabia to join the ranks" (Mackey, 1987: 69).

The *Mutawa* patrol the country's streets, bazaars, and shopping malls, which are increasingly being "invaded" by symbols of American "consumerism and decadence" like Kentucky Fried Chicken, Baskin Robbins, and Pizza Hut. They ensure that women dress according to modest Islamic tradition, do not drive cars, and are not approached by men in public; restrict mingling between the sexes; and ensure businesses close for prayer hours (LeMoyne, 1990; Mackey, 1987: 68-71). In addition, they "keep foreign books and magazines they find objectionable out of the kingdom. Offensive advertising is controlled by a legion of manual laborers armed with ink pots and brushes, who leaf through imported magazines, painting out pictures of women and ads for alcohol" (Mackey, 1987: 70).

The *Moutawin* (interchangeably spelled *Matawain, Mutawin,* or *Mutawin*), the plural of *Mutawa*, have become

> a group of vigilantes with an increasingly sophisticated bureaucracy. The government has little control over its membership or its actions. A *Matawa* is not appointed but rather rises up, by virtue of his piety, through the ranks of the local mosque. [It is] a genuine grass-roots organization and an important component of the backbone of the House of Saud's political support--the religious fundamentalists.

Therefore, it has tremendous power. Although mostly free of political control by the House of Saud, the religious organization is largely dependent on government financing since the practice of Wahhabism does not include contributions to the local mosque (Mackey, 1987: 69).

In sum, "in the face of the onslaught of wealth, materialism, foreign influences, and the ever-escalating press of change, the *matawain* stand in defense of a way of life. They are there to enforce the rules that have measured life in Saudi Arabia since Mohammed" (Mackey, 1987: 72).

Furthermore,

the mutawain patrol the public morals and the police enforce civil law. But [in Saudi Arabia] since all law is ultimately religious, there is a constant overlapping of jurisdictions. And in any jurisdictional conflict with the matawain, the civil police are rendered powerless. No one in the political sphere is willing to back its own police in a confrontation with the religious authorities. Therefore, the religious police dominate unless the parties involved have sufficient political power to appeal the matter to a higher authority. This sets in motion the consensus process, which can reach the highest level of government and which, at some point, may or may not settle the matter (Mackey, 1987: 276).

Immediately before the Gulf Conflict, Islamic fundamentalists, "were criticizing the puritanical leadership of the Government appointed religious hierarchy as insufficiently pious. In sermons from mosques and in cassette-recorded homilies, these extremists attacked the Government as corrupt in a way that no other force dared do" (Miller, 1991: 31). Criticism of this sort increased during the Conflict, after the foreign troops, particularly the Americans, established bases in Saudi Arabia.

## THE EFFECT OF THE GULF CONFLICT

In 1990, shortly after Iraq invaded Kuwait, close to 200,000 U.S. troops arrived in Saudi Arabia. The *Mutawa*, feeling spiritually threatened, "launched an intensive drive against such affronts to Islam as alcohol, home videos, rock music, dancing and female drivers." One of the more dramatic cases involved "gun and club toting mutawin storm[ing] private homes and arrest[ing] dozens of prominent Saudis and foreigners on charges of drinking alcohol and chatting casually with members of the opposite sex." This response was "highly unusual--and shocking even to some fairly conservative Saudis--that the religious police would break into private homes, considered to be sacrosanct by Arab custom, and brandish weapons in the faces of terrified citizens and foreigners" (Nickerson, 1991: D4). Almost as a reaction to this heightened fundamentalism, "King Fahd... named a new head of the mutawin and gave him cabinet rank reflecting the force's enhanced stature..." (Perrin, 1990: A12).

During the Conflict, there was also "widespread internal unrest and criticism of the Saudi legal system" (Tarazi, 1993: 260). On November 6, 1990, the now famous drive-in by 50 Saudi women took place. These sentiments inspired two important "reformist" petitions being presented to King Fahd: one "religious" and the other "secular." In order to diffuse the situation, the King needed to "draft a Basic Law that balanced the interests of both movements. In other words, he would have to create a basic law which would expand and guarantee fundamental rights under the precepts of Islam" (Tarazi, 1993: 263).

On March 1, 1992, Saudi Arabia issued two new major laws: the Basic Law of Government and the Consultative Council Law. These "supplemented... the 1958 Regulation of the Council of Ministers," and "represent the first extensive written constitutional system." The Basic Law included measures which insured "civil and human rights in the context of pre-trial arrest and detention." Nevertheless, these laws are "subordinate" to the *Shari'a*, which is the official constitution of Saudi Arabia (Tarazi, 1993: 258). Moreover, according to Middle East Watch, the law governing arrest and detention gives inadequate protection to detainees, who may only obtain counsel at the discretion of the Ministry of the Interior...." (Tarazi, 1993: 269). In the long run, the supposed changes in the laws probably will not have a major effect on how police conduct their affairs.

After the Gulf Conflict, the demands for change increased. "Amongst the most argued topics are the creation of a larger, professional army, an expanded role for women, more democracy, press freedom and an international security to protect gulf oilfields" (LeMoyne, 1990: A, 17). The ruling Saud family has, with American support,

> proved able to weather radical demands over several decades...the Saudi monarchy is one of the most resilient and conservative governing institutions in the modern world, choosing the pace to permit innovation by pragmatically wielding the oil wealth needed to buy reality at home and acceptance abroad. Among the luxuries that almost unimaginable oil wealth and geographic isolation have permitted this Arab kingdom, perhaps the most striking has been the effort to resist unwanted social innovation (LeMoyne, 1990: A, 17).

### *SUMMARY*

Despite this apparent liberalization, Saudi police are still complicitous in violating international human rights standards. For example, in September 1992, "authorities beheaded 23-year old Sadiq Abd al-Karim Malallah after he was found guilty of insulting Muhammad and the Quran" (*Middle East Journal*, Vol. 47, No. 1, Winter, 1993: 109). Additionally, in May 1993 police raided a "university campus in Riyadh" and arrested Mohammed Mas'ari, a professor and the spokesman of the "Committee for the Defense of Legitimate Rights," a banned human rights group which "has expressed a desire to meet with the country's liberal factions to find common ground on human rights and democracy issues" (Evans, 1993: 8).

### CONCLUSION

In sum, there have been numerous responses to the Gulf Conflict in each of the countries reviewed. The Conflict challenged the devout, puritanical, and conservative elements of societies in Yemen, Kuwait, and Saudi Arabia. Iraq's invasion of Kuwait on August 2, 1990 increased each country's instability and served as a catalyst for change. So long as municipal police have the greatest contact with citizens among any arm of government, they must also respond to these changes.

This overview is a starting point. Due to problems with access to sources, many of the changes which have taken place with police forces in these countries can only be inferred. More in-depth and resource intensive analysis might be achieved by consulting Arabic language sources, interviewing those individuals working for or having some connection with the police of each country, and conducting field research. Until then, we must rely on open source academic and popular materials and make cautious conclusions keeping in mind their inherent contributions and shortcomings.

## NOTES

1. An earlier version of this chapter was presented at the Annual Meeting of the American Society of Criminology, Phoenix, Arizona, October 30, 1993. Special thanks to Nawal Ammar, Paul Bond, Charles Dunbar, Gregory Gause, Sam Matheson, and others whose positions and organizations may be compromised by citing them for research assistance. Additional appreciation for comments is extended to Paul Bond, Otwin Marenin and Natasha J. Cabrera.

Points of view are those of the author and do not necessarily represent the view of the U.S. Department of Justice or the National Institute of Justice.

2. All future references to the Republic of Yemen will use the much shorter Yemen, unless the author is referring to the preunification states.

3. These countries were selected because it is argued that they experienced the greatest changes as a result of the Gulf Conflict.

4. In this respect, the author subscribes to Simon's (1991: 305-310) travel theorem. Nevertheless, should funding be obtained, field research in the respective states will be conducted.

5. For a more detailed examination of Shari'a law see, for example, Amin (1987); Anderson (1959); El-Awa (1982); Moore (1987); Rahmatian (1993); Schacht (1964); Souryal (1988).

6. This interpretation is echoed by Andrade (1985: 234).

7. "The CSF were under the Ministry of the Interior. They were separate from the police and operated under an open mandate to search homes, monitor telephone conversations, read personal correspondence, or otherwise intrude into the private lives when they believed that the security of the state was jeopardized.... According to the United States Department of State's *Country Reports on Human Rights Practices for 1984*, there had been credible reports that the CSF occasionally resorted to secret arrests and clandestine detention. There was no indication that the CSF had been guilty of political killings in 1984" (Krieger et al. 1985a: 211).

8. This perception is echoed by Kurian (1989: 477).

9. Based on an interview with Charles Dunbar, former U.S. Ambassador to Yemen from July 1988-May 1991, conducted on October 20, 1994.

10. Over the past two decades, the majority of Yemeni migrants emigrated "to neighboring oil states. With up to 30 percent of adult men abroad at a time, migration affected virtually every household. The earnings of roughly 1.25 million expatriates, coupled with heavy foreign assistance, fuelled the region's socioeconomic transformation" (Stevenson, 1993: 15).

11. The country had a number of economic problems beyond the incorporation of the returning guest workers which led to discontent. Some of these challenges included "few goods which could be offered in the international arena for foreign exchange; relative overpopulation; no real economic development or diversification; a relatively high percentage of the national budget devoted to military expenditure...and a rather high...budget support and development activities provided by other states" (Werner, 1993: 173).

# SOURCES

Abir, Mordechai (1988), *Saudi Arabia in the Oil Era*, Boulder, CO: Westview.

Al-Enezi, Mehar (1991), "The Effect of Occupational Socialization on Attitudes Related to Police Occupational Culture: A Case Study of the Cadets in the Police Academy of the State of Kuwait," Ph.D. Dissertation, Michigan State University.

Al-Fahed, Mohammed (1989), "An Historical Analysis of Police in Kuwait: Prospects for the Future," Ph.D. Dissertation, University of Exeter.

Alobied, Abdullah (1987), "Police Functions and Organization in Saudi Arabia," *Police Studies*, 10, 2, Summer, 80-84.

Al-Shunaber, Khalid Fahad (1984), "Toward the Modernization of Law Enforcement Education in Saudi Arabia," Master's Thesis, California State University, Chico.

Al-Yassini, Ayman (1985), *Religion and State in the Kingdom of Saudi Arabia*, Boulder: Westview.

Amin, S.H. (1987), *Law and Justice in Contemporary Yemen: People's Democratic Republic of Yemen and Yemen Arab Republic*, Glasgow: Royston Ltd.

Anderson, J.N.D. (1959), *Islamic Law in the Modern World*, New York: New York University Press.

Andrade, John (1985), *World Police and Paramilitary Forces*, New York: Stockton Press.

Assiri, Abdul-Reda (1990), *Kuwait's Foreign Policy*, Boulder: Westview Press.

Attia, M., M.K.Y. Mustafa, M. Khogali, N.A.Mahmoud, and E.I. Arar (1985), "Optimization of night and shiftwork plans among policemen in Kuwait: A field experiment," *International Archives of Occupational and Environmental Health*, 56, 81-90.

Batal, Abdullah M. (1973), "The Influence of Islamic Law on Police Administration in Saudi Arabia," Master's Thesis, Central Missouri State University.

Becker, Harold and Donna Lee Becker (1986), *Handbook of the World's Police*, Metuchen, N.J: The Scarecrow Press.

Carapico, Sheila (1993a), "Elections and Mass Politics in Yemen," *Middle East Report*, November-December, 2-7.

------ (1993b), "The Economic Dimension of Yemeni Unity,"
    *Middle East Report*, September-October, 9-14.

Ceasar, Judith (1990), "Rumblings Under the Throne," *The Nation*,
    251, 21, December 17, 762-764.

Ceasar, Judith (1992), "Foreigners and Demons," *The
    Progressive*, November, 56, 43.

Cramer, James (1964), *The World's Police*, London: Cassell.

Crystal, Jill (1990), *Oil and Politics in the Gulf: Rulers and Merchants
    in Kuwait and Quatar*, New York: Cambridge University
    Press.

El-Awa, Mohamed (1982), *Punishment in Islamic Law: a Comparative
    Study*, Indianapolis: American Trust Publications.

Evans, Kathy (1993), "Saudi Rights Group Seeks Dialogue with
    Opposition as Police Question Leaders," *The Guardian*, May
    17, 8.

Graz, Liesl (1992), *The Turbulent Gulf: People, Politics and Power*,
    New York: I.B.Tavris and Co., Ltd.

Greene, Marilyn (1991), "U.S. Soldiers Help Rebuild Police Force,"
    *USA Today*, March 12, A, 5.

Halliday, Fred (1992), "San'a Diary," *New Statesmen and
    Society*, October 16, 26.

Hepburn, Bob (1991), "A Bitter Legacy for Kuwait," *The Toronto
    Star*, July 28, H, 2.

Hudson, Michael C. (1991), "After the Gulf War: Prospects for
    Democratization in the Arab World," *Middle East Journal*,
    45, 3, Summer, 407-426.

Hundley, Tom (1992), "Yemen Set to Forge First Arab Democracy,"
    *The Toronto Star*, July 19, F, 8.

Ibrahim, Saad Eddin (1993), "Crisis, Elites, and Democratization in the
    Arab World," *Middle East Journal*, 47, 2, Spring, 292-306.

Janowitz, Morris (1977), *Military Institutions and Coercion in the
    Developing Nations*, Chicago: The University of Chicago
    Press.

Kelly, Jack (1991), "Kuwait Slow to Deal with Rapes," *USA Today*,
    July 29, A, 9.

Khalidi, Walid (1991), "The Gulf Crisis: Origins and Consequences,"
    *Journal of Palestine Studies*, 20, 2, Winter, 5-28.

Klien, Nathan (1963), "Psychiatry in Kuwait," *British Journal of
    Psychiatry*, 109, 766-774.

Krieger, Laurie et al. (1985a), "North Yemen," in Foreign Area Studies, *The Yemen Country Studies*, Washington, DC: The American University.

Krieger, Laurie et al. (1985b), "South Yemen," in Foreign Area Studies, *The Yemen Country Studies*, Washington, DC: The American University.

Kurian, George Thomas (1989), *World Encyclopedia of Police Forces and Penal Systems*, New York: Facts on File.

*Law and Order* (1991a), "Gun Amnesty Unsuccessful," October, 39, 10, 4.

*Law and Order* (1991b), "Traffic Offenses Big Problem," October, 39, 10, 4.

*Law and Order* (1992), "Hidden Arms Crackdown," September, 40, 9, 8.

Lawyers Committee for Human Rights (1992), *Kuwait: Building the Rule of Law: Human Rights in Kuwait After the Occupation*, New York: Lawyers Committee for Human Rights.

LeMoyne, James (1990), "Fuel for Saudi Debate Opening Society without Causing Strife," *The New York Times*, October 31, A, 17.

Lerner, Daniel (1964), *The Passing of Traditional Society: Modernizing the Middle East*, New York: Free Press.

Lesch, Ann M. (1991), "Palestinians in Kuwait," *Journal of Palestine Studies*, 20, 4, Summer, 42-54.

Lief, Louise (1991), "Kuwait's Other Cloud," *U.S. News and World Report*, 110, 12, April 1, 40-45.

Lipsky, George A. (1959), *Saudi Arabia: Its People Its Society Its Culture*, New Haven: Hraf Press.

Mackey, Sandra (1987), *The Saudis: Inside the Desert Kingdom*, New York: Meridian Book.

Messick, Brinkley (1983), "Prosecution in Yemen: The Introduction of the *Niyaba*," *International Journal of Middle Eastern Studies*, 15, 507-518.

*Middle East Journal* (1993), 47, 1, Winter, 109.

Middle East Watch (1991), *A Victory Turned Sour: Human Rights in Kuwait Since Liberation*, new york: middle east watch.

Miller, Judith (1991), "The Struggle Within," *The New York Times Magazine*, March 10, 46, 27-39.

Minnesota Lawyers International Human Rights Committee (1992), *Shame in the House of Saud: Contempt for Human Rights in the Kingdom of Saudi Arabia*, Minneapolis: Minnesota Lawyers International Human Rights Committee.

Moore, Richter H., Jr. (1987), "Courts, Law, Justice, and Criminal Trials in Saudi Arabia," *International Journal of Comparative and Applied Criminal Justice*, 11, 1, 61-67.

*The New York Times* (1993), March 24, 19.

Nickerson, Colin (1991), "Saudi's Religious Police in Frenzy over Foreigners," *The Toronto Star*, January 5, D, 4.

Norton, Augustus Richard (1993), "The Future of Civil Society in the Middle East," *Middle East Journal*, 47, 2, Spring, 205-216.

Perrin, Jean-Pierre (1990), "Troops Test Saudi Faith," *The Gazette*, December 20, A, 12.

Qatash, Soudan (1988), "Education, Training, Motivation Effect on Job Performance of the Police of the State of Kuwait," Ph.D. Dissertation, Rensselaer Polytechnic Institute.

Rahmatian, Ali Akbar (1993), "Issues of Law and Punishment in Islam Theory, Practice, Discussion," Ph.D. Dissertation, Florida State University.

Rajehi, Mohammad Owayedh R. (1977), "Saudi Arabian Students' Attitudes Toward Police: An Exploratory Study with Some Comparison of American Students' Attitudes Toward Police," Master's Thesis, Michigan State University.

Rajehi, Mohammad Owayedh R. (1981), "The Impact of Social Change on Police Development in Saudi Arabia: A Case Study of Riyadh Police Department," Ph.D. Dissertation, Michigan State University.

Salem Ali, Amir (1991), "The Role of Police in Society: A Survey of Attitudes Toward this Role Among Civilians and Police Patrol Officers in Kuwait," Ph.D. Dissertation, The American University.

Saud, Jawad Askar (1987), "Comparison of a Specially Designed Circuit Training Program with the Traditional Calisthenics Training Program on the Physical Fitness Levels of the Officer Candidates at the Kuwait Police Academy," Ph.D. Dissertation, Michigan State University.

Schacht, Joseph (1964), *Islamic Law*, London: University Press.

Sherry, Virginia N. (1990), "What the Democratic Forces Want," *The Nation*, November 5, 251, 509.

Simon, Herbert (1991), *Models of My Life*, New York: Basic Books.

Souryal, Sam S. (1988), "The Role of Shariah Law in Deterring Criminality in Saudi Arabia," *International Journal of Comparative and Applied Criminal Justice*, 12, 1, Spring, 1-25.

Stevenson, Thomas B. (1993), "Yemini Workers Come Home: Reabsorbing One Million Migrants," *Middle East Report*, March-April, 15-20.

Sultan, Nabil Ahmed (1993), "Bureaucratic Corruption as a Consequence of the Gulf Migration," *Crime, Law and Social Change*, 19, 4, June, 379-390.

Tarazi, Michael A. (1993), "Saudi Arabia's New Basic Laws: The Struggle for Participatory Islamic Government," *Harvard International Law Journal*, 34, 258-275.

Tétreault, Mary Ann (1993), "Civil Society in Kuwait: Protected Spaces and Women's Rights," *Middle East Journal*, 47, 2, Spring, 275-291.

Warren, Peter (1991), "Police Join in Kuwait Crime Wave," *The Guardian*, May 20, 8:3.

Werner, Manfred W. (1993), "National Integration and National Security: The Case of Yemen," in Bahgat Korany, Paul Noble, and Rex Bryan (eds.), *The Many Faces of National Security in the Arab World*, Houndsmills, Basingstoke: The Macmillan Press Ltd., 169-184.

# THE LEGITIMATIONS OF POLICING IN HONG KONG: A NON-DEMOCRATIC PERSPECTIVE

## Jon Vagg[1]

This paper makes three broad arguments about the nature of police legitimacy and the way in which it can change over time. First, "police legitimacy" should not be treated as a unitary concept. It comprises a number of distinct elements, of which the most important appear to be those of legitimating accounts presented by the state, the extent to which those accounts command public acceptance, and the level of "consent to policing" or "compliance with police" that occurs in practice. Second, compliance with or consent to policing may have little to do with those legitimating accounts or their credibility. But third, both legitimation practices, and compliance and consent, are likely to be affected by broader shifts in the nature of the state, particularly those shifts which highlight questions such as "whose law?" and "whose order?"

These three arguments are advanced using Hong Kong as a case study. Hong Kong, on the Pearl River delta in southern China, became a British colony in 1841 and will become a Special Administrative Region of China in 1997. The history of the territory between these two years can be broadly divided into three phases, each illustrating different patterns of police legitimacy and consent. It was, first, a colonial administration with limited and selective participation from expatriate and local Chinese individuals and organizations. The second phase, beginning after World War II, saw a progressive incorporation of community organizations and pressure groups into governmental processes. More recently, there have been limited moves towards representative democracy, despite warnings from China that such reforms will be defined as impediments to a smooth transfer of sovereignty. During the shifts from one phase to another--and,

admittedly, these shifts took place relatively slowly, over periods of
around 20 years--definitions of police legitimacy have been contested,
with varying results.

The next section of this paper addresses some of the
complexities masked by broad terms such as "legitimation" and
"consent." It is followed by a discussion of policing in Hong Kong,
which broadly follows the historical development of policing in the
territory and the issues of legitimation and consent which have surfaced
over time. The final part of the paper offers some observations which,
while based on the experience of a single colonial territory, may have
a more general application.

## LEGITIMATION AND CONSENT

Police legitimacy and "consent to policing" are distinct yet
related phenomena. In a narrow sense, police legitimacy simply implies
"that the police are granted some degree of monopoly within society by
those with the power to so authorize, be they an elite within the
society, an occupying power, or the community as a whole" (Mawby,
1990: 3). In a wider sense, however, a great deal flows from the issues
of who has the power to authorize that monopoly, what exactly it is a
monopoly over, whether the claim of legitimacy is accepted by the
population being policed, and that population's reaction to policing on
the ground.

In most countries worldwide, the power to establish the police
force and determine its powers lies with governments and is a matter
of law. Moreover, most governments, of all political persuasions,
allege that they are acting on behalf of a people and expressing its will.
The more critical issues are whether legitimating accounts are bolstered
by mechanisms which can show the "people's will" and whether they
have any relevance to the way policing is conducted and received on
the ground.

In Britain, for example, the legitimations of policing are based
upon the accountability of police forces to law, local police authorities,
and national government. The mechanics of these accountabilities,
admittedly very imperfect, in principle allow public opinion to
influence policing over the long term and in general, if not over
specific incidents. In addition there was, until the early 1980s at any
rate, a high level of cross-party support for the police and a general
belief among large segments of the population that the police were

fundamentally impartial and honest (Morgan, 1991).[2] In so far as anybody believed that legitimation mattered, governmental accounts of police legitimacy were accepted. And in practice, policing was conducted largely by consent, in the sense that the broad mass of the population believed that the police acted on behalf of society as a whole, co-operated and gave respect from to the police, and were usually disposed to believe police accounts of their actions unless clear evidence to the contrary emerged.

This brief example of British policing does, however, underline the need to consider legitimation in terms of three rather separate issues. First is the question of whether the constitutional, legal, and political arrangements for policing offer a credible account of the police role which is internally consistent, consistent with broader political principles on which the state is based, and shows the police to be ultimately within government control--that is, supervised and controlled by the courts and law, parliament, municipal authorities, watchdog bodies, or any combination of these. Second, there is the question of whether these legitimating accounts are in fact believed by any reasonably large segment of the public and, if so, whether such beliefs lead the public to co-operate with the police. Yet both these questions are ultimately less crucial than the third: is there in fact a level of uncoerced co-operation and popular consent or at least a lack of active dissent to the police mandate and the way it is implemented even in the absence of any legitimating accounts?

Answers to such questions can become rather complex. Policing encompasses a broad range of activities, from uniformed patrol and "community policing" to quasi-military anti-riot operations and from traffic control to the surveillance of political activists. These have to be evaluated separately. The problem of whether consent is simply hegemony--"consent to domination"--must also be addressed. Bearing in mind that totalitarian as well as democratic states have, on paper, extensive safeguards against police abuse of power, we need to consider when and how concepts such as the "rule of law" become convenient fictions rather than serious controls on police practices.

Changes over time in social and political structures can both require and produce changes in the legitimating accounts and the extent to which there is support for the police. One factor in this may have to do with the broader structure of the state and the presence or absence of a popular belief that the police--even if they act within the law--are enforcing laws in ways that support narrow sectional interests.

Moreover, it may well be that even in times of political turmoil and crisis, when constitutional legitimacy breaks down, the police are able to carry on their "bread and butter" work of catching petty offenders, directing traffic, dealing with minor administrative matters, and so on, because they can rely on continuing public support for such tasks. One can thus envisage a police force operating illegitimately in the narrow sense of the word but enjoying a popular legitimacy. In addition, it may be that certain illegitimate police activities are widely thought to be socially useful and to that extent legitimate. Small-scale corruption, for example, may be seen as a way of bridging the gap between laws and social needs.[3] If, on the other hand, there is a popular belief that police corruption is self-serving, it may be censured.

Even more importantly, behind the practicalities of "consent" there are questions about the motivations for consent or dissent. These are likely to depend on perceptions of whether the police have right on their side, irrespective of whether or not they are within the law. There are some situations where even very extreme illegal acts - extrajudicial killings, for example - may be supported by large sections of the public because they deal with pressing crime problems.[4]

Along with these theoretical issues, there is also a methodological problem. As Morgan comments (1991: 9), it is quite likely that most people do not think deeply about the legitimations of policing, and a public survey of attitudes may turn out to be little more than a survey of patriotic feelings. These general attitudes may be at variance with the kinds of concerns that emerge over specific incidents which come to acquire a wider symbolic significance. Data relating to police legitimacy are therefore rather slippery. We often do not know what people's attitudes are; we have to infer them, and the extent and strength to which they are held, from a range of secondary phenomena such as demonstrations, media reporting and other contemporary accounts, claims and counter-claims made in public or legislative debates, specific incidents, and indeed police reactions to events such as public inquiries. Most of our data are makeshift, and the onus is on the researcher to come up with internally consistent and coherent assessments of the situation.

The observations above can be summarized as follows. Formal legitimacy and "popular legitimacy" are not necessarily related, and the latter is more likely to be influenced by popular views of police behavior than by the legitimating accounts and processes of governments. Police handling of particular situations may well come to be seen as symbolic and have wider ramifications for questions of popular legitimacy than the police actions in themselves would warrant. And a failure to explain, justify, or otherwise ground police actions in culturally acceptable ways can lead to public alienation, loss of credibility, and a loss of popular legitimacy which may have implications for everyday police practice. With these points in mind, the following sections consider, in the context of Hong Kong, how social and political change have affected the different forms of police legitimacy outlined above.

## HONG KONG AS A COLONY

Hong Kong was ceded to the British by China in 1841 as part of the outcome of the Sino-British Opium Wars. Roughly 98 percent of the population is Chinese, but only in the last few years has the locally-born population outnumbered those who came from the mainland as migrants in 1945-1949, the mid-1960s, and the early 1970s. Its "head of state" is a governor with wide executive powers, appointed from Britain. This leads to a kind of contradiction. The police are, formally and legally, an arm of state; yet the British doctrine of "policing by consent" has been held to apply in various, and changing, ways over the years.

Unusually for a colony, the population at the time the British took it over was very small--about 4,000 people. However, the intention was to use the island as a military base and trading station, and in line with the laissez-faire economic doctrines of that period it was open to trade from any source and by any person. It quickly attracted a large Chinese population, some in search of employment but others seeking to evade the Chinese authorities. Moreover, the non-Chinese population, though small, included many deserting seamen and adventurers. This led the Governor, Sir John Davis, to complain in 1844 "that it was more difficult to govern the few hundred British than the thousands of Chinese" (Endacott, 1964: 16).

A police force was set up within a few months of Britain's taking possession of the island, with an initial establishment of eleven Europeans and 21 Chinese. Questions of political legitimacy were superfluous since there was no electorate. It was not until 1845 that a rate was levied on property, and then only on the few major property owners, to support the police.[5] And most persons in the territory might best be described as economic migrants or fugitives from Chinese justice who had no strong claims to political representation. Though there were discussions in 1845 about the creation of a municipal authority, which would have control over roads, sewers, and policing, the Governor refused the proposal on the grounds that it would result in ratepayers--a small elite of mainly expatriate businessmen--exercising control over a Chinese majority (Endacott, 1964: 75). A municipal authority was subsequently created (the Sanitary Board in 1883, which became the Urban Council in 1936), but policing remains a function of central government.

The police force was set up largely because of concern over levels of crime in the territory. In this period the very idea of a police force was novel. The first force in England, the London Metropolitan Police, had been established only 12 years earlier, in 1829. An earlier model existed, however: the Royal Irish Constabulary, a highly centralized and semi-military force, with a mandate to pacify and police a territory hostile to British rule. Although it is unclear whether this was a consciously followed model, the Hong Kong police exhibited many characteristics of the RIC; they were armed (though initially firearms were restricted to European officers), lived in barracks, and were officered mainly by expatriates with a military background.

Support for the police, among expatriate elites at least, depended crucially upon its ability to control crime. It was, however, generally perceived as ineffective. Recruitment was difficult and staff turnover was high, the expatriates spoke no Cantonese, corruption quickly became a problem, and there were numerous complaints from those who paid police rates about the inefficiency of policing.[6]

But the police were also handicapped by the legal framework. On the one hand, formal and legal police legitimacy could only derive from the fact of British rule. On the other, questions of law and punishment were treated with some delicacy. There was a colonial tradition of keeping local law and custom in so far as it did not conflict with British values and, in this case, there were also differing Chinese and British interpretations of the relevant diplomatic agreements. Endacott (1964: 32) observes that in 1843-44, correspondence between Hong Kong and the Colonial Office in London resulted in the Governor being instructed that "there will of course be a large body of Chinese persons to whom the law of England would be a rule of action and a measure of right equally unintelligible and vexatious." With some exceptions, English law should apply only to non-Chinese, with the

Chinese population being subject to Chinese law and a Chinese magistrate stationed in a small fort in Kowloon (which was not then a part of Hong Kong) for the purpose.[7] However, the British would have police jurisdiction over all persons in the territory. These arrangements caused further diplomatic arguments between China and Britain, but the key point is that while the police were an English force, the laws they were enforcing were, for the bulk of the population, Chinese. It is unclear whether or how this worked in practice. Endacott (1964: 36-38) notes that it created constitutional problems in matters such as access to the Supreme Court, while attempts to set up a Hong Kong Chinese administration to deal with assistance to the police and dispute resolution foundered.

The two-track legal system was unilaterally dropped around 1858-61, though Chinese customs and some aspects of customary law continued to be respected. In the meantime, however, various punishments allowed under Chinese law were prohibited in Hong Kong, and the magistrate (who was also the chief of police) was restricted to punishments of fines, imprisonment, or flogging. The result was that the powers of punishment were widely perceived as inadequate, since offenses which in Hong Kong resulted in short prison sentences would routinely be dealt with by capital punishment in China.

This picture differs sharply from the English and American experiences, where police forces were set up at city, borough, or county level; were subject to control by local elites; and were (in England) often resisted by an indigenous population or (in America) had a primary mandate to maintain order among migrants moving into and through settled communities.[8] In Hong Kong, policing was a central government function precisely because of fears that municipalization would lead to control of the police by expatriate elites. There was no credible popular electorate, and neither were there moves to create one; most Chinese, like their British rulers, were not indigenous to the territory. In the absence of any of the trappings of representative democracy and what appears to be the indifference of the mainly immigrant population, questions about legitimacy during this period revolved around three issues; the inefficiency of the police in fighting crime, the cost of the police, especially in view of their inefficiency, and the political issue of whose law--both criminal and civil--the Chinese population should be subject to.

## HONG KONG AS AN ADMINISTRATIVE STATE

In 1880, the first Chinese member of Hong Kong's Legislative Council was appointed; in 1982 the first elections were held, albeit for municipal rather than legislative positions. In the period between these two events, Hong Kong was gradually transformed from an administered state into an "administrative state" (King, 1981) in which, in the absence of full democracy, "established or emerging socio-economic elites" were "co-opted into the polity through appointments to government councils and boards, thus creating an elite-consensual community that helps to sustain legitimacy and integration" (Cheung and Louie 1991: 2).

Miners (1986: 198) has explained the rationale for this structure in more detail:

> However benevolent and efficient the bureaucracy may be, it still remains in the eyes of the Chinese a government by foreigners whose motives are always regarded with suspicion.... [Y]et government can only carry out its policies efficiently and cheaply with the willing co-operation of the population. Since it cannot assert its rule because it won an election, government takes great pains to emphasize that changes in policy are not the arbitrary dictates of an imperial master, but are rather the outcome of the fullest possible discussion with the groups most likely to be affected. The people participate in decision-making, it is claimed, not by voting for the candidates of their choice, but through their group spokesmen who sit on the councils and advisory boards which government has established.

Such views probably overstate the degree to which local Chinese interests are represented in reality. The government's paternalistic authoritarianism led it to consider seriously what it conceived of as Chinese interests, but the "insiders" in the consultation process have historically not been conduits for popular opinion. They have included the Hong Kong and Shanghai Bank, the Royal Hong Kong Jockey Club (with a monopoly on gambling, and the largest charitable fund in the territory), the General Chamber of Commerce and some manufacturing associations, various professional bodies such as the Law Society, and the Heung Yee Kuk, a body which originated in 1926 as a government-sponsored organization of village heads and was subsequently recognized as representative of, as Endacott (1964: 208) puts it, "responsible opinion" in the New Territories.[9]

What are the implications of this mode of government for police legitimacy? An answer to this question in the Hong Kong context would have to make four points.

First, in 1967 the territory experienced a series of major disturbances, which were initiated by communist agitators during the period of the Cultural Revolution in China. When the mass campaign faltered, the agitators embarked on a series of bombings which ran until early 1968 and targeted everyday locations such as trams, bus stops, and traffic junctions.

It seems unlikely that police legitimacy, whether in terms of acceptance of legitimating accounts or "consent to policing," was much of an issue prior to the riots. Lau (1982: 74) speaking of the period until around the end of the 1960s, suggested that the social and political environment was one in which "individuals and their familial group actively pursue their own best interests....Passive adaptation to the existing institutional structure is the norm, and efforts to transform the social order are frowned upon, particularly if they lead to disruption of social stability." This is probably overstating the case, especially in view of the presence of pro-China trade unions and periodic labor unrest.

However it is fair to say that outside of labor disputes, the major bases of collective action prior to 1967 were the family, the village or neighbourhood, occupational groups (hawkers, fishermen, etc.), and clan associations. Many people acknowledged that serious problems, notably corruption, existed in the police but this appears to have generated no overt challenge to police legitimacy. Indeed, the only major public accusations of corruption arose out of the bizarre mishandling of a public inquiry, discussed below. Many people were involved in the 1967 demonstrations but, it now appears, participated under pressure from mainland-led and -financed trades unions which lost much of their popular support after 1967.[10] These undoubtedly damaged popular support for communism, while the police were widely seen as defending Hong Kong's political stability in a period of massive social and political upheaval in China. The success of the police in coping with the 1967 disturbances and, more importantly, the subsequent bombings undoubtedly brought them widespread public respect.

Second, the development of government by (selected) consultation seems to have created relatively few practical problems. The process of outsiders becoming insiders is one of otherwise unrepresented groups bringing pressure to bear on government and thus mesh with questions of public order. To win the "right" of being consulted, any group must show that it commands a reasonable level of support. While this process can begin with press conferences, petitions, and the like, it may end with public demonstrations. The police may thus become embroiled in defending "public order" against groups which have achieved widespread public support and which may in future years emerge as parties in the political consultation processes.

It is fair to say that police perceptions of the importance of these processes is varied. For one thing, their political implications are likely to be rather remote from the concerns of front-line officers. However, workers in fields such as police-public relations and senior operational officers acknowledge that the policing of protests is a delicate area. Today's demonstrators may be tomorrow's legislators. The production of legitimating accounts which will help maintain "consent to policing" is taken seriously, and the police have by and large taken care not to be placed in positions which could be interpreted as attempts to suppress movements with wide public support. In several cases, the police have decided not to enforce laws relating to public demonstrations because of their assessment of the consequences on public opinion.[11] Moreover, the Hong Kong police were among the first worldwide to establish a press liaison office (in 1965) and this is now one of the largest such offices to be found in any police force.[12]

Third, however, the process of outsiders becoming insiders has operated in ways that have minimized the likelihood of police legitimacy becoming an issue. It has often been individuals rather than their groups that have made the transition into District Board, municipal council, or government committee members. Currently available evidence supports the contention that these ex-activists, although maintaining links with their old constituencies, begin to adopt an elitist view towards them while remaining marginal players in government policy formation (Chui, 1993). Moreover, one of the functions of District Officers has been to collect community opinion and defuse issues that have threatened to become contentious. Thus pressure groups have tended over time to lose their leadership and to have their campaigning issues dispersed and dissolved. Although the policing of protests is done with care (and an eye to media interpretations of the events) the result has been that since the early 1970s few campaigns have attracted mass support or interest, and those that have have not usually disturbed public attitudes about policing.[13] The weight of the police public relations machinery is also there to support police versions of events, and despite occasional criticisms of the police, the press has by and large been compliant. It enjoys a high degree of access to the police, depends on it for a large part of its local news, and thus has an incentive to keep on good terms with the police.

Fourth, in stark contrast to the generally emollient stance of government and the lack of incidents which could truly be said to put pressure on police-public relations, it should be noted that some groups have been excluded from the consultation machinery and have been policed against. In the early 1980s it became public knowledge that the government had set up a Standing Committee on Pressure Groups (SCOPG), which used information generated by Special Branch--the police department concerned with internal security--to monitor the activities of pressure groups, and in some cases attempts had been made to destabilize them. The list of 11 groups under surveillance, when leaked, provoked some mirth. It included the Hong Kong Heritage Society and the Conservancy Association (apparently on the grounds that they opposed the interests of major property developers yet had no economic interests at stake).

However the key groups it was concerned with appeared to be those which were self-funding or received funds from overseas, were active on a number of fronts, and whose leaders received no immediate personal benefits from their actions. The three leading such groups were the Hong Kong Observers, a 51-strong group of intellectuals who jointly wrote a regular newspaper column dealing with social problems ranging from police corruption to health policy and road planning; the Christian Industrial Committee, active in promoting workplace rights and in campaigns on issues such as bus fares and tax allowances; and the Society for Community Organization, a largely Catholic-based grassroots organization working on a range of issues in relation to poverty. In addition, one Urban Councillor, Elsie Elliott (later Elsie Tu) had been under surveillance as a suspected subversive.[14]

In some respects, the example of SCOPG does reflect the way in which critics of the government have been brought into the political process. The Conservancy Association and the Heritage Society were subsequently invited to consult with a newly-formed Environmental Protection Committee, while Elsie Tu became a Legislative Councillor. SCOPG was wound up in 1983.

It is unclear how far the revelations of undercover surveillance and "dirty tricks" damaged confidence in the police. On the one hand they had clearly been shown to operate as an executive arm of government, used among other things to monitor, intimidate, or destabilize community groups thought by government to be "unhelpful." On the other, while contemporary press reports were clearly hostile, their criticism was directed at central government rather than the police, and those under surveillance expressed studied surprise rather than anger. No mass campaign against SCOPG was mounted, and it may be--though no evidence on the point exists--that many people, especially if they had come from the Mainland post-1949, saw political surveillance and dirty tricks as a normal and unremarkable state of affairs that had little bearing on legitimacy.

## CORRUPTION

Immediately prior to the 1967 disturbances a major public enquiry into the 1966 "Star Ferry" riots (Hong Kong Government, 1967) had, inadvertently as it happened, highlighted the depth and pervasiveness of police corruption. Yet there were few traces of any widespread unease about this and the police emerged from the 1967 disturbances with a high level of public support. There was, we might say, consent to corrupt policing.[15] Yet six years later, public concern about police corruption had become the single major political issue in the territory, with repercussions for questions of legitimating accounts and public attitudes towards the police.

It remains unclear when and how routine police corruption became "syndicated," that is, organized into groups and hierarchies whereby protection money was routinely passed up the chain of command so that most officers, local and expatriate, benefitted from it. Nor is it clear when or how promotion by corruption became the norm. Local officers paid their seniors to have promotion examinations and decisions and transfers fixed in their favor in the expectation that their new position would enable them to recoup the bribes they paid. However, this system was entrenched by the 1960s.[16]

In retrospect it seems that organized corruption was compromised by two factors. One was greed. The amounts of money demanded and collected increased sharply in the 1960s, perhaps because the price of promotion--the internal demands of the system--increased. So long as the amounts of money were relatively small for any individual shop or restaurant owner and so long as payments did in fact buy good relations with the police, there were few complaints. When the demand for cash increased, those being squeezed began to complain.

The other factor was the apparent complicity between police and triads. It became increasingly clear that various "scams" were operating, for example with triads organizing minor offenders such as street hawkers so that particular individuals took turns at being arrested and were paid for it. This was done quite openly; individuals would appear at court as defendants, perhaps two or three times in one session, under different names, to "take the rap" and pay the fine. In this period, police detection rates were often around 70 percent, because triads would determine who the offenders were and deliver them to the police, in some cases paying them to undergo prison sentences. In short, ordinary citizens knew that offenders enjoyed triad protection; those who were involved in profitable and organized offending were able to pay others to go to jail for them; the criminal justice system was a facade; and the system was being paid for out of the squeeze money extorted from them.[17]

The attempt to re-take control over the system was sparked by a single incident, the "Godber affair," in 1973-4. Godber, a senior official at the Kowloon Regional Headquarters, was found to have assets of about HK$4.3 million--about six times his total salary for the entire time he had been a police officer. (He was, however, charged with the more specific offense of accepting HK$25,000 to arrange the posting of a superintendent to Wanchai police station, at that time one of the more "fertile" areas for corruption.) He was able to evade arrest and flew to England, from where he could not be extradited since the specific offence he was charged with did not exist in English law. He was, after a year of negotiations, brought back to face charges and in 1975 received a four-year prison sentence.

This need not necessarily have created a scandal. A number of Chinese officers had been found in similar positions and had evaded arrest by going to Taiwan, which has no extradition agreement with Hong Kong. However, the fact that Godber was not only an expatriate, but was able to evade justice by returning to Britain, created massive problems in offering any credible account not only of police legitimacy but of government legitimacy as a whole. There were, as both Lethbridge (1985) and Lo (1993: 89) recount, mass public rallies against police corruption, in which the single case of Godber came to symbolize the factual and moral corruption of the whole system of government. The popular slogan was "Fight corruption, catch Godber." His eventual trial was, in Lo's words, a "dramatization of evil" (1993: 92).

One part of the strategy to regain control over the police was the introduction of the Independent Commission Against Corruption, an investigatory agency reporting directly to the Governor and specifically mandated to attack police corruption. It was resisted. There were police demonstrations against it, and on one occasion its offices were ransacked by persons believed to be off-duty police officers. However, within the relatively short period of five or six years, syndicated police corruption was brought to an end.

What, then, were the costs of regaining control? Was it possible to revalidate legitimating accounts and win back the ground lost in the early 1970s? The costs of the fight against corruption were significant; in essence, once the force could no longer rely on its old and corrupt practices, it came to be seen as incapable of fighting crime. The fight against corruption entailed the end of a cosy police-triad relationship, disrupted informal aspects of the maintenance of public security, and dried up police sources of information. At the same time, the public became more willing to report crime. The crime rate rose, from 39,778 reports (928 per 100,000 population) in 1973 to 55,911 reports (1,278 per 100,000) in 1974. However, detection levels fell from around 76 percent in the period 1968-71, to 59 percent in 1972 and below 50 percent in most years thereafter.

## HONG KONG AS A NEAR-DEMOCRACY

Hong Kong is not a democracy. However, throughout the 1980s and early 1990s there were several moves towards greater democratic representation in government, largely by the extension of voting rights and representation to legislative bodies. Despite the lack of a thoroughgoing "one person one vote" system, there has clearly been some degree of political change over the last two decades. The question this raises is whether the increasing level of democratization has resulted in any changes in the processes of police legitimacy. The answer is that it has had some--though only a very small--impact, part of which has perhaps ironically been in favor of stronger rather than weaker public order policing.

First, the directly elected members are themselves, for the most part, members of fledgling political parties--the two main parties being a liberal democratic grouping and a conservative, pro-business group. In view of the impending resumption of Chinese sovereignty in 1997, both parties have come to be identified principally with their positions on China. In so far as the parties have developed coherent views on criminal justice, those views are linked to the wider issue of 1997 and debates about the importance of protecting human rights after the Chinese resumption of sovereignty. While this has led to discussion of matters such as police powers, the moral high ground in relation to wider criminal justice issues has largely been taken by advocates of crime control.

This situation has been replicated at local government level. Since the early 1980s District Boards have had subcommittees, known as District Fight Crime Committees, which advise the police at local level about neighborhood crime concerns. Scrutiny of their reports suggests that most such advice involves relatively minor offending and, in some cases, "undesirable" rather than criminal behaviour. They routinely note that the police have acceded to requests for more intensive policing of "blackspots" where shoplifting, juvenile crime, or simply complaints of youths "hanging around" had come to their attention. While the usual circumstances of juvenile crime in Hong Kong--in particular the influence of a triad-based street culture on juvenile delinquents--may make such requests understandable, there is concern that demands for more intensive street policing may have led to net-widening (Gray, 1991; see more generally Vagg, 1993).

Second, the gradual creation of a democratic political system required the police to open up part of their organization to scrutiny by elected politicians. In 1973, a centralized Force Complaints Office had been created to encourage "greater public confidence in the impartiality of investigations" (Commissioner of Police, 1975: 9). A centralized office, however, could be monitored by a committee of legislators, and in 1977, a joint office of the "unofficial" legislative and executive councillors (that is, those who were not government officials) created a "Police Group" to monitor and review police complaints. Following the now-traditional pattern in Hong Kong, this "unofficial" body was gradually absorbed into the structure of government; in 1986 it became the Police Complaints Committee, with a formal mandate to review the results of complaints investigations, and in 1993, it was put on a statutory footing as a subcommittee of the Legislative Council.[18]

A third impact of the wider democratic base and one which follows from the first point above seems to have been a demand for more rather than less public order policing. The most important such demand arose out of a crowd accident on New Year's Day 1993, in which 21 people died. The street on which this took place, Lan Kwai Fong, is a popular nightlife center. However the street is narrow and very steep. A public pop concert had been organized for midnight; the street was very crowded, and the street surface had become slippery from a combination of aerosol streamers and beer. Some people lost their footing and ultimately about 150-200 people fell in a pile around five persons deep. The crush of people made rescue impossible and those at the bottom of the pile died.

The disaster resulted in massive pressure on the police from legislators and the public. It was widely argued that the police should have done something to prevent the crowd building up to the level it did, so that rescue would have been easier. The police responded by suggesting that attempts to limit the crowd would have been interpreted by those present, especially on an occasion such as a New Year celebration, as an unwarranted restriction on the freedom of the public.

The subsequent inquiry and report, while not recommending legal changes, did note that the police could have used their existing powers more forcefully (Hong Kong Government, 1993). It recommended inter alia that the police should patrol large crowds, using as a measure of crowd density the pragmatic issue of whether they could move freely through the crowd; barriers should be erected so that the flow of persons into and out of the area could be controlled; and one-way pedestrian systems should be imposed on such occasions. Such measures were in fact taken at subsequent festivals.

In summary, the extension of democracy in Hong Kong has had three identifiable impacts on police legitimacy. First, the investigation of complaints against the police has come to be supervised by a statutory body the membership of which includes elected legislative councillors. Despite this, there remains controversy over the extent to which supervision is effective. None of the data published by the police, the police department dealing with complaints, or the supervisory body is of much assistance in settling this question.

Second, in the absence of alternative models, a philosophy of crime control seems to have taken root at all levels of government, and local government bodies now call on the police to address relatively trivial and sometimes non-criminal "disorder" in their areas, some of it simply juveniles hanging around in public places. Hence police legitimacy at all levels, from the Legislative Council to local municipal boards, appears to have become tied more explicitly to crime control. Greater democracy has, ironically, resulted in calls for more intensive and intrusive policing of groups such as young people. And third, one particular disaster led to widespread demands for more, rather than less, crowd control and public order policing.

## THE RUN-UP TO 1997 AND THE BILL OF RIGHTS

The British rule of Hong Kong will be superseded by Chinese rule on June 30, 1997. This has a large number of implications, only one of which I shall discuss here. In an attempt to boost public confidence in the future of Hong Kong, the government decided in 1991 to implement a Bill of Rights based on the International Covenant on Civil and Political Rights. This was, on humanitarian grounds, a welcome and long-overdue reform. However it did nothing for public confidence since it incurred criticism from the Chinese government, despite creating a situation which would occur in any case since the Basic Law for Hong Kong proposed by China includes recognition of the ICCPR. [19] What the Bill also created, however, was a large number of problems for policing--some of which, to be sure, should have been faced much earlier.

The principal problems were those of legal presumptions. Under previous legislation, the courts were entitled to presume that possession of drugs of more than a certain quantity constituted evidence of trafficking unless the defendant could rebut the assumption. Similarly, possession of keys to a property where drugs were found led to a presumption that the keyholder was in possession of the drugs unless the defendant could produce evidence to rebut the presumption. Article 11(1) of the Bill of Rights requires defendants to be considered innocent until proven guilty. The presumptions contained in the Dangerous Drugs Ordinance were thus progressively struck down as they were challenged, the first such case being *R v Sin Yau Ming* (HC No. 289 of 1990, September 30, 1991). A further problem related to the Independent Commission Against Corruption, the body set up in 1974 to combat police corruption. The Prevention of Bribery Ordinance allowed the possession of assets in excess of those which could be shown to be legally obtained (for example, from an official salary) to be presumed to be the result of corruption unless the defendant could present evidence as to the source of the assets.

Both the police and the ICAC complained that the striking down of these presumptions left them fighting crime with one hand tied behind their backs. Although the Bill of Rights had passed through the Legislative Council, there appeared to be sympathy from legislators, and to some extent from the public, for this view. A measure which had been intended to strengthen individual legal rights thus opened discussion about both police powers and ICAC powers in relation to police and other corruption. Subsequently, a number of other problems emerged, ranging from stop and search provisions and ID card checks to police powers in relation to demonstrations.

The repeal of the presumptions, the consequent need for the police and ICAC to produce a higher quality of evidence to the prosecuting authorities, and the tightening of legal controls over the police in relation to public order ought, in principle, to have strengthened legal and constitutional police legitimacy. Yet it remains unclear whether these changes have met with public approval. There have been several moral panics about rising crime rates in recent years, mainly in relation to armed robbery, which in the early 1990s become a symbol of increased lawlessness.[20] It seems likely--though there is little hard evidence--that the primary public demand and therefore the basis for attitudinal consent is effective rather than procedurally legitimate policing.[21]

## IRONIES OF LEGITIMACY IN POLICING

This paper began with three propositions. The first proposition was that police legitimacy comprises a number of distinct elements; the legitimating accounts presented by the state, the extent to which those accounts command public acceptance, and the actual level of "consent to policing" or "compliance with police."

The second was that these different types of legitimacy may be only distantly related to each other. We tend to assume that the accounts are directed at the public, and that public acceptance of them will assist the police in their work. On the basis of the material presented here this seems to be a moot point. It is equally if not more likely that the public, insofar as it considers those accounts in the first place, disregards them. Different segments of the public base their decisions on police legitimacy on more or less privately-formulated criteria, which in Hong Kong appear to be based on factors such as police compliance with public wishes, the maintenance of public order, and crime control. It is perfectly possible, therefore, that legitimating accounts have nothing to do with questions of consent to policing. Not only can an illegitimate force--for example a corrupt one--command public support, but one that has revised its working practices to accommodate human rights concerns may lose public support on the grounds of loss of effectiveness. However, the argument in relation to corruption only appears to hold so long as individuals not only feel they get value for money but retain some confidence that criminals (as opposed to illegal hawkers and other "administrative" offenders) end up being sent to jail. Moreover, specific events can take on a symbolic meaning which extends far beyond its intrinsic significance. Such was the case with Godber's flight to England to evade corruption charges.

The third proposition was that both legitimating accounts and compliance and consent are likely to be affected by broader shifts in the nature of the state, particularly those shifts which highlight questions such as "whose law?" and "whose order?" Hong Kong has seen three different periods in which these questions have had to be answered differently.

The first period was strictly Colonial. During this period, both legitimacy and operational control flowed directly from government. To have attempted to create other structures would probably have resulted in control over the police being exercised by a small group of self-interested businessmen, most of whom were opium traders. And ironically, many of the problems of legitimacy --leaving aside questions of efficiency--arose from efforts to accommodate well-intentioned, if Colonial and paternalistic, concepts such as the retention of Chinese law for the Chinese population.

The second period was that of the "administrative state," governed by consultation. With hindsight, we can conclude that consultation meant in practice little more than informing groups of policies and offering justifications for them. This form of government was in principle likely to lead to public disorder as "outsiders" tried to become "insiders." Yet this did not happen, because on the whole the leaders of pressure groups were co-opted into consultative positions and had then to control their groups. Police legitimacy, which could have been endangered by the demands of public order policing, was never really at stake although government legitimacy was undermined by revelations of "dirty tricks" applied to selected and critical groups of "outsiders. "

The third period, the current one, has seen increasing levels of democratic participation in government, even though Hong Kong cannot in truth be called a democratic state. The presence of elected members of the legislature has resulted in some realignments of political power; investigations of police complaints are now overseen by a committee of government officials and elected legislators, although the practical results are much as they ever were--hardly any complaints are substantiated, and the reasons for this remain the subject of sharply differing accounts. Meanwhile, the newly elected members have been flexing their political muscles by providing the police with greater powers and requiring more stringent law enforcement across a range of areas from juvenile crime to public order situations. This may in part be attributable to a conformist and pro-order outlook which has developed in the territory and is sometimes argued to derive from Confucian values. Certainly many individuals believe that such values are widely held, though there is ambiguity about their precise content and about who holds them. And it may in part be due to the lack of a well-developed party political structure, the lack of party political criminal justice agendas, and the consequent uncritical acceptance of a crime control outlook.

However, bearing in mind the 1997 handover of sovereignty to China, most democratic aspects of Hong Kong's political system will almost certainly be swept aside. Police legitimacy is in these circumstances not the most pressing political concern. But so far as it is concerned, the best we can expect is that crime control will continue to be the key ground for police legitimacy. The worst is that the crime control model will be supplemented by more overtly political legitimations such as the maintenance of political stability. Meanwhile, as noted above, public opinion surveys report a widespread belief that public order will decline and corruption will increase.[22] This gives rise to some pessimism about the prospects for police legitimacy even in the best case, since in Hong Kong, beliefs about police legitimacy appear to revolve crucially around issues of corruption and crime control.

## NOTES

1. An earlier version of this paper was presented at the American Society of Criminology 45th Annual Conference, October 26-31, 1993, Phoenix, Arizona. The paper has benefitted from my discussions with my colleague Carol Jones and my postgraduate students. Some parts of the paper rely heavily on historical materials and newspaper clippings collected until the early 1980s by the late James Lethbridge, Reader in Sociology at the University of Hong Kong. Responsibility for any mistakes, etc., is mine.

2. These mechanisms were close to breaking in the mid-1980s. There were major disputes about the role of the police in maintaining public order, espcially concerning strikes, young blacks and Asian minorities. See, for example, Loader (1993), Morgan and Smith (1989), Reiner (1985), Scraton (1985), and Smith and Gray (1985).

3. This argument has been advanced by functionalist writers among others, and is discussed in Lethbridge (1985).

4. For example, commenting on Indonesia, Bourchier (1990) notes that in 1982-3, rising violent crime rates were dealt with by "mysterious gunmen"--in actuality squads of military and national police--who carried out killings of known criminals. Public opinion polls found support for such actions. In the face of a major crime problem, a sense that the police were acting with legitimacy outweighed concern that the killings were illegal, until it became apparent that mistakes were being made.

5. However, the imposition of a police rate was fiercely resisted by the business community: Endacott (1964: 75-6).

6. In later years attempts were made to recruit police from non-local but supposedly dependable sources, such as the Indian Army. A large number of officers were recruited in this way, but they too became involved in corruption (see, for example, Crisswell and Watson, 1982).

7. When Kowloon became a part of the colony, the fort continued to be regarded as Chinese territory. Consequently known as the "Kowloon Walled City," it became a haven for wanted persons who believed that Hong Kong law did not extend to it. While in the 1950s, the British de facto ceased to regard the Walled City as Chinese territory, policing it was extremely difficult partly because of the grip of organized crime and partly because of its complicated internal layout. The Walled City was finally demolished in 1992-3 and is now under redevelopment as a park.

8. On America, see for example Monkkonen (1981); and on England, Reiner (1985) and Storch (1975).

9. The New Territories is the area to the north of the Kowloon peninsula which came under British control, on a 99-year lease, in 1898. The creation of the Heung Yee Kuk was an attempt by the British to bring traditional clan heads into the system of government. A brief review of the Kuk's history appears in Endacott (1964), but since the 1970s, with the development of new towns in the New Territories, the Kuk has come to represent an increasingly narrow band of New Territories residents' opinions, while at the same time representing itself as the repository of local tradition. Most recently it has been active in opposing the extension of property inheritance rights to women in the New Territories.

10. On the post-1967 decline in trade unionism in Hong Kong, see England and Rear (1975) and Leung and Chiu (1992). For a more general and overtly pro-police account of the demonstrations and bombing campaign, see Cooper (1970).

11. Conversations with senior police officers.

12. For a fuller account of the Hong Kong Police Public Information Bureau, see Traver and Gaylord (1981).

13. Certain public protests have been able to bring quick results; for example in 1971 a public demonstration by the Hong Kong Society for the Blind against new pay scales in government-run sheltered workshops created such negative publicity that the government capitulated within 48 hours (Miners, 1986: 200-201). Others, such as

campaigns in the 1970s to press the government to remedy structural deficiencies in public housing, were less successful (Lui, 1984; Lo, 1993). While the policing of demonstrations and public meetings was generally restrained, Lui (1984: 190) comments that the processes of consultation with and absorption of interest groups that these protests initiated were "ineffective to tackle problems which require a change in the principle of the government policy and to accommodate demands that go far beyond the limits of consultation."

14. On SCOPG, see in particular Campbell (1980), and Hong Kong Observers (1983). Contemporary newspaper reports include "Secret Plan for Dictatorship in Hong Kong--Claim" (*South China Morning Post*, December 12, 1980), "Conspiracy to Control the Critics" (*Hong Kong Standard*, December 13, 1980), "Spy Group Row Grows" (*Hong Kong Standard*, January 17, 1981), "SCOPG: Hazard Politicians in Civilized Countries Do Not Face" (*Hong Kong Standard*, January 28, 1981), and "SCOPG Poses a Frightening Trend" (*Hong Kong Standard*, February 2, 1981).

15. In her autobiography and elsewhere, Tu states that many individuals complained to her about police corruption. She was however in a rather unique position, since she had acquired a reputation for campaigning specifically on corruption issues (Elliott, 1971, 1988).

16. For further discussion of this system, see Cheung and Lau (1981), Lee (1981), and Lethbridge (1985).

17. See Lethbridge (1985), Sinclair (1983), and Vagg (1991).

18. In recent years, about 3,000-3,500 complaints have been recorded per annum. The publicly available information suggests that only a very small proportion of even potentially serious complaints are substantiated. Almost certainly fewer than 10 percent of all investigations result in a substantiated complaint, and data from the PCC annual reports suggest that in potentially serious cases, such as complaints of assault by the police, the level of substantiated cases is very low (Commissioner of Police, 1993; Complaints Against Police Office, 1990).

19. The Bill of Rights has generated a large legal literature, of which the most pertinant items are Byrnes and Chan (1991a, 1991b; 1992a, 1991b, 1991c; 1993) and Wacks (1993).

20. See for example Chung et al. (1992). This opinion survey showed the majority of the population, at a time when there was a spate of armed robberies, to believe that public order was in bad or very bad condition. The majority also believed that the situation would deteriorate, supported increased policing in areas with large numbers of goldsmiths' shops, and supported the restoration of the death penalty notwithstanding the fact that armed robbery per se has never been subject to this penalty, no executions have been carried out since 1966, and the penalty was abolished by the Legislative Council in 1992.

21. There is a mass of data to suggest that Hong Kong people have tended historically to be conservative and pro-order, though not necessarily pro-law. Whether those data tap popular or elite opinion is open to debate. Many writers have argued that Chinese cultural values, influenced by Confucianism, stress the concept of social harmony; the rights of the social group to be protected from outside threats take precedence over the right of accused individuals to be treated fairly. Moreover, some anthropological studies suggest that in the New Territories at least, the government and the police are sometimes seen as threats to harmony rather than guarantors of it (Ward, 1989; Watson, 1989). However, recent thinking sees "Chineseness" and Confucian traditions as cultural resources to be manipulated by ideologues, rather than settled bodies of widely-accepted values and principles (see, for example, the discussion in Evans, 1993). What remains unclear is therefore the extent to which conservative and crime-control attitudes are representative of popular opinion and whether there have been shifts in attitudes over recent years.

22. See note 20 above. In addition, a poll conducted by Hong Kong Baptist College indicated that 78 percent of those polled believed that there would be corruption in Hong Kong post-1997 (*South China Morning Post*, September 17, 1993).

## SOURCES

Bourchier, D. (1990), "Crime, Law, and State Authority in Indonesia," in A. Budiman (ed.), *State and Civil Society in Indonesia*. Monash Papers on Southeast Asia 22. Clayton, Victoria: Monash University Centre of Southeast Asian Studies.

Byrnes, A., and J.M.M.Chan (1991a), *Bill of Rights Bulletin*, Vol. 1, No. 1, October. Hong Kong: University of Hong Kong Faculty of Law.

Byrnes, A., and J.M.M.Chan (1991b), *Bill of Rights Bulletin*, Vol. 1, No. 2, December. Hong Kong: University of Hong Kong Faculty of Law.

Byrnes, A., and J.M.M.Chan (1992a), *Bill of Rights Bulletin*, Vol. 1, No. 3, April. Hong Kong: University of Hong Kong Faculty of Law.

Byrnes, A., and J.M.M. Chan (1992b), *Bill of Rights Bulletin*, Vol. 1, No. 4, August. Hong Kong: University of Hong Kong Faculty of Law.

Byrnes, A., and J.M.M.Chan (1992c), *Bill of Rights Bulletin*, Vol. 2, No. 1, November/December. Hong Kong: University of Hong Kong Faculty of Law.

Byrnes, A., and J.M.M.Chan (1993), *Bill of Rights Bulletin*, Vol. 2, No. 2, March/April. Hong Kong: University of Hong Kong Faculty of Law.

Campbell, D. (1980), "A Secret Plan for Dictatorship," *New Statesman*, 12 December, 8-12.

Cheung, A.B.L., and K.S. Louie (1991), *Social Conflicts in Hong Kong 1975-1986: Trends and Implications*, Hong Kong Institute of Asia-Pacific Studies Occasional Paper 3. Hong Kong, Chinese University of Hong Kong Institute of Asia-Pacific Studies.

Cheung, T.S., and C.C. Lau (1981), "A Profile of Syndicate Corruption in the Police Force," in R.P.L. Lee (ed.), *Corruption and Its Control in Hong Kong*, Hong Kong: Chinese University Press.

Chui, E.W.T. (1993), *Elite Mass Relationships in Hong Kong: A Look into the Perception of Local Level Political Representatives*, Hong Kong Institute of Asia-Pacific Studies Occasional Paper 24. Hong Kong, Chinese University of Hong Kong Institute of Asia-Pacific Studies.

Chung, R.T.Y., M.C.F. Tong, and R.K.M. Lui (1992), *Public Opinion Programme Poll 30 April-2 May 1992: Hong Kong People's Opinion on Law and Order, Summary Report*, Hong Kong: University of Hong Kong Social Sciences Research Centre.

Commissioner of Police (1975), *Royal Hong Kong Police Review 1974*, Hong Kong: Government Printer.

Commissioner of Police (1993), *Royal Hong Kong Police Review 1992*, Hong Kong: Government Printer.

Complaints Against Police Office (1990), *Complaints Against Police. Annual Report 1989*, Hong Kong: Royal Hong Kong Police.

Cooper, J. (1970), *Colony in Conflict: The Hong Kong Disturbances May 1967-January 1968*, Hong Kong: Swindon.

Crisswell, C., and M.Watson (1982), *The Royal Hong Kong Police 1841-1945*, Hong Kong: Macmillan.

Elliot, E. (1971), *The Avarice, Bureaucracy and Corruption of Hong Kong*, Hong Kong: Friends Commercial Printing Factory.

Elliott, E. (1988), *Elsie Tu: An Autobiography*, Hong Kong: Longman.

Endacott, G.B. (1964), *Government and People in Hong Kong 1841-1962: A Constitutional History*, Hong Kong: Hong Kong University Press.

England, J., and J. Rear (1975), *Chinese Labour under British Rule*, Hong Kong: Oxford University Press.

Evans, G. (1993), "Introduction: Asia and the Anthropological Imagination," in G. Evans (ed.), *Asia's Cultural Mosaic*, Englewood Cliffs, NJ: Prentice Hall.

Gray, P. (1991), "Juvenile Crime and Disciplinary Welfare," in H. Traver and J. Vagg (eds.), *Crime and Justice in Hong Kong*, Hong Kong: Oxford University Press.

Hong Kong Government (1967), *Kowloon Disturbances 1966: Report of Commission of Inquiry*, Hong Kong: Government Printer.

Hong Kong Government (1993), *The Lan Kwai Fong Disaster on January 1, 1993: Inquiry by the Honourable Mr Justice Bokhary. Final Report*, Hong Kong: Hong Kong Government.

King, A.Y.C. (1981), "Administrative Absorption of Politics in Hong Kong: Emphasis on the Grass Roots Level," in A.Y.C. King and R.R.L. Lee (eds.), *Social Life and Development in Hong Kong*, Hong Kong: Chinese University Press.

Lau, S.K. (1982), *Society and Politics in Hong Kong*, Hong Kong: Chinese University Press.

Lee, R.P.L. (ed.) (1981), *Corruption and Its Control in Hong Kong*, Hong Kong: Chinese University Press.

Lethbridge, H.J. (1985), *Hard Craft in Hong Kong: Scandal, Corruption, the ICAC*, Hong Kong: Oxford University Press.

Leung, B.K.P., and S. Chiu (1992), *Industrial Strikes and Labour Movement in Hong Kong 1946-1989*, Social Sciences Research Centre Occasional Paper 3. Hong Kong: University of Hong Kong Social Sciences Research Centre.

Lo, T.W. (1993), *Corruption and Politics in Hong Kong and China*, Buckingham: Open University Press.

Loader, I. (1993), "Democracy, Justice and the Limits of Policing: Rethinking Police Accountability," paper to the British Criminology Conference, Cardiff, July.

Lui, T.L. (1984), *Urban Protests in Hong Kong: A Sociological Study of Housing Conflicts*, M.Phil thesis. Hong Kong: University of Hong Kong.

Mawby, R.I. (1990), *Comparative Policing Issues: The British and American Experience in International Perspective*, London: Unwin Hyman.

Miners, N. (1986), *The Government and Politics of Hong Kong*. 4th ed., Hong Kong: Oxford University Press.

Monkkonen, E. (1981), *Police in Urban America 1860-1920*, Cambridge: Cambridge University Press.

Morgan, R. (1991), *Policing by Consent: Current Thinking on Police Accountability in Great Britain*, Social Sciences Research Centre Occasional Paper 1. Hong Kong: University of Hong Kong Social Sciences Research Centre.

Morgan, R., and D. Smith (eds.) (1989), *Coming to Terms with Policing: Perspectives on Policy*, London: Routledge.

Reiner, R. (1985), *The Politics of Police*, Brighton: Wheatsheaf.

Scraton, P. (1985), "The State v The People: An Introduction,"
    *Journal of Law and Society*, 12, 3, 251-66.
Sinclair, K. (1983), *Asia's Finest: An Illustrated Account of the Royal
    Hong Kong Police*, Hong Kong: Unicorn Press.
Smith, D., and J. Gray (1985), *Police and People in London*,
    London: Gower.
Storch, R.D. (1975), "The Plague of Blue Locusts: Police Reform and
    Popular Resistance in Northern England 1840-57,"
    *International Review of Social History*, 20, 61-90.
Traver, H., and M.S. Gaylord (1991), "The Royal Hong Kong
    Police," in H. Traver and J. Vagg (eds.), *Crime and Justice
    in Hong Kong*, Hong Kong: Oxford University Press.
Vagg, J. (1991), "Policing Hong Kong," *Policing and Society*,
    1, 235-47.
------ (1993), "Context and Linkage: Reflections on Comparative
    Research and 'Internationalism' in Criminology," *British
    Journal of Criminology*, 33, 4, Autumn.
Wacks, R. (ed.) (1993), *Police Powers in Hong Kong: Problems and
    Prospects*, Hong Kong: University of Hong Kong Faculty of
    Law.
Ward, B.E. (1989), "Temper Tantrums in Kau Sai: Some Speculations
    Upon Their Effects," in Ward, B.E., *Through Other Eyes: An
    Anthropologist's View of Hong Kong*, Hong Kong: Chinese
    University Press.
Watson, J.L. (1989), "Self Defense Corps, Violence and the Bachelor
    Sub-culture in South China: Two Case Studies," *Proceedings
    of the Second International Congress of Sinology*, Taipei:
    Academica Sinica.

# *FORZA POLIZIA*: TIME TO CHANGE THE ITALIAN POLICING SYSTEM?[1]

## Monica den Boer

### INTRODUCTION

For all that Italy is a modern and well-integrated West European state, not much literature is available in English about its law enforcement agencies. One reason for this may be the sheer complexity of the Italian policing system, which is multidimensional and extremely bureaucratic. Another reason may be that Italy's internal security situation is in constant flux: terrorism had priority on the security agenda during the seventies and early eighties, the Mafia and organized crime during the late eighties and early nineties. Other problems have been added since then, such as unprecedented numbers of immigrants, corruption and bribery scandals at the heart of the Italian administration, a crisis in the security services, and a changing political map. With the exception of the security services, law enforcement organizations have remained remarkably stable throughout the volatile periods of Italian governance. They have also begun to lift the lid: the Italian police are opening up, making it easier for researchers to fathom the vast amount of expert knowledge and opinion.

Due to its strategic southern geographical position and the imminent exportation of Mafia activities to other parts of Europe (Calvi, 1993; Parisi, 1993: 428), Italy occupies a crucial place within the emerging security community of the European Union. Of all the western democracies, Italy has the reputation of being particularly affected by overt insecurity and diffuse illegality, mainly caused by terrorism, organized crime, and conspiracies (Palidda, 1992: 235). Recently also, the whole of Italy has been plagued by a spate of corruption scandals.[2] Former Prime Ministers Craxi and Andreotti stand accused, respectively, of taking bribes in Milan for the amount of $29 million and of being the reference of the Mafia in Rome. More than other states in the European Union, Italy has experienced various forms of violence. Some blame this on Italy's ambiguous evolution, on a vacuum caused by its rapid transition from a rural society into advanced capitalism, and an increasing emphasis on individualism rather than on collectivity (Ferrarotti, 1979).

## THE EVOLUTION OF ITALIAN POLICING

After the Second World War, the constitutional monarchy was replaced by a new republican form of government. A Constitution was drafted in 1947 and took effect in January 1948 (Wilson, 1990: 316f). There was a strong emphasis on centralization in order to prevent the fragmentation of the past but also to counterbalance the influence of the Catholic Church, the traditional forces in the south, and social revolutionaries. Modelled on the Napoleonic idea of centralization and hierarchy, the Italian Republic retained control over the police. However, the centralization has also had its drawbacks: Italy's bureaucracy is massive, employing four million people out of a total working population of 19 million. The bureaucracy works at a slow pace and is often called inefficient (Wilson, 1990: 378f).

### THE NINETEENTH CENTURY: THE BIRTH OF A MODEL
At the beginning of the nineteenth century, an organizational basis was laid for the municipal or "city" police, which worked in cities with more than 100,000 inhabitants; the *gendarmerie* covered the smaller municipalities in the countryside (Canosa, 1976: 17; Tarrow, 1989: 105). In 1802, after the Napoleonic conquest of the Italian peninsula, the king of Piedmont created a version of the French *gendarmerie*, and reorganized preexisting police forces into the corps of the *carabinieri* (Collin, 1985: 188; Davis, 1988: 71). The Piedmontese government was the first to develop a modern cabinet system of government and to assign law enforcement to the Interior Ministry, at the time of the *Risorgimento* (unification). A dual system of policing was installed, and old "pre-unitary" police forces were integrated in the *carabinieri* and the *guardia di pubblica sicurezza*. Among those integrated were the Roman gendarmes and the municipal police: their first competence was the execution of decisions taken by tribunals, which were ruled by *bargelli* (heads of police, or captains)

(Gleizal et al., 1993: 114; Monet, 1993: 52). The dual system of policing--which Italy has in common with France and Luxembourg-- never became "pluralist," because of a firm line of command which always departed from the *Viminale* (the Ministry of the Interior's headquarters) in Rome. Even though multiple (e.g., municipal) police forces exist, they do not have general powers and as such do not enter the essential framework of the police forces (Monet, 1993: 73).

In the second half of the nineteenth century, trade unionism and strikes became a regular phenomenon. A crisis of confidence within the police forces resulted from a combination of this sociopolitical situation and from understaffing: there were about 7,000 Interior Ministry Police and 18,000 *carabinieri* to police all of Italy. Meanwhile, Italy had the highest rate of violent crimes in Europe (Davis, 1988: 314). Palidda (1992: 252) claims that in the middle of the nineteenth century there were four police officers per 1,000 inhabitants. Britain and France each had about four times as many police per capita during the same period and substantially lower crime rates (Palidda, 1992: 190, 191; Davis, 1988: 240). The number of *carabinieri* was increased subsequently, and in 1887, the forces numbered a total of 47,000 men, of whom 24,600 were *carabinieri* and 4,500 *pubblica sicurezza* guards; the rest was divided up between the municipal guards and the forest police (Gleizal et al., 1993: 116).

## THE TWENTIETH CENTURY: GROWTH AND TRANSFORMATION

In the course of the twentieth century, the police forces mainly concentrated on internal security rather than criminality and focused on various revolutionaries (Collin, 1985: 188). The democratic liberal Giolitti who dominated the political scene between 1901 and 1922 set out to increase public confidence in the police and to familiarize the police with the idea that they were the keepers of the peace on a neutral basis (Collin, 1985: 191). After initial success, the police forces underwent another crisis during the years of the First World War. Prime Minister Nitti dealt with this crisis by "doubling the size of the *carabinieri* and re-building the Interior Ministry police" (Collin, 1985: 192). Not only did the violence continue. The fascist movement was becoming stronger and recruited support from the police ranks. The immunity mechanism became law in 1930,[3] which meant that the public could not pursue legal proceedings against police officers for facts relative to the use of arms and other means of physical violence performed under service duty (Bernardi, 1979: 22; Collin, 1985: 192).

It was at the beginning of the 1920s that the *carabinieri* started to openly sympathize with the fascists (Canosa, 1976: 61f; Collin, 1985: 192). During the fascist regime, Mussolini himself took the Interior Ministry portfolio and appointed loyal General De Bono as his Chief of Police (Collin, 1985: 193). The fascist period meant a promotion of police powers and tasks,[4] because of changes in the penal law (special norms, also in the war law) and the prefect apparatus: from 1926 onward, the prefect became the most important state authority at provincial level (D'Orsi, 1972: 28, 34, 35).

By 1943, the *carabinieri* and the Interior Ministry cooperated in plans to have Mussolini removed from power, against the background of growing opposition from the Italian citizens and a deteriorating war record. Mussolini's removal was accomplished at the King's instructions in 1943. After the Germans invaded Rome, both police forces straightened their image by participating in the Resistance movement (Collin, 1985: 194, 195). A purge process was set in motion by the appointment of a Higher Commissioner for national purge in 1944. At the same time, the police organization found itself to be disintegrated and morale was low (Canosa, 1976: 106). In the areas of Italy liberated by the partisans, political battles were fought inside the police forces (Reiter, 1993: 10). The Allies had an advisory role and recommended a profound reform of the Italian security forces. They also decided the quantitative level of the police forces and helped to rehabilitate the police forces. Concrete plans with an emphasis on demilitarization and decentralization were only formulated in 1947 but never materialized (Reiter, 1993: 12).

Social unrest and political tension predominated after the War, and the new Minister of the Interior Scelba formed rapid-response units as an (often violent) answer to these phenomena (Collin, 1985: 196; Reiter, 1993: 15). This type of response was reiterated at the end of the sixties, when both the Interior Ministry and the *carabinieri* adopted a hard-line approach to student and civil rights demonstrations. The image of the police suffered from this repressive policy into the next decade (Collin, 1985: 198). Not only civil disorders but also terrorism proved a problem for Italy's internal security towards the end of the sixties. Neofascist elements carried out a bombing in 1969 at the Piazza Fontana in Milano; according to Collin (1985: 198), the police "ignored evidence leading to the right and arrested a harmless group of anarchists." Until today, the case is still a mystery and is still a subject of investigation.

The capacity of the police forces expanded substantially since the nineteenth century. In 1945, the *pubblica sicurezza* counted more than 44,000 men, of whom 20,000 were "auxiliaries" (most of these were partisans); the *carabinieri* counted 75,000 men in 1946 (Gleizal et al., 1993: 116).[5] Hence, at the moment the picture looks dramatically different from that of a century ago: there are now in Italy 445[6] police officers per 100,000 inhabitants, which is much higher than the European average of 338 (Monet, 1993: 122). The average in the European Union is 257 people per police officer--the one extreme is Italy, with 191 people per police officer and the other extreme is Denmark with 499 people per police officer (Benyon et al., 1993: 68). With over 300,000 officers spread out over the different forces, an important part of the Italian National Budget (BNP) is spent on the internal security "industry" (Palidda, 1992: 258).

## POLICE AND PUBLIC CONFIDENCE

Policing activities have always been met with suspicion and *antipatia* in Italy (Canosa, 1976: 16). The public has had good reasons to adopt this attitude, particularly because of the large number of casualties caused by aggressive police action at demonstrations, the lethal use of weapons, and the disrespect for human rights in interrogations. The concern for public order led to a restriction of civil liberties.[7] A large number of conflicts between public and police occurred in the context of industrial protest. Some confrontations escalated in violence, with killings on both sides (Sassoon, 1986: 129). Canosa's (1976) systematic listing of these killings leaves the reader with a rather grim impression of the culture of the Italian police. The discussion about police violence in Parliament and Senate resulted in trial proceedings against the judiciary police and a parliamentary commission ordered the improvement of rules for the interrogation of suspects (Canosa, 1976: 166-170).

The repressive model of policing became more sophisticated during the beginning of the sixties: more modern methods were used and killings became far less frequent (Canosa, 1976: 273). Towards the end of the sixties, at the time of the student demonstrations and hightened industrial conflict, law enforcement authorities adopted a "strategy of tension," leading to an "emergency period" in the second half of the seventies, when--in the context of a radicalized climate of the terrorist emergency--"the policing of protest became extremely repressive" (Della Porta, 1992: 6, 10; see also Tarrow, 1989). In 1972, the police mounted a massive operation when during one single night 163,000 people were checked, of whom 469 were arrested on suspicion of terrorist activities. Later it also became apparent that police tapped telephones (Canosa, 1976: 288, 332).

After the many clashes with demonstrators and "subversives," there was a reorientation within the police forces and growing emphasis on preventive strategies. In the light of this reorientation, the police forces adopted a more professional and psychological approach, refined and clarified ideological and military instructions, considered the introduction of modern technology, and improved and perfectionalized physical coercion (D'Orsi, 1972: 66). Following the 1981 reform, police officers are said to have cultivated better contacts with the public (Palidda, 1992), predominantly in a sphere of "national reconciliation" (Della Porta, 1992: 11-12), although this seems to have been counteracted for a while by the *Reale* law of 1975, which introduced draconian powers and had a dramatic effect on the escalation of police violence and the display of police potency.

Accounts about Italy's human rights record diverge. One report claims Italy's record is worse than Britain's.[8] This stands in sharp contrast with Wilson (1990: 397), who says that Italy has a very good record in observing basic human rights. However, Wilson (1990: 399) also comments that the threat posed by terrorism led to the introduction of "draconian laws to combat it," as anti-terrorist police were provided with "important powers of arrest, preventive detention, search and seizure, detention without trial when judicial proceedings were disrupted, interference in client-attorney relations, and a variety of other powers."

## SYNDICALIZATION, DEMILITARIZATION, AND "FEMINIZATION"

Public confidence improved slightly as a result of two drastic reforms: syndicalization and demilitarization. The movement toward syndicalization was initiated by a group of militant police officers, who petitioned and demonstrated (Monet, 1993: 142). Because both the Interior Ministry police and the *carabinieri* used to be militarized, the Ministry argued against syndicalization. However, as Canosa (1976: 347) says, there was actually a syndicate for military officers, called the SINAM (*Sindicato Nazionale Autonomo Militari*). This right of syndicalization was denied until the early eighties, when the police organization was reformed as a consequence of the new bill in 1981.[9] Canosa (1976: 349) also says that syndicalization is not a guarantee for improved standards of policing. For example, the reputation of the police has not improved despite intense syndicalization. The same may be true for accountability. A general, comparative observation is that unlike most other West European countries, there is no Police Complaints Board or ombudsman in Italy, which has severe repercussions for the social legitimacy of policing.

The public face of the Italian police has also changed as a result of women[10] entering the State Police force following a parliamentary decision. For more than three years after this decision in 1981, however only men kept being recruited into the force. Furthermore, the *concorsi*[11] were not opened up for women, and the incorporation of former female police assistants was considered "objectionable."[12] However, with time, female officers started to appear but mainly as traffic constables and transport police officers. As such, there has been considerable recruitment of women into the lower ranks, although women are discouraged at the top. In 1987, the total percentage of women in the State Police was about 5 percent (2,025 were appointed in the course of that year). Only two of these occupied the post of chief inspector, while there were 431 inspectors, 147 deputy inspectors, and 50 first inspectors.[13] At the beginning of the nineties, however, this percentage had risen to over 50 percent, which is quite an achievement for any European police force (Monet, 1993: 127).[14] However, female police officers leave their job more frequently than their male counterparts, primarily for marriage or alternative employment. Although there are no differences in arming women, female officers are excluded from taking part in the Special Patrol Groups.[15] Women are not allowed in the *carabinieri* or the *guardia di finanza*, although this will change in the near future.

## ORGANIZATION OF THE ITALIAN POLICE

The organization of the Italian police can be seen along two axes. The first is the functional distinction between the *polizia di sicurezza* (security police) or administrative policing and the *polizia giudiziaria* (judicial police). The function of the security police is to maintain the public order and to prevent crimes, and the function of the judicial police is repressive vis-à-vis crime and public order. The axis between prevention and repression roughly parallels the distinction between magistrature and police. The judicial police are accountable to the Directorate of the Judicial Authority. The distinction between security police and judicial police runs through all of Italy's police forces. The second organizational axis of the Italian police is the distinction between different police forces (D'Orsi, 1972: 72; Scandone and Atzori, 1990: 166).

There are currently six different police forces in Italy, two of which are the most important, namely the *polizia di stato* (State Police, or also translated as Public Security Police), and the *carabinieri*. This marks one of the principal characteristics of the Italian police, namely its structural duality (Bernardi, 1979: 4, 10; Collin, 1985: 185, 191), causing numerous turf battles and a chronic lack of coordination despite attempts by the Department of Public Security to remove obstacles to improved cooperation.

The other police forces are the *guardia di finanza*, which numbers about 42,000 men; it assists the Ministry of Finance in enforcing tax, excise customs, and tariff legislation; the *corpo forestale*, which started as an element of the fascist militia, survived the demise of Mussolini, and is now a 6,000 man enforcement agency for the Ministry of Agriculture and Forests; the *prison guards*, who are subordinated to the Ministry of Justice and numbered around 12,000 in 1985 (Collin, 1985: 188); and the *vigili urbani*, local police forces working in city centers (D'Orsi, 1972: 106). The post office and the state railways have their own small police forces, and the local police forces are active in most of the *comune*. Collin (1985: 188) notes that these forces have historically been troubled by inefficiency and corruption and have been marginal in law enforcement. Also important are the private police forces: according to some data there were 241 private police forces in 1956, all of which were a member of FEDERPOL, which at the time was directed by the (then) Director of the Italian Interpol (NCB). One of these private forces belonged to FIAT, which in 1951 already employed 1,500 people (D'Orsi, 1972: 105). It is claimed that the role of the private police has increased as a result of the failure of the Italian state to guarantee security (Bernardi, 1979: 42, 169).

The three largest police forces are accountable to three

different parliamentary committees of inquiry: the *carabinieri* to the Committee of Defence, the *guardia di finanza* to the Committee of Finance, and the *polizia di stato* to the Committee of the Interior. The Council of Ministers nominates the commander of the armed forces, the commander of each of the security forces, the chief of police and the chiefs of the two secret security services, the SISMI and the SISDE (see below) (Palidda, 1992: 246). The security interests of various ministries are connected within an Interministerial Security Committee, which is presided by the Prime Minister and which gathers the Ministers of Foreign Affairs, Interior, Justice, Defense, and Finance (Monet, 1993: 117).

The forces are coordinated on two levels, the national and the provincial. At the national level, one finds the National Committee for Public Order and Security, which is composed of the Minister of Interior (who chairs it), an undersecretary of state, the director general of the *pubblica sicurezza*, the chief commander of the *carabinieri* and the chief commander of the *guardia di finanza*. The committee seeks to promote mutual coordination and consultation between the police forces. The committee deals with general aspects of the policing mandate but more specifically functional and territorial competences, financial aspects, logistic and administrative aspects, dislocation and co-ordination, and training and formation (Scandone and Atzori, 1990: 172). The committee's activities are shadowed at the provincial level where, under the authority of the prefect, one finds the Provincial Committee for Public Order and Security (CPOSP). This functions as an auxiliary body for consultation composed of the prefect, the *questore* and the provincial commanders of the *carabinieri* and the *guardia di finanza* (Palidda, 1992: 248).

### POLIZIA DI STATO

The *polizia di stato* (State Police) is a national organization and its title was introduced with the reform bill of 1981. The organization employs approximately 100,000 people (Palidda, 1992: 253; Benyon et al., 1993: 67). Between 1938 and 1949 its predecessor, the *pubblica sicurezza*, grew from 17,565 officers to 75,604 officers. The biggest leap occurred between 1943 and 1946, when the *polizia dell'Africa Italiana* and many partisans were absorbed into the force (D'Orsi, 1972: 40). A substantial recruitment, both into the *polizia di stato* and the *carabinieri*, took place in central-southern parts of Italy between 1961 and 1968. At the end of the sixties, more than two-thirds of the recruited police officers came from four regions (Boatti, 1978: 113; Monet, 1993: 129). The slogan in southern Italy became *Germania o polizia* (Germany or the Police), which symbolized a hard choice between working within the police force or being a "guest worker" in Germany (D'Orsi, 1972: 243).

The *polizia di stato* is immediately accountable to the Department of Public Security (*Dipartimento di Pubblica Sicurezza*) of the Ministry of the Interior and has branches in all major communities of the provinces. Police work in the 92 provinces of the country is chiefly the responsibility of the local prefect, who is directly answerable to the Minister of the Interior (Collin, 1985: 186); the *prefettura* is a remnant of Napoleonic government and was installed by law on July 24, 1802; the powers of the prefect were fixed in a law issued on October 23, 1859 (Bernardi, 1979: 45). Parallel with this system of government is the police hierarchy. The prefect has to maintain contact with the *questore* (comparable with a British Chief Constable) and with the Provincial Commander of the Carabinieri corps (Scandone and Atzori, 1990: 171). The Chief of Police instructs these senior police officials. In turn the *questore* directs and coordinates--at the technical-operational level--the regional state police force, and can dispose of other forces if necessary.[16] This requires regular contact with the local commanders of the *carabinieri* and the *guardia di finanza* (Scandone and Atzori, 1990: 171). Under the *questore* serves a hierarchy of high-ranking civilian officials, and each major city is supervised by a *commissario* (or chief superintendent) with more junior officials for other less important population centers (Collin, 1985: 186). A steady decentralization of policing tasks has taken place since 1972. A decree in 1977 provided the transfer of administrative tasks of state to local units and entities, primarily because the central level found it impossible to know what the needs were at the local level (Bernardi, 1979: 161, 162).

The task of the Department of Public Security (*Dipartimento di Pubblica Sicurezza*) is to classify, analyse, and evaluate the information and data about public order and public security furnished by its services, i.e., the state police; to perform scientific and technological research; to gather documentation, research reports, and statistics; to plan common logistic and administrative services; to coordinate budgets of the single police forces; and to maintain and develop international and communitarian contacts (Scandone and Atzori, 1990: 169). The head of this department is at the same time *capo della polizia di stato* (head of the state police), who is assisted by two *vice capi* (deputy directors). The Director of the department has a dual function, namely a political one (the formulation of public order and security strategies), and a technical-operational one (the coordination of the police forces and the direction and administration of the *polizia di stato*) (Scandone and Atzori, 1990: 174-175).

The tasks of the *polizia di stato* include patrol, traffic surveillance, criminal investigations, intelligence, and the combating of organized crime; all these tasks are undertaken to ensure the liberty and rights of citizens, to enforce the observance of laws, rules and provisions, to control public order and security, to prevent and repress crime, and to provide help in the event of casualties (Scandone and Atzori, 1990: 174). The officers of the *polizia di stato* are armed with rifles and machine guns.[17]

One of the most important moments in the history of the *polizia di stato* was the 1981 law to reform the police. There had been calls for a profound reform since the end of the sixties, when the demands included the radical and democratic reform of the laws on *pubblica sicurezza*, the democratization of relations between the officers and the *questura* (i.e., the abolition of authoritarianism), and the application of civil service rules and norms to police officers (Bernardi, 1979: 66). Although the demonstrations and hunger strikes in support of these demands were met by sanctions, convictions, and widespread repression, it was quietly acknowledged that the police was ineffective, in particular because of the tensions between police and civil servant officials and between civil and military police (Bernardi, 1979: 69; Canosa, 1976: 343-345). The reform of 1981 brought about the demilitarization of the National Police and syndicalization (unionization),[18] which are the fundamental reference points for the democratic evolution of the Italian police. A civil tradition has always been present in other European countries, notably Great Britain (except for the Royal Ulster Constabulary), Denmark, Sweden, and Norway, and in countries like the Netherlands, Germany, Switzerland, and Finland a military police is at least always accompanied by a civil police force (Canosa, 1976: 105). The reform also introduced the integration of police ranks to create a new generation of officers and agents, which opened up the organization for women and younger officers (see above; also Palidda, 1992: 257).

## CARABINIERI

The *carabinieri* are a paramilitary organization, created in 1814 by Vittorio Emanuele I, King of Sardinia (D'Orsi, 1972: 5). The mission it was given included the protection of public order within the state and, alongside the royal army, to maintain order and to enforce laws in the countryside (Monet, 1993: 51). While it employed 800 men then, it now employs over 100,000 men (Benyon et al., 1993: 68). All *carabinieri* troops were nationally integrated as a result of a decree in 1861. After having been changed a few times since its inception,[19] the force is under dual responsibility of the Ministry of the Interior (concerning public order and security tasks) and the Ministry of Defence (concerning military tasks). *Carabinieri* are employed in rural areas and in most urban communities. Its functions resemble those of the *polizia di stato*: prevention and repression of crime, vigilation of the observance of laws and normative provisions, controlling public order and security, guarding prisoners, and participating in border control (Scandone and Atzori, 1990: 199). Hence, the remit of the *carabinieri* includes standard police work and crime detection (patrol, traffic regulation, criminal investigation, and intelligence), anti-drug and narcotics investigations, disarmament of bombs, accuracy controls of weights, measures, and advertisements, investigations into food and drink adulteration, inspection of industrial establishments for worker safety, services to the judiciary for assorted tasks, protection of the President of the Republic, supply of trained personnel for intelligence and counterespionage services, and numerous other duties (Collin, 1985: 186). A degree of overlap between the activities of the *carabinieri* with those of the *polizia di stato* is therefore no surprise. Canosa (1976: 400) emphasizes that although the *carabinieri* are comparable to the *guardia civil* in Spain and the *gendarmerie* in France, the *carabinieri* have a much larger remit: in territorial terms, both countryside and cities are covered and, in functional terms, both the maintenance of public order and the gathering of information and intelligence are included (see also Boatti, 1978: 143f).

As its paramilitary constitution suggests, *carabinieri* officers are armed and have both civilian and military vehicles, armored cars, and tanks. Weapons include light infantry capability, and the force employs fixed-wing aircraft and helicopters for surveillance and rescue operations.[20]

## GUARDIA DI FINANZA

The history of the *guardia di finanza* goes back to the creation of the Legion of Light Troops in Sardinia by Vittorio Amedeo III in 1774. It was a special corps with tasks which included vigilance and the military defence of frontiers. The organization therefore has its origin in early military units, whose task it was to control frontiers and prevent and suppress contraband. In 1862, the Italian state instituted a military corps of customs officers, and they were called the *guardia di finanza* from 1881 (Canosa, 1976: 24).[21] The *guardia* became a military state corps in 1907 and in 1959 was made directly accountable to the Ministry of Finance. The *guardia di finanza* is led by a General Commander, who is supported by a Second Commander. The tasks of the *guardia di finanza*, laid down in the Law No. 189 of April 23, 1958, include the prevention and suppression of tax evasion, contraband, economic fraud and economic criminality (fight against drug trafficking and organized crime) (Palidda, 1992: 254). The principal task is therefore the enforcement of fiscal law. This implies surveillance tasks, support of the maritime police and the military-political defence of the borders (Scandone and Atzori, 1990: 217). The fact that the powers and competences of the *guardia* are statutorily provided makes it a unique form of administration. There is no comparable, military organization in other countries which carries out fiscal and criminal law enforcement tasks. Preventive and repressive controls are performed by the *guardia di finanza* in the customs areas of ports, airports, and land frontiers. It controls the flow of currencies, drugs, arms, and works of art and has assumed new authority with the formation of the European Union and the Customs Union, namely, the repression of EU frauds and the misuse of EU subsidy funds. For this purpose, the *guardia* actively cooperates with foreign collateral services in applying mutual assistance conventions and EU regulations. Again, one cannot avoid the impression of functional overlap when looking at the formidable inventory of the tasks of this force. These include traffic law enforcement, the protection of archaeological, historical, and artistic patrimony, assistance in the maintenance of public order, and cooperation in the political-military defence of the frontiers and in military operations. The *guardia di finanza* effectively employs 55,000 men (Palidda, 1992: 254; Benyon et al., 1993: 68).

In recent years, the *guardia di finanza* has geared itself into the fight against drugs and organized crime. For these purposes, drug investigation units were strengthened and extended beyond the normal port, airport, and frontier checkpoints. It also plays a fundamental role in the fight against organized crime. In particular, it directs tax investigations of people suspected of being involved in organized crime; it identifies the origin of real-estate and assets, refers criminal charges to the competent judicial and law enforcement authorities, and carries out investigations into money-laundering activities.

## INTELLIGENCE SERVICES

Two new intelligence services were created in 1977,[22] namely SISDE (*Servizio per le Informazioni e la Sicurezza Democratica*) and SISMI (*Servizio per le Informazione e la Sicurezza Militare*), respectively representing the "civil" intelligence service and the "military" intelligence service. The SISDE is the intelligence service dependent on the Ministry of Interior and is in charge of the centralization of all information necessary for the protection of the democratic state and institutions (Monet, 1993: 117). The CESIS (*Comitato Esecutivo per i Servizi de Informazione di Sicurezza*) is a technical platform for the exchange of information between the intelligence directors which ensures a minimum of collaboration and coordination between them (Monet, 1993: 117).

A parliamentary commission was set up in August 1993 to examine the workings of the secret services after explosions in Rome and Milan,[23] which followed a bombing campaign that had started in May 1993 with explosions in Florence[24] and Rome. The Commission recommended that the Italian Official Secrets Act be lifted for investigations into terrorist acts. This recommendation was regarded as a dramatic admission by the state that secret service officers may have been linked with the bombings.[25] If this allegation is true, it means that the secret service which should have protected the Italian state against subversion is itself responsible for undermining it by means of anti-democratic activities. The head of the domestic intelligence service SISDE, Mr. Malpica, had quit by the end of July 1993--immediately after the bombings--after strong criticism by politicians of the lax control of Italy's security services. A reorganization of the security services was already announced by Prime Minister Ciampi at the annual commemoration of the Bologna station bombing of 1980.[26] A reform of the secret services was agreed to by cabinet ministers on November 2, 1993. The reorganization plans included making the secret services better structured, more efficient and more accountable.[27] The resigned director of SISDE, Mr. Malpica, was arrested and another top official gave himself up to authorities. The police suspects that they and four others stole 49bn lire (£20 million) from the secret service's funds, although other reports allege the diversion of 14bn lire (£5.8 million) for private use.[28] Other allegations included claims by senior secret service officers that President Scalfaro illegally took money from the secret services at the time he held the Interior Ministry portfolio, a claim which sent a shock wave throughout the whole of Italy.[29] In July 1994, Gaetano Marino, a *carabinieri* general was appointed director of SISDE after it was discovered that the service had compiled secret dossiers on politicians and political parties without relating these to intelligence questions; presumably the dossiers were employed to exercise political pressure.

Earlier controversies had come to light in the sixties when it emerged that the SIFAR (*Servizio Informazioni Forze Armate*) had expanded its activities beyond reasonable proportion. These activities mainly covered the collection of dossiers; in 1960, the service had about 157,000 of those. Meanwhile, the service had also changed in qualitative terms, as it had moved from counterespionage to gathering intelligence on persons who were considered to be a danger to state security and it also gathered more "indirect information" in relation to state security, such as intimate details about the lives of so-called "extremists." It is no surprise therefore that concerns were expressed about the implications for constitutional liberties of SIFAR's activities (Canosa, 1976: 319-323). The Italian Parliament concluded in 1974 that SIFAR was unique in Europe, but that it and the other intelligence service (the SID) should perhaps be better coordinated. This is when the possibility of a unified organization was raised (Canosa, 1976: 326). Therefore in 1993, Prime Minister Ciampi's proposal to merge SISDE and SISMI[30] is historically not original. The proposed shake-up is said to be both controversial and dramatic as it constitutes a fundamental political challenge to the heart of the Italian state.

## SECURITY THREATS IN ITALY

Italy has been plagued by various forms of violence, resulting in a multitude of contradictory security demands (Palidda, 1992: 236). The internal security agenda in Italy has been notoriously dynamic. Although the severity of indigenous and imported terrorism has declined, Italy still lives under the threat of terrorist attacks. Clutterbuck (1990: 26) reports that between 1969 and 1987 14,599 terrorist incidents were recorded, of which 359 caused death or injury: "A total of 419 people were killed and 1,182 were injured.... Of the 359 attacks involving death or injury, 267 (74.5 percent) were attributed to left-wing terrorists, 27 (7.5 percent) to right-wing terrorists, and 65 (18 percent) to Arabs and others." Numerous injuries and deaths have also been caused by or associated with Mafia activities. Although successes were obtained in the fight against the Mafia, the impact of the murders of General Dalla Chiesa and judges Falcone and Borsellino, as well as that of the 1993 bombings in Florence and Rome, has been huge. Recently a new security issue has been added to the agenda: illegal immigration.

### SECURITY THREAT I: TERRORISM

Left-wing terrorism--mostly represented by the *Brigate Rosse* (BR)--is often related to the Italian Communist Party's (PCI) abandonment of its revolutionary tradition, the student movement's failure to achieve profound reforms, and a general decline in popular mobilization (Collin, 1985: 199; Tarrow, 1989: 297; Wilson, 1990: 394). The BR started by infiltrating factories in the north, pamphleteering, committing acts of sabotage, and kidnapping personnel managers (Collin, 1985: 199; Clutterbuck, 1990: 30). The aim gradually became the toppling of the existing regime. Wilson (1990: 342) regards BR's objective as having been more realistic than that of the *Rote Armee Faktion* in Germany, given the "apparent fragility of the Italian state and the seeming low levels of popular support." It was the threat to the existing regime rather than the death toll that made the authorities nervous.

Police and government did not react immediately, as they saw these moves as a part of the "strategy of tension," which they themselves had staged. The government did, however, create a General Inspectorate for Action against Terrorism in 1974, but the *carabinieri* and the Interior Ministry Police did not collaborate very well (Collin, 1985: 199). Terrorist activities were waning by 1974. Links were broken between senior police and military figures and neo-fascist bombers, and law enforcement authorities managed to take two senior BR-terrorists out of circulation. After these events, BR moved into its second, more violent phase and was joined by the *Nuclei Armati Proletari* (NAP from Naples) and the *Primea Linea* (Turin). The BR were successful in striking at Italian society, as discipline, hierarchy and morale were strong. The BR infiltrated police ranks and financed its operations by bank robberies and kidnappings. The climax of BR's activities occurred in 1978, when Aldo Moro, who had been Prime Minister several times, was abducted and killed. This action was explained as an attempt to sabotage the "Historic Compromise" between the Christian Democratic party (DC) and the Italian Communist Party (PCI) negotiated by Moro (Collin, 1985: 200). Today, there is still controversy as to whether senior Christian Democrats were involved in blocking attempts to release Moro.[31]

The response to surging terrorism was a series of legislative and organizational reforms. New anti-terrorist legislation in 1975 (*Legge Reale*) tightened sanctions against terrorism, restricted the rights of the suspect, and increased police powers such as the interrogation of suspects for the duration of 48 hours without the presence of a lawyer and the bugging of telephones with a simple verbal authorization of a magistrate (Collin, 1985: 200; Monet, 1993: 243). In subsequent years, more anti-terrorist laws were publicly endorsed and introduced, giving police greater freedom to conduct searches of premises linked with suspected terrorists, extending the policeman's right to carry and use firearms, lengthening the time a suspect could be held without trial when legal proceedings were disrupted by violence, and allowing the preventive arrest of people of whom it was suspected they would commit a crime (Della Porta, 1992: 10).[32] A new anti-terrorist task force was established, called the *Direzione per le investigazione generali e per le operazioni speciali* (DIGOS) (Collin, 1985: 200). The regional anti-terrorist squads, which had been created in 1974 and which were performing judicial policing tasks, were disbanded in 1979 by a ministerial decree (Bernardi, 1979: 43). Ranks of terrorist units were infiltrated and paid informants were used to obtain the location of terrorist bases and names of members (Wilson, 1990: 396).

The organizational response was a request to Carabinieri

General Carlo Dalla Chiesa in 1974 to direct all anti-terrorist operations. He was given numerous facilities and was answerable directly to the Interior Minister; he was not obliged to keep the judiciary informed of his activities and his powers were kept secret from Parliament for a year (Clutterbuck, 1990: 31; Collin, 1985: 200). His controversial tactics proved successful: BR base apartments in Rome and Milan were raided; important *brigatisti* were arrested; crucial documents were captured. Despite his bad civil rights record, Dalla Chiesa was reappointed in 1978. After an initial resurgence of BR violence, Dalla Chiesa adopted other tactics, namely arresting senior members of the parliamentary left who could reveal information, and extracting information from BR terrorists in exchange for a reduced sentence (*pentiti*, a tactic which was later employed to obtain information from *mafiosi* and turned into law).[33] Dalla Chiesa was backed by the *Cossiga* Law (Law 15 of 6 February 1980), which introduced the concepts of "association with the aim of terrorism and of subversion of the democratic order" and "attack for subversive or terrorist purposes." Police powers were extended even further. Around the same time, intelligence-gathering was facilitated by setting up a computerized database in the Ministry of Interior, and police coordination was improved by allocating a magistrate to each terrorist incident (Clutterbuck, 1990: 38, 39). By the end of 1982, the authorities declared that both right- and left-wing terrorism were under control (Collin, 1985: 200). In the same year, the use of *pentiti* became legal as a controversial law was approved by parliament (Monet, 1993: 243). From this time onward, BR started to fragment into smaller, autonomous groups, and although left-wing terrorism maintained its presence in Italy, it gradually lost political support (Monet, 1993: 241).

Right-wing terrorist attacks claimed more lives than those of the left-wing, particularly because actions of the former were less specifically targeted at individuals. The most notorious right-wing actions have been the Piazza Fontana bombing in 1969, the Bologna railway station bombing in 1980, and the Bologna train bombing in 1984. Wilson (1990: 395) claims that right-wing terrorism was a much more shadowy subject because terrorists from the far right were much less willing to claim responsibility for their attacks, and they sought less publicity than the left-wing terrorists. International or "imported" terrorist attacks have been vicious, in particular the 1985 shooting by Middle Eastern terrorists at the Rome Airport (Wilson, 1990: 342).

Anti-terrorist experts relate the general decline in terrorism to events in East Europe. Antagonism and right-wing extremism have become the ascendent themes. It is felt that the terrorist threat now predominantly comes from separatist groups, such as the IRA in Northern Ireland and ETA in Spain. But in Italy itself, the criminal organizations with contacts in the higher echelons of society are believed to undermine the state and its citizens. The bombings in Rome and Florence earlier in 1993 may have been evidence of the widening of the "Mafia-concept," and this is used as further justification by the Anti-Terrorist police units in Italy to widen their remit to organized crime.[34] This "widening" could also be interpreted as a strategic diversion as it helps to obscure the fact that the law enforcement authorities have so far failed to clarify the possible links between terrorism and the Mafia.

### SECURITY THREAT II: THE MAFIA AND ORGANIZED CRIME

The word "mafia" was for the first time used in an official document in 1865 by Count Gualterio, who was appointed prefect of Palermo (Duggan, 1989: 26). At the time of the *Risorgimento*, the early Mafia resisted attempts by the Italian police to impose control over Sicilian arrests, but Sicilian landowners backed law enforcement authorities in the 1870s when they discovered that the Italian government was prepared to protect bourgeois interests as it feared popular unrest in the region (Collin, 1985: 202; Duggan, 1989: 37). The Mafia exploited the weakness of the government after the First World War but were countered by police chief Mori who sought to outlaw the organization (Duggan, 1989: 59). Fifteen mass trials were held between 1927 and 1929, and all but six of the 154 defendants were convicted. After a short retreat, the Mafia returned to the scene after the Second World War (Sterling, 1991: 61).

A thesis held by Pino Arlacchi (1986: 40) is that Mafia power is essentially complementary to the power of the state.[35] In essence, the Mafia echoes or shadows roles and functions of a state in three main areas: protection, repression, and mediation. First, the Mafia embodies the institutionalization of the protection against thieves and bandits, which has resulted in a system of taxation and racketeering. Second, the Mafia has its origins in the repression of nonconformist behavior, particularly that of thieves, robbers, vagabonds, homosexuals, bandits, and prostitutes. And third, the Mafia embodies a substitute for official justice by mediating in conflicts within the local society and the society's relations with the outside world (Arlacchi, 1986: 27-29). Gambetta (1993) claims, in contrast, that conceptualizing the Mafia as a legal system in its own right ought to be reconsidered-- the demise of the Mafia depends on whether the Italian state will choose to deliver genuine protection.

After the Second World War, Mafia activities became not only internationalized (trans-Atlantic connections),[36] but also moved into serious and organized crime, involving drug trafficking, arms trafficking, money laundering, protection rackets, and kidnapping (Collin, 1985: 203; Sassoon, 1986: 253; Sterling, 1991: 39). Although the Mafia was still at the service of politicians by delivering votes and financing political campaigns, the organization went into business during the 1970s, and violence became more endemic (Sassoon, 1986: 252). Its entrepreneurial activity is characterized by the discouragement of competition; by setting up a protection umbrella in the field in which the Mafia is trading; the holding down of wages and the erosion of social security rules; and the gaining of access to financial resources (contacts in the banking world, money laundering activities) (Arlacchi, 1986: 89ff). As a business enterprise--with the availability of capital and division of labor--the Mafia can hire personnel to get rid of inconvenient witnesses, police informers, magistrates, and police officers (Arlacchi, 1986: 195, 214).

In the past, two problems have hampered effective operations against the Mafia, and their rival organizations (the Neapolitan *Camorra*, Calabrean *N'drangheta*, and Sardinian banditism). First, the two police organizations did not manage to collaborate properly until police reorganization in the beginning of the eighties. Second, the Sicilian population regarded the *carabinieri* and police as foreigners, which has had negative repercussions on the relations between police and the Sicilian population, a problem aggravated by the *omertà* rule (i.e., Collin, 1985: 204; Duggan, 1989: 55, 59, 60, 61; Sterling, 1991: 45). One of the tactics used by the police has been to accept truces, but they have lost popularity since senior police officers and lawyers have been killed by the Mafia.

An important anti-Mafia law is the law of May 31, 1965, n. 575, which is called "Dispositions against the Mafia." The main measure of the law is to enable the prosecutor of the Republic to have suspects of Mafia-crimes placed under special surveillance. Also, the anti-Mafia law was expanded to include those who commit preparatory crimes. In 1975, this measure was extended to include people who were suspected of involvement in terrorism or subversive activities and other dangerous crimes, such as drug trafficking. The law of 1982 provided new preventive measures, and association with a criminal organization (Mafioso association) can in itself be sufficient for detention. The burden of proof became much lighter, as the prosecutors only had to demonstrate the suspect's habitual involvement in crime. With the law of March 31, 1990, n. 575, the ambit of the anti-Mafia legislation was widened to include those who appear to have links with Mafioso associations, with socially dangerous people, and with people involved in preparatory acts of *eversione* and terrorism. Inclusions were accumulative, for a more effective prosecution; it prompted the start of a process of "auto-generation" with a tendency of expansion (Nanula, 1992). New laws were passed in 1992 to establish a new witness protection program in line with that of the USA.[37] The killings of Judge Falcone in May 1992 and Judge Borsellino two months later put pressure on the Amato government to pass laws allowing police to tap telephones and the courts to seize the assets of suspected *Mafiosi*. To guarantee people's safety, 7,000 troops were sent to Sicily.[38] A special national anti-Mafia police investigation unit has been created, the DIA (*Direzione Investigativa Antimafia*), and confiscation of assets has enabled law enforcement authorities to hit the Mafia "where it hurts."[39] One of these instruments is the anti-money laundering law of 1990, which anticipated the 1991 EC Directive on Prevention of Use of the Financial System for the Purpose of Money Laundering. This law introduced a mandatory reporting system of suspicious transactions by financial institutions; failure to report can lead to the imposition of criminal charges, conviction of which may lead from anything like a fine to imprisonment.[40] Within the Interior Ministry, there is a high Commissariat for the coordination against organized crime, which is now a business claimed to jointly generate $17 billion in annual revenue.[41] The Commissariat is a special agency which consists of mixed units of the three main security forces and was created by law in 1981. It is directed by a director general of the public security (*pubblica sicurezza*) who is appointed by the Council of Ministers (Palidda, 1992: 247). Attempts to set up a national anti-Mafia pool of magistrates have been cumbersome because of tensions between the national and the regional magistrature, between the magistrates and the political parties, and between traditional and innovative systems of investigation.

Has the mood in Italy changed sufficiently to form a strong offensive against the Mafia? Giorgio Musio, the police chief (prefect) of Palermo, thinks that particularly the mood among the young has changed. People are beginning to stand up against the *omertà* tradition, and within Mafia organizations themselves, some have turned against the honored society.[42] The Italian state, meanwhile, has reopened the war with the Mafia and law enforcement authorities have been successful recently in arresting and trying some of the top members of the Cosa Nostra hierarchy, "Toto" Riina and Nitto Santapaola.[43] The witness protection programme has so far encouraged 400 *pentiti* to cooperate, and their evidence has already been used to incriminate a top police intelligence officer who was supposedly working against the Mafia and to expose corrupt justice officials and police officers. One of the most important *pentiti* has been Tommasso Buscetta, a repentant *Mafioso* who lives in America and benefits from the witness-protection scheme (Sterling, 1991: 82-101). He has alleged that journalist Pecorelli in 1979 and General Dalla Chiesa in 1982 were executed by the Mafia to protect Mr Andreotti.[44] Meanwhile, there have been a number of mass trials, leading to hundreds of convictions. One may wonder whether the role of the *pentiti* and the growing anti-Mafia sentiment in Italy are signals of an imminent change of balance or to what extent these signals are related to the collapse of the Christian-Democratic Party, the *tangentopoli,* and the end of the Cold War? The murder of Salvatore Lima, the Christian Democrat leader in Sicily, is generally regarded as a warning to Mr. Andreotti for failing to protect the Mafia.[45] The discovery that the Mafia has had contacts in the higher echelons of the DC party is not new. A final report of the parliamentary commission "Antimafia"--instituted in 1962--showed already in 1976 that there were multi-level contacts between the High Mafia and the DC, which were "the primary obstacles to police operations against criminality" (Collin, 1985: 204). At the moment, Mr. Andreotti, "seven times prime minister, life senator and the longest-serving, wiliest and probably the most powerful statesman in the country," stands accused of being the Mafia's reference in Rome.[46] As he has been a key person in the Italian government for a long time, he may have been the manager of a permanent appeasement which included guarding the boundaries between the territory of the Italian state and that of the Mafia, between the legitimate and the illegitimate arena.

It is striking that most solutions with regard to the Mafia have been sought in the criminal justice sphere, rather than within the economic and political. Gambetta (1993) suggests a whole battery of possible solutions: liberalization of the drugs market, abolition of state control over the price of cigarettes, simplification of the procedure for assigning public contracts, improvement of antitrust legislation, and a redesign of the voting process to minimize the opportunities for selling votes. In other words: remove the incentives.

### SECURITY THREAT III: ILLEGAL IMMIGRATION

Immigration is a relatively new phenomenon in Italy. Once one of the poorer countries in the European region, it used to produce emigrants: between 1861 and 1973, 26 million Italians left the country. Between 1876 and 1910 emigration was from the Veneto region to South America, in particular Argentina and Brazil, and from southern Italy to the United States (Sassoon, 1986: 98). After the Second World War, migrants would either move from south to north Italy because of Italy's "economic" or "territorial" dualism (Sassoon, 1986: 17, 36), or from south Italy to foreign countries, in particular Switzerland, France, and (West) Germany. This picture changed when Italy became a more prosperous country after experiencing an economic boom (Sassoon, 1986: 28) and started to receive immigrants, in particular from the Maghreb. But even at the beginning of the eighties, the number of immigrants that moved to Italy was small in comparison with other West European countries. At the beginning of 1991, 633,000 non-EC nationals legally resided in the country (compared with 391,000 in the middle of the eighties).[47] The number of aliens in Italy is now estimated at one million due to the continuing presence of unregistered aliens. One of the most spectacular events in Italy's immigration record was the arrival of 20,000 shipborne Albanians in the southern Italian ports of Brindisi, Otranto, and Bari in the spring of 1991; this is likely to be the reason for this remarkable rise in applications.[48] In the late summer of 1991, many Albanians were repatriated with the help of police, who were using batons and firing tear gas. This reaction demonstrates that illegal immigration is indeed perceived as a "threat" to Italy's internal security.[49]

On December 22, 1989 Bill No. 414/89 was approved; it included provisions on the regularization of labor, the entry of non-EC nationals, residence permits, etc. (Pastore, 1990: 334). All illegal immigrants present in Italy on December 31, 1989 were offered the "legalization" or "regularization" of their position, except those who had a criminal record (Pastore, 1990: 336). Due to the coming into force of this so-called "Martelli-law" in February 1990, police controls on immigration became more structured and centralized. Police powers particularly related to refusal of entry, flagging, and a new expulsion discipline (Pastore, 1990: 342).

The presence of immigrants in Italy unfortunately provoked a spate of racist attacks in various Italian regions (Furlong, 1992: 345). Two nights of violent clashes in Genoa between local inhabitants and African immigrants prompted Dr. Parisi, head of the *polizia di stato*, to say that the violence was caused by a battle between gangs of Italian and immigrant drug traffickers, but others said that local resentment against the thousands of Moroccans, Tunisians, Senegalese, Sudanese, and Nigerians had been used by the gangs as a pretext to launch their attacks.[50] In Puglia, 400 African migrant workers fled Stornara after attacks by locals, as unemployment and economic hardship in the region have caused friction between locals and migrants.[51] Significant is the rising popularity of extreme right-wing parties within the mainstream political culture and neo-fascist political parties (Husbands, 1991: 8; 1992: 272). In particular, the parties in Northern Italy have experienced a growing membership and are now represented in government.

Two members of Parliament demanded an inquiry into the case of Daud Addawe Ali, a Somali asylum-seeker who had been resident in Italy for a year and who had been beaten unconscious by police after having been blamed for causing consternation outside the aliens registration office in Rome (Amnesty International, 1992: 18). Notwithstanding these infringements of human rights by the police, law enforcement authorities are getting tougher on extreme right-wing persons and the threat of organised attacks against immigrants led to the introduction of a law which made racism, antisemitism and xenophobia a criminal offence.[52] In July 1993, the right-wing extremist Franco Freda--acquitted in 1985 of involvement in the bombing of the Piazza Fontana in Milan--was arrested by police for organizing a neo-Nazi party and for racism. Although the organization of a neo-Nazi party has been a crime since 1952, this was the first time that the law against racism had been used after it was approved in June 1993.[53]

## RATIONALES FOR CHANGE

The question which remains to be answered is the one raised by Marenin in the introductory chapter to this volume: is or can the Italian police be actively involved in the change of its own organization or in more fundamental societal changes? The answer to that question tends to be negative. The reasons are two-fold. First, one cannot avoid the impression that the Italian police organization remains firmly entangled in the power play between law and politics which reached its climax during the summer of 1994. A governmental decree issued in July determined that the power of investigating judges to order pre-trial detention in corruption cases would be limited, for fear of it being misused as a means of pressure.[54] The decree resulted in serious protests by investigating judges after the release of businessmen and other individuals who were suspected of corruption. In fact, Milan's anti-corruption team resigned entirely,[55] resulting in the abolishment of the decree. The Minister of Justice, Alfredo Biondi, then threatened to resign if his substitute proposal--to decrease the number of prisoners by means of alternative sentences (including house arrest)--were not accepted. As a consequence of the many aberrations in Italian society, wider police powers and *ad hoc* legislation have always been justified by both the political and the legal side. Hence it would be untactful for law enforcement agencies to take an independent stance. This paralysis is further reinforced by the firm line of command from the Interior Ministry. Organizational hierarchy, combined with a vast bureaucracy and fragmentary units, causes organic obscurity and a relative lack of autonomy, making it nearly impossible to mobilize individuals within the police organization. A top-down transformation is thus only realistic if it occurs in parallel with a wider transformation of the nature and organization of the Italian administration.

Change can therefore only be expected at the "thin blue line" between the police organization and citizens. Rather than the pursuit of social legitimacy, individual police officers may succeed in strengthening their social credibility by putting more effort into preventive policing, community policing, and improved accountability procedures, and by putting a human face to the practice of law enforcement--a case so well illustrated in the film *Il ladro dei bambini* by Gianni Amelio. The Italian police will have to move from a position of being tolerated by society to a position of being accepted. But this bottom-up change--the demystification of the cop's enigma--will be hard to achieve as long as the wide occurrence of organized crime results in a persistent demand for repressive and proactive policing. Furthermore, it is hard to quietly contemplate innovative organizational scenarios and criminal justice strategies in the context of a perpetual distraction by political and criminal crises. In the absence of bottom-up transformations, the Italian police organization may do nothing more than reproduce the status quo. The existing order will remain unchallenged, and rather than acting as a semi-autonomous actor within the social matrix (Falk Moore, 1978), Italian police officers will remain the face of state sovereignty.

The constant preoccupation with internal security crises tends to overshadow the crucial position of Italian law enforcement agencies in regional, European, and global policing initiatives. More than any other member state of the European Union, the Italians have welcomed international cooperation against drug trafficking and the Mafia, in particular with the American Drug Enforcement Administration. Hence, the Italians have built up considerable expertise in the fight against organized crime which could be exploited by the other EU Member States and be further developed in the context of the new European Police Office (Europol).

The question is whether this influence can be reversed as well. Already visible within the EU is a north-south divide (Zanders, 1994: 14), which is largely caused by the wide divergence between the predominantly civil policing styles in northern Europe (especially within the candidate Nordic states) and the still strongly military-oriented styles of policing in southern Europe. It remains to be seen whether increased cross-border police cooperation results in an approximation of policing styles, cultures and modus operandi. The Italian police organization could--if it desires these changes--profit from the vast experience in the northern European countries with forms of community policing (cutting the distance between police and citizen), preventive criminal justice programmes, decentralized police organizations, and accountability systems (ombudsman and police complaint boards).

Apart from an increased participation in international law enforcement training programs (e.g., the Police Summer Course and perhaps a future European Police Academy), international exchange programs and language courses, this may require firm reorientations within the Italian police organization. First, although Italian law enforcement agencies have been one of the strongest advocates of European integration (Hine, 1993: 286), their professional orientation has always been strongly directed towards the United States rather than towards other EU member states; this could change if Italy were to be more actively involved in the push for improved European police cooperation. Second, the Interior Ministry is probably the least likely of all other ministries to be drawn into the process of European integration. As long as the Italian police organization will not occupy a semi-autonomous position vis-à-vis the Interior Ministry, other Ministries such as Foreign Affairs could promote further integration of the Italian law enforcement administration within the EU. Finally, an international exchange of knowledge and expertise about international organized crime could contribute to falsify the perception of organized crime as a primarily indigenous affair; without cooperation with foreign police organizations, one of the worst afflictions of Italian society will remain unsolved.

## NOTES

1. Parts of this chapter were published earlier as a working paper entitled "The Italian Police and European Police Cooperation" (No. XIII, Working Paper Series "A System of European Police Cooperation after 1992," University of Edinburgh, 1993), which was written in the context of an ESRC research-project (R000 23 2639) on European police cooperation. I am grateful to Dr. David Elwood and Dottore Nicoletta Policek for their valuable comments and suggestions, and to Dr. Gaetano Picolella, who organized a tailored interview program for me at the Ministry of the Interior in Rome in June 1993. The author is responsible for the content of this text.

2. *The Economist*, June 26, 1993, Italy Survey, p. 3; see also: *The Independent*, February 4, 1993, "Italy's Avalanche of Scandals Thunders On"; *Financial Times*, February 13-14, 1993, "Something Rotten in the State of Italy."

3. Article 16 of the Law on Criminal Procedure, 1930. This norm remained in place until 1963. However, in factual terms the immunity rule remained and was only slightly modified by the *Reale* law (May 22, 1975), when it was ruled that not the procurator of the Republic but the general procurator would instruct an investigation into allegations of this nature (Bernardi, 1979: 25).

4. After the crisis preceding the First World War, fascism was attractive for policemen in both Italy and Germany as it offered a clear role and new prestige (Reiter, 1993: 6).

5. For more statistics, see Canosa (1976: 106, 131) and Boatti (1978: 29).

6. If the *guardia di finanza* and the municipal police are included, the number becomes 498 police officers per 100,000 inhabitants.

7. There was a bill which proposed that not carrying an identity card should be penalized, but this was incompatible with the Constitution (Canosa, 1976: 239).

8. *The Independent*, September 7, 1993, "Britain Faces Hearing on SAS Killings."

9. Law of April 1, 1981, n. 121, *Nuovo ordinamento dell'Amministrazione della pubblica sicurezza.*

10. We will not here discuss the "Female Police," which was created in 1959 and which monitored public morality and dress (Bernardi, 1979: 48).

11. Application procedure where all candidates have to take a test. D.P.R. December 23, 1983, n. 904.

12. *Facts, Figures and General Information*, page 61.

13. *Facts, Figures and General Information*, page 62.

14. In Spain for instance, the number of female police officers in the national corps is 400, which makes up a total of less than 1 percent (Monet, 1993: 128).

15. Art. 33 of Act. no. 121/82, clause 3. In *Facts, Figures and General Information*, page 62.

16. For further organizational details, see Scandone and Atzori, 1990: 187-193.

17. *Facts, Figures and General Information*, page 56.

18. The militarization of the police was introduced by Rdl of June 31, 1943, n. 687, Art. 1. (Bernardi, 1979: 35). Syndicalization was partly due to the ratification in 1961 of the European Social Charter, and of the Geneva Convention in 1949 (Ibid: 81).

19. In 1919, the *carabinieri* were integrated in the army, but a decree in 1922 inserted the *carabinieri* as an *unica forza armata* under permanent service of the *pubblica sicurezza* (Canosa, 1976: 21).

20. *Facts, Figures and General Information*, page 55.

21. Brochure, *"La Guardia di Finanza."*

22. Created with the law of October 24, 1977, n. 801.

23. *The Independent*, July 31, 1993, "Italy Investigates Bombings and Buries Victims."

24. *Financial Times*, May 28, 1993, "Five Die as Car Bomb Damages Florence Art Gallery"; *Washington Post*, May 29, 1993, "Italians March in Outrage over Museum Bombing"; *Financial Times*, May 29-30, 1993, "Italy Fears Renewed Attacks"; *NRC Weekeditie*, June 1, 1993, *"Wat heeft het voor zin om een aanslag te plegen op de Uffizi."*

25. *The Independent*, August 4, 1993, "Move to Change Italy's 'State Secrets' Law."

26. *The Guardian*, August 3, 1993, "Ciampi Vows Bombers Will Be Beaten."

27. *The Independent*, November 3, 1993, "Italy's Secret Service Faces Big Shake-up."

28. *Financial Times*, October 19, 1993, "Italian Leader Acts over State Security."

29. *The Independent*, November 5, 1993, "Italians Leap to Defend President"; *The Independent On Sunday*, November 7, 1993, "Italy Still on Red Alert after Week of Alarms."

30. *Financial Times*, November 5, 1993, "Ciampi Speeds Intelligence Service Reform."

31. *The Guardian*, April 12, 1993, "Moro Murder File To Be Released."

32. "The 'emergency laws' authorized the arrest of anyone who violated the prohibition against disguising oneself (Law 533/77); abolished the maximum limit for preventive detention when a trial was suspended because it was impossible to form a jury or to exercise defence rights (Law 296/77); modified the rules for the formation of popular juries (Law 74/78); introduced a special prison system (Laws 1/77 and 450/77); increased sentences for terrorist crimes; and limited individual guarantees for citizens and defendants (Laws 191/78 and 15/80)." The latter introduced the "preventive arrest." (Della Porta, 1992: 10).

33. "Penitence Law" (Law 304) of May 29, 1982.

34. Personal interview with Mr. Fasano, Head of Directorate of Prevention, Rome, June 10, 1993.

35. See also *The Economist*, April 24, 1993, "The Sicilian Mafia. A State within a State."

36. For example, see *The Independent*, May 16, 1993, "Mafia Buys up Its Own Island in the Caribbean."

37. *Financial Times*, June 5-6, 1993; "At War with the Mafia in an Island of Fear."

38. *The Economist*, June 29, 1993, Italy Survey, p. 15.

39. *The Economist*, April 24, 1993, "The Sicilian Mafia. A State within a State." The DIA is connected with the DNA (*Direzione Nazionale Antimafia*), which is a central body within the regional offices. Another important body is the General Council for the Fight against Organized Crime (*Consiglio Generale per la Lotta Crimini Organizzati*), which is composed of the heads of state police, *carabinieri* and *guardia di finanza*, and the Director of DNA. This Council prepares strategies and guidelines against organized crime, and the coordination of these strategies is carried out at provincial and regional level.

40. *Legge* 19.3.1990, no. 55.

41. *Facts on File*, January 23, 1992, citing a report by the Italian Economic Institute (CENSIS), adds that organized crime accounts for 2 percent of the nation's gross domestic product, four-fifths of which came from illegal activities and one-fifth from legitimate enterprises connected to crime (e.g., public contracts obtained through corruption or intimidation).

42. *Financial Times*, June 5-6, 1993; "At War with the Mafia in an Island of Fear"; *Financial Times*, July 20, 1993, "Sicily Shows Way to Clean-up."

43. *The Independent*, January 16, 1993, "Mafia's 'Boss of All Bosses' Held"; *Financial Times*, January 16-17, 1993, "Italian Authorities Arrest Alleged Cosa Nostra Boss"; *The Independent*, January 18, 1993, "Mafia Chief 'Sold by His Own Driver'"; *The Independent*, May 8, 1993, "Police in Big Mafia Roundup"; *The Independent*, May 19, 1993, "Italian Police Score With Capture of a Mafia Boss"; *Financial Times*, May 19, 1993, "Italian Raid Nets Chief in Cosa Nostra"; *NRC*

*Weekeditie*, May 25, 1993, *"De mafia is nog niet verslagen"*; *The Independent*, October 9, 1993, "Mafia Kingpin Jailed for Life."

44. *The Economist*, June 29, 1993, Italy Survey, p. 9.

45. *The Economist*, June 29, 1993, Italy Survey, p. 15; *The Guardian*, March 30, 1993, "Andreotti 'Was Mafia's Man at the Heart of the State'"; *Financial Times*, March 30, 1993, "Italian Spotlight on Links to Mafia."

46. *The Independent*, March 29, 1993, "Andreotti Suspected of Links with Mafia"; *The Guardian*, March 30, 1993, "Andreotti 'Was Mafia's Man at the Heart of the State'"; *The Economist*, June 29, 1993, Italy Survey, p. 9.

47. OECD-EEC statistics, 1985-1987.

48. Keesing's *Facts on File*, 1991: 38105; see also *The Independent*, March 8, 1991, "Albanian Army Sent into Port of Exodus"; *Financial Times*, March 9-10, 1991, "Shivering Albanians Shelter in Brindisi's Cattle Trucks"; *The Independent*, March 9, 1991, "Empty Welcome for Albanians"; *Financial Times*, March 11, 1991, "Albania Declares Military Zone to Stop Refugees"; *The Independent*, March 12, 1991, "Albanians Return from a 'Foolish' Italian Escapade."

49. *Financial Times*, August 12, 1991, "Clashes Erupt as Albanian Refugees Shun Repatriation"; *The Independent*, August 12, 1991, "New Europe Rejects the Poor of Albania"; *NRC*, August 19, 1991, *"Italië stuurt ook harde kern Albanezen terug"*; *Volkskrant*, August 19, 1991, *"Verjaging Albanezen zorgvuldig voorbereid."*

50. *The Independent*, July 23, 1993, "Italian Gangsters Clash with Africans."

51. *The Independent*, August 18, 1993.

52. *Financial Times*, November 25, 1992, "The Rise of the Far Right in Europe"; *The Guardian*, November 26, 1992, "Neo-Nazis Face European Crack-down on Racism."

53. *Financial Times*, July 13, 1993, "Far-right Arrests in Italy."

54. *NRC Handelsblad*, July 16, 1994, "*Italiaanse justitie had voorarrest als wapen.*"

55. *Financial Times*, July 15, 1994, "Milan's Anti-corruption Magistrates Team Quits."

## SOURCES

Amnesty International (1992), *Racist Torture and Ill-Treatment by Police in Western Europe*, EUR 03/01/92.

Arlacchi, Pino (1986), *Mafia Business. The Mafia Ethic and the Spirit of Capitalism*, 2nd ed., translated by Martin Ryle, London: Verso.

Benyon, John, Lynne Turnbull, Andrew Willis, Rachel Woodward and Adrian Beck (1993), *Police Co-operation in Europe: An Investigation*, Leicester: University of Leicester, Centre for the Study of Public Order.

Bernardi, Alberto (1979), *La Riforma della Polizia. Smilitarizzazione e Sindacato*, Torino: Giulio Einandi (Editore).

Boatti, Giorgio (1978), *L'arma. Carabinieri da de Lorenzo a Mino 1962-1977*, Feltrinelli: Milano.

Calvi, Fabrizio (1993), *Het Europa van de Peetvaders: de Maffia Verovert een Continent*, Leuven/Kritak, Amsterdam/Balans.

Canosa, Romano (1976), *La Polizia in Italia dal 1945 a Oggi*. Il Mulino: Universale Paperbacks.

Clutterbuck, Richard (1990), *Terrorism, Drugs and Crime in Europe After 1992*, London: Routledge.

Collin, Richard O. (1985), "The Blunt Instruments: Italy and the Police," in John Roach and Jürgen Thomaneck (eds.), *Police and Public Order in Europe*, London: Croom Helm, 185-214.

Davis, John A. (1988), *Conflict and Control: Law and Order in Nineteenth-Century Italy*, London: Macmillan.

Della Porta, Donatella (1992), "Social Movements and the State. First Thoughts from a Research on the Policing of Protest," revised version of a paper presented at the conference "European/American Perspectives on Social Movements," Washington D.C., August 13-15, 1992.

D'Orsi, Angelo (1972), *La Polizia. Le Forze dell'Ordine Italiano*. Milano: Feltrinelli.

Duggan, Christopher (1989), *Fascism and the Mafia*. New Haven and London: Yale University Press.

*Facts, Figures and General Information* (1989), International Conference for Policewomen, March 19-23, 1989, The Netherlands. Compiled and Edited by Frans-Jan Mulschlegel and Marjan Stolwerk, Warnsveld.

Falk Moore, Sally (1978), *Law as Process: An Anthropological Approach*, London: Routledge and Kegan Paul.

Ferrarotti, Franco (1979), *Alle Radici della Violenza*, Milano: Rizzoli Editore.

Furlong, Paul (1992), "The Extreme Right in Italy: Old Orders and Dangerous Novelties," *Parliamentary Affairs*, 45, 3, 345-356.

Gambetta, Diego (1993), *The Sicilian Mafia. The Business of Protection*, Cambridge/London: Harvard University Press.

Gleizal, J.-J., J. Gatti-Domenach, and C. Journès (1993), *La Police. Le Cas de Démocraties Occidentales*, Paris: Presses Universitaires de France.

Hine, David (1993), *Governing Italy. The Politics of Bargained Pluralism*, Oxford: Clarendon Press.

Husbands, Christopher T. (1991), "The Extreme Right--a Brief European Overview," in *Race and Immigration*, Runnymede Trust Bulletin, No. 247, July/August, 5-14.

Husbands, Christopher T. (1992), "The Other Face of 1992: The Extreme-Right Explosion in Western Europe," *Parliamentary Affairs*, 45, 3, July, 267-284.

Monet, Jean-Claude (1993), *Police et Sociétés en Europe*, Paris: La documentation française.

Nanula, Gaetano (1992), *Lotta alla Mafia*, Milano: Giuffre.

Palidda, Salvatore (1992), "*Les forces de sécurité en Italie,*" in *Polices d'Europe*, avec la collaboration de J.M. Erbes, J.C. Monet, A. Funk, etc., Paris: IHESI, Editions de l'Harmattan, 235-266.

Parisi, Vincenzo (1993), "Round Table: Citizens and Criminal Justice," in *Understanding Crime Experiences of Crime and Crime Control*, Acts of the International Conference, Rome, November 18-20, 1992, Anna Alvazzi del Frate, Uglješa Zvekić and Jan J.M. van Dijk (eds.), Rome: UNICRI, Pub. No. 49, 427-429.

Pastore, Massimo (1990), "*La nuova legge sugli stranieri extracommunitari: disciplina innovativa o razionalizzazione dell'esistente?*" *Questione Giustizia*, 2, 331-345.

Reiter, Herbert (1993), "Reform or Restoration? The Police in Italy and Germany 1943/45-1950," paper for the meeting of the International Research Group on "Police Knowledge", June 6-7, 1993, EUI, Florence.

Sassoon, Donald (1986), *Contemporary Italy. Politics, Economy and Society Since 1945*. London and New York: Longman.

Scandone, Giuseppe, and Atzori, Pierfrancesco (1990), *Le Polizie d'Europa*, Roma: Edizioni Laurus Robuffo.

Sterling, Claire [1991 (1990)], *The Mafia. The Long Reach of the International Sicilian Mafia*, London: Grafton.

Tarrow, Sydney (1989), *Democracy and Disorder. Protest and Politics in Italy 1965-1975*, Oxford: Clarendon Press.

Wilson, Frank L. (1990), *European Politics Today. The Democratic Experience*, Englewood Cliffs: Prentice Hall.

Zanders, Patrick (1994), "*Europese Politiesamenwerking in een historisch perspektief,*" in Transpol, *Internationalisering door Grenzeloze Samenwerking*, Lelystad: Koninklijke Vermande, 7-20.

# BAD APPLES OR ROTTEN BARREL? POLICING IN NORTHERN IRELAND

## Graham Ellison and Jim Smyth

### INTRODUCTION

The erosion of the legitimacy of state power is a feature of the late twentieth century, intimately related to the questioning of the canons of the Enlightenment, the universalistic prescriptions of which were used to underpin the stability of state and society in the modern world. Civil society, the internalisation of the norms of democracy, individualism, and personal freedom have found their authority undermined in a world where the compression of time and space and the remorseless logic of capital accumulation has weakened the power of local elites--economically as well as ideologically--and threatened the social cohesion of clearly defined national entities.

Power structures gain legitimacy the hard way through a prolonged process of compromise and reform and while the resulting reality is never complete and seamless, a (sometimes precarious) socio-political consensus and stability emerges. The current preoccupation with the apparent implosion of legitimacy is not confined to western democracies, but it is here that the most anguished cries are heard. The demystification of the British monarchy, often seen by outsiders as an amusing real life soap opera, is taken seriously in a society where an implicit acceptance of hierarchy and deference has formed a pillar of stability for a long time. In the United States, the hounding of the presidency by a media which seems to have divested itself of loyalty to state and nation makes an uncomfortable parallel.

It is important to avoid the temptation of retreat into nostalgia for an imagined past of peace, security and social cohesion, to glory in the imagined "Victorian values" of Margaret Thatcher, or the "back to the futurism" of the Hollywood dream industry. Nowhere is nostalgia more prevalent than in the law-and-order debate often dominated by the specter of moral panics and a sense of bewilderment at the state of the world. This common sense and rosy-hued view of the past finds its academic expression in the Enlightenment idea of historical progress and the power of reason. Such an approach sees the law as evolving from universal principles--just laws--and that agreement about universal principles forms the basis of legitimacy including the mandate of the police.

The dilemma facing English rule in Ireland, where the legitimacy of this rule was never generally accepted, is neatly encapsulated by the nineteenth century commentator, A. V. Dicey. Dicey (1973) is in no doubt as to the problems presented by ruling Ireland, and he openly admits that coercive laws are often counter productive.

> When the enforcement of the law is called 'Coercion' not only does the criminal think himself to be in the right, or at any rate think that the law is a wrongful law, but also the society to which he belongs holds that the law breaker is maintaining a moral right against an immoral law (p.113).

Dicey's answer to this problem was to evade it by stating that a Coercion Act should not be aimed at the "direct enforcement of rules opposed to public opinion" but would focus upon deeds "in themselves condemned by the human conscience" (p.115). This appeal to universal values and "civilised" discourse prompted the Irish to recognise the validity of just laws and their embodiment in the British Constitution and to act accordingly. According to Dicey and other English commentators, the fact that the Irish did not accept the validity of the English version of the rule of law had nothing to do with the law itself but with the inherently unreasonable nature of the Irish. The central dilemma of a policy based upon a mix of reform and repression was posed: to uphold the rule of law in Ireland the state was forced to abolish it in a welter of emergency legislation (Farrell, 1986).[1]

This historical reality, which consists not just in the absence of legitimacy but in the active and often militant opposition to the state and its agents by a significant section of the population, forms the background to the organisation, rhetoric, and practice of policing in Northern Ireland. The organisation of the Royal Ulster Constabulary

(RUC) is designed, as was its predecessor the Royal Irish Constabulary (RIC), with the primary role of counterinsurgency and political control in mind, to which the activity of 'normal policing' is subordinated. The practice of policing, such as the use of lethal force, is concealed and obscured in an ideological discourse which attempts to present the police as a body serving the community as a whole in a professional and neutral manner. This discourse and the institutional framework of the law and police organisation seek to justify police practices which differ significantly from the norm in democratic societies. In this chapter we will attempt to separate the rhetoric from reality by focusing upon two crucial aspects of policing in Northern Ireland: the use of lethal force and the discourse of professionalism.

## AFTER PARTITION--THE RUC

The somewhat erratic and disorganised policing of Ireland was consolidated and centralised in 1836 with the establishment of the "Constabulary of Ireland" to be known as the Royal Irish Constabulary (RIC). A dense web of 1,400 police posts was opened and manned by an armed force of around 10,000 by the middle of the century. The RIC was to be the model for subsequent colonial police forces and its role was very definitely a political one. It was an instrument of state policy--"the eyes and ears of Dublin Castle"--and reported directly back to the central administration at the Castle (the center of British administration in Ireland). The level of resistance to British rule, and the fact that a large part of crime in nineteenth-century Ireland (in contrast to the situation in England) was made up of public order offences and acts of "collective violence" which were a direct response to the land problem and agrarian reform, meant that the RIC had as a primary function the gathering of political intelligence and the control of political violence (Palmer, 1988: 380). Given the existence of a substantial nationalist minority within the boundaries of Northern Ireland, it is hardly surprising that the Royal Ulster Constabulary was to follow the model developed by the RIC.

After partition in 1922,[2] the RUC was to become the armed agent of the Unionist state (Farrell, 1986). Clearly, all police forces--along with all other elements of the security apparatus--are there, in the last analysis, to defend the state, but the level of relative autonomy enjoyed by such institutions is crucial. A state confident of its legitimacy and political stability can allow itself the luxury of detachment from the problems of social control confident that the relationship between citizen and the agencies of control will be based upon shared assumptions and a belief in the due process of law. These assumptions could not be made in the new entity of Northern Ireland, where a significant minority were alienated from the new state and felt that their needs and aspirations were being denied. The new statelet used force to establish itself and, in 1922, passed the Civil Authorities (Special Powers) Act[3] which was to form the basis of the unionist monopoly of political power for the next half a century.[4] This piece of legislation not only transferred many powers of the judiciary to the executive but also removed the actions of the Minister of Home Affairs from parliamentary scrutiny. The Act gave the Minister the power "to take all such steps and issue all such orders as may be necessary for the preserving of peace." The Unionist dominated parliament passed the Act with only one member seeing fit to comment on the powers given to the Minister, remarking that the bill really needed only to comprise one section: "the Home Secretary should have the power to do what he likes, or else let someone else do what he likes for him" (Newark, 1955: 47).

The state, therefore, opted for a "security" response to internal dissent as opposed to one based upon the due process of law. The instrument of this response was to be the Police. By the middle of 1922 there were 50,000 police (full and part time), supported by 13 battalions of British soldiers, for a population of one and a half million, one third of which was Catholic. Opposition to the state was crushed without mercy and the Special Powers Act was the bedrock of policing in the province. As one commentator has put it:

> In Northern Ireland, the Special Powers Act, though it was occasionally used against Protestants, bore heavily on one section of the population, the Roman Catholics, for the simple reason that the IRA enjoyed a wide measure of Catholic support and, indeed, could in some areas of Belfast be regarded as defenders of the Catholic population (Boyce, 1979: 39).

Despite numerous military campaigns launched by the IRA between 1922 and 1958 and more peaceful attempts at resistance, the Stormont state, through ruthless use of its powers, managed to maintain its rule until the onset of the Civil Rights Movement in the late sixties. The Civil Rights Movement (CRM) was a child born of the union of local circumstances and global forces. It presented the state with demands which transcended the traditional irredentist terrain of conflict and which could not be brushed away by simple repression. The traditional nationalist focus upon the total abolition of the state was replaced by a reformist platform directed at the redressing of discrimination and the sectarian nature of many, tacitly sanctioned, social and economic practices. This focus upon democratic rights and the universalistic norms of social democracy and the welfare state were hardly revolutionary in the eyes of the outside world (which for the first time was party to the events on the streets of Belfast and Derry through the medium of television), but posed an insoluble dilemma for the local state.

The very stability of the state, and its legitimacy in the eyes of the Protestants the Unionist majority, was based upon the exclusion and repression of the minority and this, in turn, was the fundamental task of the RUC: the upholding of a blatantly discriminatory system. The response of the Unionist regime to the reformist demands of the CRM and the mass collective--and peaceful--actions of the demonstrators was predictably brutal and repressive. Preferring to interpret the demands of the CRM as another twist in the IRA campaign to destroy the state, it unleashed the full panoply of repressive powers against it. That this occurred under the gaze of the television cameras was enough to spur the London government into action but not before a resurgent IRA had embarked upon a new military campaign.

## THE BRITISH RESPONSE: NORMALISATION

The initial response of the British state to civil disorder in Ireland was hesitant and incoherent. It was only after the collapse of the RUC as a disciplined force in the widespread street disturbances of 1969 that British troops were sent to Northern Ireland. Given the post-war experience of the British Army's--often reluctant--withdrawal from empire, it is not surprising that the Colonial war model of counterinsurgency was adopted in Ireland (Kitson, 1971). This consisted essentially of the primacy of military, virtual martial law, and internment without trial. Apart from proving ineffective in dealing with widespread civil disturbance and an emergent IRA, the damage done to the image of Britain abroad was incalculable.

From 1972 onwards the state began to modify its counterinsurgency strategy in an attempt to "normalise" the situation. The main components of this strategy were:

a reorganisation and rearming of the police force to allow the introduction of police primacy;

the setting up of full-time interrogation centers to contain suspects arrested on the basis of a new centralised intelligence gathering system;

the establishment of special courts ("Diplock Courts") consisting of one judge to try terrorist suspects;[5] and

the professionalisation of police practice and rhetoric.

The overall strategic intention of the changes in policing was to present a picture of normalisation of a society which was, apart from the activities of a small unrepresentative minority, carrying on with its normal day to day activities under the benign eye of a professional and neutral police force. The reality of a protracted and bloody internal war was, where possible, evaded and there was constant stress upon the proposition that the IRA had no widespread support but only continued to exist through coercion and intimidation. A central plank of state rhetoric was the proposition that soldiers and police were subjected to the rule of law and were constrained to act within the law. As Brodgen (1987) has pointed out, the difference between Colonial and "normal" policing is far from distinct and to a large extent ideological. Police forces do not exist in a political and social vacuum, and organisational and other reforms are a response to a specific situation or situations and are not simply part of some abstract process of professionalisation or liberalisation.

Indeed, the policy of normalisation embarked upon in the seventies was the central element in a concerted counterinsurgency strategy designed to criminalise political violence and develop a sophisticated process of gaining convictions based upon intelligence gathering and interrogation. The objective of the reforms was not "to improve  police relations with the Catholics" (Brewer, 1990, 1991, 1994; Brewer and Magee, 1990)--indeed the effect was  quite the opposite--but to defeat the IRA both militarily and politically. The inherent contradictions in this type of policy are vividly illustrated by the controversy over the use of lethal force by the security forces.

## USE OF LETHAL FORCE BY THE SECURITY FORCES

Writing in *Discipline and Punish* on the topic of judicial executions, Foucault (1977) remarks that the public execution is not only to be understood as a judicial ritual but also as a public one--"it belongs, even in minor cases, to the ceremonies by which power is manifested" (p.14). It is Foucault's contention (but one that has been questioned in terms of historical facts--e.g., Merquior, 1991:96) that the public execution disappeared in Continental Europe at the end of the eighteenth century as a result of the unstable nature of the impact of such events upon the crowd who were likely to use it as a reason for rioting. Foucault cites the English case as a deviation from his (much criticised) periodisation, remarking that the public execution lasted longer there than in other European countries. This persistence he attributes to the need for rigor as a result of the social disturbances which took place between 1770-1820. One presumes that Foucault is referring here to such popular protests as the Corn Bill Riots of 1815-1820 and the Luddite movement of 1811-1812. But disruptive and dangerous as these popular protests were, they were mere affrays compared to the unrest in Ireland. The Rebellion of 1798 left 30,000 dead on both sides and, between March and December 1799, 231 native Irish suspected of involvement in the rebellion were condemned to death, although about a quarter of these sentences were commuted (Foster, 1988: 280). Executions were public and ritualised: a common practice was to hang rebels at cross-roads and the corpse, wrapped in sacking, was left to putrefy. The political nature of collective violence in Ireland lay at the heart of the response of the state and the construction of an extensive and dense security apparatus. The "normal" crime rate in Ireland was much lower than in England (Townshend, 1983: 6), but politically motivated crime was a source of concern to the state during the nineteenth century. By the middle of the century the density of policing was five times that of England, relative to population (Palmer, 1988: 34). This density of surveillance and control, by a centrally organised and quasi-military force, was a clear index of the absence of consensus and the conflict between the native population and the state expressed itself in ritualised encounters at fairs and other gatherings. The RIC felt compelled to fly the flag at fairs and other popular festivals, and their presence among large numbers of the recalcitrant peasantry was a recipe for violent encounters.

In the two decades after 1824, 956 peasants were killed in

encounters with the RIC, the majority shot at fairs or other situations conductive to riots. During the same period, 44 police were killed, 13 of them in one incident. While those suspected of involvement in the killing of policemen were hunted down with great persistence, we can find no evidence that any policeman was convicted of murder in the courts, and in the one documented case of two members of the RIC being charged with the murder of civilians, an acquittal followed. The charging of the two constables moved the Chief Secretary for Ireland to comment that "the police may as well be broken up at once" if they were found guilty (Palmer, 1988). The justifications for the use of lethal force by the RIC have a contemporary ring: the peasantry were engaged in a conspiracy against the police, there was widespread intimidation, and, given the situation, the police had little option but to open fire. The majority of the deaths during this period were the result of ritualised collective violence against the representatives of the state. On the other hand, the state itself was using the police in an equally ritualised fashion to try and convince the rural population that resistance was futile and potentially fatal for the participants. If consent was not forthcoming, the state would settle for compliance, and such compliance however brutally imposed and grudgingly given, would have to suffice.

## LETHAL FORCE IN THE CURRENT CONFLICT

Since 1969, over 350 people have been killed by the security forces in Northern Ireland. Over 300 of these deaths have been of members of the nationalist community and have been predominantly male, young, and working class. Since 1982, 80 state killings have taken place, and all but five were of Catholics (Committee for the Administration of Justice, 1993a: 7). A large proportion of those killed, of both religions, died in disputed circumstances or were unarmed. More than half, or 190, were civilians uninvolved in paramilitary activity. Over the same period, 27 policemen or soldiers have been prosecuted for incidents involving the deaths of civilians by the use of firearms. Three prosecutions have resulted in a suspended sentence and two convictions for murder. The first soldier to be convicted for murder was sentenced to life imprisonment for the killing of an unarmed civilian in 1983. He was released after two and a half years and allowed to rejoin his regiment. This is the only known case of a convicted murderer being allowed to serve in the British Army.

The third soldier was convicted in 1993 (and lost an appeal in 1994), but the judge did not impose even a minimum sentence. No police officer has been convicted of murder while on duty and in the case of members of specialised undercover units--such as the SAS (Special Air Services)--which have been responsible for at least 67 deaths, not one prosecution has ensued.

In the context of the total number of people who have died as a result of the conflict in Northern Ireland--over 3,500--the numbers killed by the security forces in disputed circumstances may well appear to be a regrettable but inevitable side effect of what has become Europe's longest-lasting armed conflict this century. It is perhaps unfortunate that, while all deaths are to be regretted, some assume a particular political resonance and effect the political process in a significant fashion both directly and indirectly by drawing attention to the broader implications of state practices.

As far as the British state is concerned, the prime objective of security policy is the "eradication of terrorism," and, given the protracted nature of the conflict, security policy tends to dominate official thinking and become an end in itself. This has led to a situation where a clear discrepancy has emerged between international legal standards concerning the prevention of the arbitrary taking of life and the law as applied in Northern Ireland (Amnesty International, 1994; Liberty, 1993). The present legal framework (based upon the Criminal Law Act of 1967) rests upon the concept of "reasonable force" in the circumstances in which the disputed killing took place. This allows the defence in such cases to make hypothetical arguments such as the fear in the mind of a member of the security forces that the victim might be armed, or be reaching for a weapon or, in a crucial House of Lords judgement, might pose a threat to the lives of soldiers or police at some future date.[6]

The state continues to maintain that there is no "shoot to kill" policy and that police and soldiers are subjected to the same law as civilians and have no immunity from prosecutions. The question of whether there is a "shoot to kill" policy in operation in Northern Ireland is of great political sensitivity. It is clear that the state, for both ideological and legal reasons, must continue to deny the existence of such a policy, and it is safe to assume that no such policy has ever been formally adopted, minuted, and documented (Liberty, 1993: 24).

However, even if such documents do not exist, policy can be inferred from a pattern of events and the response of the agencies of the state to such events. If the British state were at war in Ireland, the question would be redundant, and it is the impossibility of declaring war in a province of one's own country that forms one parameter of the ambiguous stance of the state. In the absence of a state of war, or even of the declaration of a state of emergency or martial law, the state is forced to fall back upon the idea of normalisation: as in the last century, it is a small minority who are subverting and intimidating a peace-loving majority.

The state finds it difficult to admit the full extent of resistance to its presence in Ireland and any such admission would undermine crucial parameters of policy. The state may not believe that it actually can defeat the IRA, but in the absence of a political solution it is forced to act as though such a defeat is possible both for reasons involving its own self-understanding and the morale of the security forces. The use of lethal force is a crucial dimension in this balancing act. The state must be seen to be actively pursuing the type of enemy it has socially constructed: the IRA member on active service intent on murder or the destruction of property. The demonisation of the "terrorist" has the effect of depolitising the failure of the state to establish a workable level of legitimacy and opens up a spiral of resistance and repression. Given the need of the state to avoid public and administrative acceptance of the extent of the nature of the problem, it is forced to envelop the use of lethal force in a cloak of studied ambiguity.

Although the state continues to deny the existence of a policy of "shoot to kill," an examination of the practice of counterinsurgency operations makes it clear that this is a questionable denial. As mentioned above, the law governing the use of lethal force is inadequate in that it ultimately rests upon the acceptance of the courts of the subjective impressions of the soldier or policeman involved. The concept of "such force as is reasonable in the circumstances" which underpins the actions of the security forces allows considerable latitude to soldiers and policemen, and it does not refer specifically to the use of lethal force. This concept, in the view of Amnesty International and others (Amnesty International, 1994: 13), is too vague and flexible to impose a standard of behavior which would prevent the excessive use of force. Indeed, this law does not comply with international standards as laid down in the UN Basic Principles on Summary and Arbitrary Executions or, in the eyes of many observers, with Article 2 of the European Convention for the Protection of Human Rights. The European Convention speaks (Article 2) of "absolute necessity" and "strict necessity" to justify the deprivation of life. Although Britain ratified the Convention in 1951, it did not incorporate it into domestic law.

The British government has consistently ignored calls that it should introduce legislation to bring the law on the use of lethal force into line with the UN Basic Principles. In 1991, Amnesty International sought clarification on the government's intentions in this regard but a reply has not been forthcoming (Amnesty International, 1994: I3).

Despite protestations to the contrary, the use of lethal force by the police and Army in Northern Ireland is not random or accidental, and it is unfortunate. A clear pattern has emerged over the years suggesting that a set of informal rules and tacit consent has emerged to permit the execution of those thought to pose a particular danger to the security forces. The Report of the Northern Ireland Human Rights Assembly and the 1994 Amnesty report on Political Killings in Northern Ireland are the most recent in a long line of reports and investigations which have evaluated the evidence and have come to the conclusion that such a policy exists. The report of the Human Rights Assembly (Liberty, 1993) includes a list of factors--some 25 elements in all--which are characteristic of situations, not just in Northern Ireland, where a shoot-to-kill policy is in operation. The clustering of these factors in the Irish situation leads the Report to the following conclusion:

> The evidence submitted to the Assembly, displaying as it does different combinations of all the factors mentioned above, overwhelmingly suggests the utilisation of a shoot-to kill policy in Northern Ireland. It is virtually impossible to determine whether such a policy is officially sanctioned, but what is beyond doubt is that, in failing to adhere to internationally agreed human rights standards, the UK Government has left itself open to the accusation that, at the very least, it tacitly condones a policy of shoot to kill (Liberty, 1993: 26).

But the problem of the use of lethal force does not end here. During the last three years the number of killings in the North has been dominated by the murder of (mostly uninvolved) Catholics by Protestant paramilitary groups. These killings are seemingly motivated by the desire to strike terror and fear into the minds of Catholics, particularly those living in isolated rural areas, and nationalists have persistently claimed that there is collusion between the security forces and the loyalist murder gangs. There is clear and convincing evidence of collusion between individual members of the security forces and Loyalist murder gangs spanning the passing of information on IRA suspects to direct involvement in armed attacks.[7]

It is more difficult to assess the evidence for collusion at official or semi-official levels, but a recent Amnesty International Report accepts the existence of collusion and suggests that the state has shown a marked reluctance to deal with the problem:

> Amnesty international has not been convinced that the government has taken adequate steps to halt collusion, to investigate thoroughly and make known the full truth about political killings of suspected government opponents, to bring to justice the perpetrators and dismantle "pro-state" organisations dedicated to political violence or otherwise deter such killings. Allegations of collusion range from direct involvement of security force personnel in Loyalist "death squads," complicity by authorities in such killings, to aiding and abetting such actions through the passing on of intelligence information (Amnesty International, 1994:30).

## THE ROLE OF THE COURTS

It is the responsibility of the states' legal officers (the Director of Public Prosecutions) to decide whether a prosecution should take place on the basis of information supplied by the police and the courts in order to implement the law concerning the use of lethal force by members of the security forces. The courts have shown a marked reluctance to convict soldiers and policemen brought before them under the Criminal Law Act, despite the small number sent forward by the DPP for trial. The courts have shown extreme flexibility in the interpretation of the concept of "reasonable force" and the landmark House of Lords judgement makes it clear that lethal force can be used if there is a possibility that the suspect might, in the mind of the officer concerned, pose a threat to the security forces at some later date. Lord Diplock, in handing down the leading judgement, said:

> Are we satisfied that no reasonable man (a) with
> knowledge of such facts that were known to the
> accused or reasonably believed by him to exist (b) in
> the circumstances and the time available for reflection
> (c) could be of the opinion that the prevention of the
> risk of harm to which others might be exposed if the
> suspect were allowed to escape justified exposing the
> suspect to the risk of harm to him that might result
> from the kind of force that the accused contemplated
> using?[8]

This judgement, translated into normal language, seems to endorse the right of the security forces to use lethal force as a form of preventative policing. The spirit of the House of Lords ruling was endorsed with enthusiasm by judges in Northern Ireland. In the wake of the killing of two suspected members of a Republican paramilitary organisation in 1982, a police constable was charged with murder. The judge, in acquitting him had this to say:

> While policemen are required to act within the law
> they are not required to be supermen and one does
> not use jeweller's scales to measure what is
> reasonable in the circumstances (Jennings, 1988b:
> 115).

In a case concerning the killing of two other suspects in the same year, the same judge again acquitted the police officers stating that the prosecution had not "the slightest chance in sustaining a conviction" and commended the policemen for their "courage and determination in bringing the three deceased to justice, in this case, to the final court of justice." It was during this trial that the first concrete indications of official policy on the use of lethal force began to emerge. A Deputy Chief Constable told the trial that the training of police officers placed the emphasis on "firepower, speed and aggression" and that the basic principle was "once you have decided to fire, you shoot to take on the enemy." In reply to a question from the judge he agreed that this meant taking the suspect "permanently out of action" (Jennings, 1988b: 116). These shootings in 1982 were the source of considerable controversy and became the focus of an investigation by the Assistant Chief Constable of Greater Manchester, John Stalker.

Although he was removed from the inquiry before its completion--and the completed report was never published--Stalker, in a subsequent book, said:

> The circumstances of those shootings pointed to a police inclination, if not a policy, to shoot suspects dead without warning rather than to arrest them. Coming as these incidents did, so close together, the suspicion of deliberate assassination was not unreasonable....(Stalker, 1988: 253).

The inability of the British state to face up to the nature of the conflict in Northern Ireland and confront the necessity of addressing the grievances of the minority has deep cultural and historical roots stretching back through centuries of colonial rule. In the course of the last century a complex web of constitutional principles and political and ideological dogmas backed up by a dense and highly organised system of surveillance and control emerged in Ireland. The failure of this apparatus to remove or dilute significantly the rise of Irish nationalism was manifested in the partition of Ireland in 1922 and the system of control, in an even more accentuated form, remained intact in Northern Ireland. Despite a number of half hearted attempts at reform, the state remained firmly committed to the established structures and, until relatively recently, seemed incapable of accepting the real basis of resistance and political violence--the fact that the state had ruled through coercion and repression. The RUC is an integral part of this system of control and repression and could only operate with impunity in the context of overall state policy. The use of lethal force is symptomatic of this process. For reasons to do with British and international public opinion, the existence of a shoot to kill policy must be emphatically denied and members of the security forces protected from the consequences of their actions.

This protection is institutionalised at a number of interacting levels. The studied ambiguity of the law--which the state has consistently refused to reform in line with international standards--allows the DPP to exclude most cases from reaching the courts and the judiciary (normally a judge sitting alone) have been notoriously unwilling to convict.

Other options of potential redress in such cases, such as inquests and the complaints procedure against the police, have been systematically emasculated and have little credibility among human rights organisations.

## POLICE PROFESSIONALISM

A number of commentators have assessed whether or not the police occupation can be considered professional vis-a-vis what are termed the "established professions" such as law or medicine (Crank, 1990; Regoli et al, 1988). Generally, this involves an attempt to "fit" the perceived characteristics of the established professions--theoretical knowledge, specialised training, autonomy, and a service ideal--to the police occupation in a fairly mechanistic and quantifiable fashion. However, it is not the intention here to enter into this debate except to note that studies such as these have been criticised for their atheoretical nature and their idealism (Johnson, 1972; 1979). Nevertheless, if professionalisation is about the establishment of a particular form of institutional control to improve the terms and conditions of work within a particular occupation then it is factually true that the police organisation has historically undergone a degree of professionalisation (e.g., Brogden, Jefferson & Walklate, 1988). Since the 1960s a number of institutional developments have taken place within policing--specialisation, centralisation, civilianisation, improved training, higher entrance requirements, the adoption of new technology, codes of ethics, management techniques--all of which on a purely objective basis can be taken to illustrate professionalisation of the police organisation. However, in a more specific sense, the concept of police professionalism has been treated somewhat "ambiguously and disparately" in the academic literature (Uildriks & van Mastrigt, 1991).

Nevertheless, there would appear to be a general consensus that professionalisation is both positive and desirable since it will lead to a more efficient organisation and to an overall improvement in the quality and standard of policing (for example, Reiner, 1985; Skolnick, 1975). For some commentators, however, the utility of professionalism is advanced in even stronger terms as a solution to the problem of police legitimacy and in particular to improve police-community relations (Mark, 1977). Likewise, Brewer (1991, 1993a, 1993b, 1994), Brewer and Magee (1990), Ryder (1989) and Weitzer (1985, 1987, 1990) suggest that professionalism as an institutional mechanism of reform has been relatively successful in transforming the Royal Ulster

Constabulary (RUC) from a biased, "sectarian bludgeon" of the Unionist government into a modern, professional force which performs a wide number of routine and normal police duties. The secret to this transformation has been to reconstruct the RUC in line with a set of abstract and idealised principles with are said to guide policing in liberal democratic societies and which for the RUC have been incorporated within a discourse of professional policing (for example, Brewer, 1994: 195).

## PROFESSIONALISM IN THE RUC

Much official RUC documentation stresses the increasingly "professional" nature of the force. This official discourse of professionalism is not monolithic however, but is comprised of three distinct though ultimately interrelated components. Firstly, there is a legal professionalism which stresses a commitment to the rule of law, the principle of consent and democratic accountability. This stance is supported by the ethical and valuational guidelines enshrined in the RUC's *Principles of Professional Policing Ethics* and reiterated in the RUC Charter *Raising the Standard* (1993) which emphasise a commitment to religious impartiality and the forces' assurance to serve the "whole community."

Secondly, there is a managerialist professionalism whereby force policy and specific organisational requirements are formulated in terms of goals, strategies, and objectives. In common with many UK forces the RUC have placed considerable emphasis upon managerialist and policy making strategies, such as Management by Objectives (MBO), environmental scanning, and psychometric evaluation.[9] A Strategic Plan has been produced annually since 1990, while a three-year Strategic Statement covering the period 1992-1995 was published in January 1992.[10] Additionally, in line with the national corporate philosophy of Quality of Service, a Citizens' Charter was published in January 1993 which sets performance targets for the force.[11]

Finally, there is a technical professionalism based around the adoption and utilisation of new technology that has been developed to cope with the exigencies of modern law enforcement and in particular the problem of political violence. This technical professionalism is manifested at a number of levels. All officers are routinely trained in public-order tactics and are armed with Smith & Weston .38 revolvers and the Special Air Services (SAS) issue Heckler & Koch submachine guns and have ready access to baton rounds. Highly trained and equipped Mobile Support Units (MSUs) have been formed, which operate from RUC Headquarters in Belfast and also at a divisional level and whose function is to intervene in crisis situations by providing backup to regular RUC patrols. Likewise a number of undercover RUC units trained in SAS tactics were formed in the early 1980s. Additionally, the RUC is believed to have access to one of the most sophisticated data retrieval systems (for the collation and relay of intelligence data) of any police force in Western Europe. Computers are widely used as an aid to policy formation and the force has a well equipped and staffed statistics and operational research department. Likewise, the force has access to a simulator that uses the latest interactive CD ROM technology to recreate any given situation for firearms training purposes.

Brogden and Shearing (1993) note that police professionalisation has provided a solution to two interrelated problems which have traditionally afflicted the police organisation. Firstly, it is "perceived to be a solution to the political problem of creating 'impartial' policing free of assumed partisan communal influences" (p.107). Secondly, it has provided a rule-tightening mechanism to control the "malign influence of the police occupational culture" (p.108). For the RUC these features are related. The close historical association between the Unionist government and the RUC prior to direct rule meant that partisan control of the force was manifested in sectarian and partial law enforcement by the rank and file. Allegations of political partiality have persisted, however. To counter this a discourse of professionalism has been mobilised extensively to emphasise the political impartiality of the force on two levels--the organisational structure itself and rank-and-file practice. With regard to the former a recent government White Paper to examine the structure of policing in the province reemphasised a commitment to "maintaining the operational independence of the Chief Constable and to the avoidance of political direction of the force."[12] By concentrating upon the notion of operational independence the Chief Constable and senior officers acting with his authority can be depicted as "expert" and "professional" administrators who can be trusted to use their "independent judgement" to make the correct policy decisions free from political interference. These officers are accountable to the law and to the law alone. They are not political actors advancing a political agenda but disinterested observers who make "professional policing decisions" which are themselves the product of a neutral and value-free decision-making process.[13] The use of technology in the decision-making process contributes to the view that decisions are formulated with reference to "neutral" and "scientific" criteria. This is based on the assumption that such technology "has a built in objectivity that cannot easily be corrupted by agent intervention" (Brogden & Shearing, 1993: 111).

Professionalism also provides a means to influence the behavior of the rank and file to counter the particularly troublesome aspect of rank and file deviance. The "professional" solution to this problem is to manipulate the rank and file "in ways which are more sensitive to organisational demands and pressures" (Brogden & Shearing, 1993: 96). By elevating the status of the occupation, through higher educational requirements, improved training, accelerated promotion, better working conditions and by fostering a commitment amongst the rank and file to a set of alternative goals and values (via ethical and valuational codes) it is held that the wider values of the organisation can be assimilated. There is an implicit assumption within this argument, however, that insofar as such deviance is acknowledged at all, it is perceived in terms of the individual pathology of a few "rogue" officers (bad apples) who have not yet managed to assimilate the values of professional policing and who bring the force into disrepute.

### NORMAL POLICING

One British Government MP has spoken of the RUC as a "strictly British force," performing a wide range of normal duties, with a high level of public acceptability and which operates according to the principles of impartiality, consent, the rule of law, and democratic accountability.[14] However, the extent to which these principles have ever existed in relation to police forces in socially integrated societies is a matter of some debate (Gordon, 1987; Hillyard, 1988; Jefferson, 1990). In relation to the RUC they are equally problematic. Whether or not the RUC act within or are constrained by the rule of law is academic if *the law* itself enables many of the oppressive practices of the RUC to take place. Additionally, the extent to which the RUC can be said to be accountable under the law remains dubious if we consider that in respect of allegations of wrong-doing the police investigate themselves. Equally, there would appear to be a reluctance for the

Director of Public Prosecutions (DPP) to initiate proceedings against police officers who have been charged with a criminal offence and even if such proceedings are initiated, the courts show a marked reluctance to convict. For example, in 1992 a total of 3,041 complaint cases were recorded against the RUC comprising 4,663 separate allegations.[15] A total of 2,547 cases were referred to the Independent Commission of Police Complaints by the RUC Chief Constable under the 1987 Police (Northern Ireland) Order, of which 908 cases were simultaneously referred to the Director of Public Prosecutions (DPP).[16] The DPP ruled that criminal charges be laid against officers in 8 cases, of which two were found guilty and six were acquitted in court. Overall, only 46 out of a total 4,663 (0.9%) complaints were found to be substantiated against the RUC in 1992.[17] Ironically, this low substantiation rate was cited by one senior RUC officer as proof that officers rarely engage in wrong-doing and for the general competence of the complaints system.[18] (For similar evidence relating to the British police, see Maguire & Corbett, 1989.)

Similarly, it is impossible to talk about public acceptability enshrined in the principle of consent if a substantial section of the Catholic population neither owe nor display any normative loyalty to either the state or the RUC. Although opinion poll evidence should be treated with some caution, in general it would appear that traditional Catholic antipathy to the RUC has not been modified to any significant extent (O'Connor, 1993; Stringer & Robinson, 1992). This feature is not just confined to Republicans who have historically viewed the RUC "as the repressive arm of an alien British state," but seems to be reflected in all shades of Nationalist opinion (Walker, 1990). Even the main Nationalist party in Northern Ireland, the moderate Social Democratic and Labour Party (SDLP), has been a persistent critic of police operations and has taken a policy decision to refuse nominations to the Northern Ireland Police Authority and the Police Liaison Committees organised in local council districts. Additionally, the force has consistently been unable to attract Catholic recruits. Officially, the percentage of Catholic officers in the force is just under 7 percent.[19] However, this figure appears to be skewed towards senior officers, so it is probably safe to assume that the figure for Catholic recruits and rank-and-file officers is less than 5 percent.[20] In any case the particularly low percentage of Catholic officers distinguishes the RUC as a predominantly Protestant force. Although there is no official explanation given for the reluctance of Catholics to join the RUC, the views of a number of senior officers suggest that the reason is because of intimidation by Republican paramilitaries.[21] However, while there is some evidence to support this thesis (Walker, 1990: 117), it is nevertheless based on the assumption that members of the Catholic community would be keen to join in the absence of such threats.

Formally a tripartite structure of accountability exists in Northern Ireland between the RUC Chief Constable, the Secretary of State, and the Police Authority for Northern Ireland. In theory this system is supposed to provide a three-way system of checks and balances to ensure that policing cannot be dominated by any single element and that it is representative of the needs of government, the community, and the RUC themselves. In practice, however it is heavily weighted in favor of the RUC and the government. A combination of factors has meant that the Police Authority has generally been unwilling or unable to effectively influence policing, a point which is noted in a recent government White Paper to consider the structure of policing in Northern Ireland.[22] While the government has pledged itself to modifying the relationship between the RUC, the Police Authority, and the Secretary of State, it is committed to doing so only within the existing tripartite structure. However, since the government and the RUC share the same ultimate objective in the defeat of terrorism, this has effectively granted the Chief Constable a wide remit to take whatever steps he considers necessary to deal with the security situation: in other words he had been granted *more* not *less* operational autonomy. Since the Police Authority is statutorily prohibited from intervening in areas concerning "security policy objectives or related matters"--an exclusion which is often interpreted liberally--this further isolates the Chief Constable from effective scrutiny. The checks built into the tripartite structure do not act as checks at all but further institutionalise the relationship between the government (vis-a-vis the Secretary of State) and the Chief Constable. In fact regular, top-level meetings take place between the Secretary of State and the Chief Constable, who also liaise with the Army GOC and members of the security services (Walker, 1990: 115). It is difficult to argue in any meaningful sense then that the RUC as an institution is free from political pressures and influences, contrary to the view of the ex-Chief Constable, Sir John Hermon:

> I hold firmly to the principle that the police should be
> free from political interference and direction. I do not
> intend to compromise that principle in any way, nor
> is there any pressure on me to do so....It is a
> powerful guarantee against political policing, which
> would be contrary to the public good and abhorrent
> to professional police officers.[23]

The extent to which individual officers abide by the principles of political impartiality on the ground is more difficult to ascertain since there are no (available) statistics which give a breakdown of arrests, for example, by religion. Nonetheless, a number of civil rights groups, community groups, local politicians, and clergy have all made persistent allegations of RUC harassment in Nationalist areas of the province (Liberty, 1993). Additionally, research conducted by one of the authors found that a number of officers interviewed for the study made repeated sectarian and derogatory remarks about members of the Catholic community.[24] Again, the extent to which the force as a whole is characterised by a degree of latent sectarianism is difficult to assess.[25] However, what is not in doubt is that the RUC has been involved in a number of incidents which have done little to inspire the confidence of the Catholic community in the political impartiality of the force. We have discussed the issue of lethal force, and the religious composition of the RUC but there are a number of other areas of concern such as harassment, the use of informers, brutality in police custody, and differential standards of policing applied to Republican and Loyalist paramilitary funerals, parades, and demonstrations.

There have been claims by a number of commentators that the RUC is becoming increasingly even-handed in dealing with Protestant and Catholic violence. For example, Brewer (1991) referring to the violent clashes which took place between the RUC and loyalist demonstrators in the aftermath of the signing of the Anglo-Irish Agreement notes that "...Protestant hostility to the RUC has provided policemen and women with an experimental basis to the ethos of impartiality and professionalism" (cited in Moloney, 1991). However, it would appear that even the Chief Constable himself was slightly concerned about testing the allegiance of his officers since he took the precaution of issuing a statement to the force reassuring them that the Agreement did not represent a capitulation to Nationalist demands and that "the Royal Ulster Constabulary will continue to be the Royal Ulster

Ulster Constabulary as presently constituted, with sole responsibility for policing Northern Ireland. The Uniform of the RUC will continue to be dark green and existing badges will remain."[26] A recently declassified US State Department telegram suggests however, that the attitude of the RUC may have been rather more ambivalent towards the Loyalist protesters. The telegram describes a conversation at an official dinner party held one week after the Loyalist Day of Action in March 1986 in protest at the Anglo Irish Agreement. The dinner party was attended by officials from the American Consulate in Belfast and the Northern Ireland Office. The telegram reads:

> The conversation at the dinner table was wide-ranging and informal. One area of discussion was the RUC's performance--or lack thereof--during Monday's strike. _____ in particular was scathing, saying he had refused to use a prepared text praising the force. He said sarcastically that one had to take into account the seriousness of what the RUC was up against: three or four felled trees and a strong south-easterly breeze. The Northern Ireland Office people were more reserved in their comments, but did not disagree with _____ and in fact seemed to be in accord (Moloney, 1991).

## PROFESSIONALISM AND POLICE DEVIANCE

Allegations of police deviance and misconduct, such as oppressive practices, harassment, corruption, and partial law enforcement have been widespread in Northern Ireland over the last decades of the conflict (CAJ, 1992a, 1992b, 1993). The police authorities have consistently denied the existence of any system of inherent deviance and have constantly stressed the professionalism of the force in the face of a protracted internal war. When the authorities are forced to confront the existence of police misconduct, it is invariably explained away as the isolated actions of individual officers. This "bad apple" approach was reiterated by the Chief Constable at the recent press conference to launch the RUC Annual Report for 1993. Responding to allegations of collusion between the security forces and the Loyalist paramilitaries he had this to say:

I am absolutely satisfied that collusion is neither widespread nor institutionalised. From time to time, however, there will be some bad apples in every barrel (*Irish Times*, July 5, 1994).

This view, central to the professional ideology of the RUC, needs to be treated with some skepticism. Recent research in the sociology of policing indicates that by focusing on the rank and file as *the problem* (i.e., in terms of individual pathology; e.g., McConville & Shepherd, 1993: 197), the structural and organisational determinants of police deviance are often overlooked (cf. Shearing, 1981; Grimshaw & Jefferson, 1987; McBarnet, 1979, 1983;, Lustgarten, 1986, 1987).

Much literature in the sociology of police work assumes a schism between the rank and· file and senior officers within the organisation. This schism is said to be the result of a conflict between two competing value systems: that of the occupational culture of the rank and file and that of the organisational structure itself, manifested in official policy, rules, procedures, and the command structure. This conflict has allowed a number of commentators to suggest that the occupational culture and the organisational structure "represent *rival* sets of determination on police behavior--with the former mostly winning out" (Grimshaw & Jefferson, 1987: 19). Reuss-Ianni & Ianni (1983) for example, speak about a "conflict" between *cop culture* and *management culture*. Similarly, Holdaway (1977) concludes that the *practical professionalism* of the rank and file deviates from the *managerial professionalism* of senior officers. The problem here, however, is that because such conclusions are derived from ethnographic studies of the rank and file, they are necessarily skewed towards a "bottom up" perspective. Effectively all they demonstrate is a *perception* of the organisational structure (senior officers, official policy, rules, procedures) as seen through the eyes of the rank and file.

In truth however, little is known about the workings of the organisational structure or how official policy is formulated. Possibly, this is because as *Punch* has noted "the politics of access [into the organisation] tend to deflect researchers downwards, away from the powerful" (cited in Grimshaw & Jefferson, 1987: 18). In any case, in much of the academic literature the organisational structure is treated as relatively unproblematic. It is a given entity, something for the rank and file to subvert or deviate from. Nonetheless, it is difficult, if not spurious to generalise about an assumed relationship between the rank and file and the organisational structure simply on the basis of what the rank and file perceive this relationship to be. In addition, since senior officers have risen through the rank structure themselves they often are well aware of the values and ideologies which sustain the occupational culture of the rank and file (McConville & Shepherd, 1993; Brogden & Shearing, 1993). On this basis, Grimshaw & Jefferson (1987: 19) note that in the absence of any firm evidence to the contrary, the occupational culture and the organisational structure might "not be universally in conflict."

It can no longer be assumed, therefore, that organisational deviance is simply a "rank and file" problem. Indeed, there is considerable evidence to support the view that senior officers often give their support to, or are complicit in, organisational deviance by the rank and file if it is perceived to be in line with the goals of the organisation or a response to external (political) pressures facing the organisation, for example, the pressure to get results (Shearing, 1990; Ericson, 1981; Lee, 1981; Grimshaw & Jefferson, 1987; Brogden & Shearing, 1993; McConville & Shepherd, 1993). This is not to exaggerate the extent to which the organisational structure concurs with the occupational culture to condone or justify particular kinds of behavior, but neither is it to exaggerate the "gap" between official policy and unofficial practice that the ethnomethodologists do. Rather it is to suggest that the occupational culture and the organisational structure have a symbiotic relationship in which organisational deviance by the rank and file will be tolerated under certain conditions and in certain circumstances if it is perceived to be in line with more general organisational goals. For example, in relation to the South African Police (SAP) under apartheid, Brogden & Shearing (1993) have demonstrated a clear link between the cultural practices of the SAP and the wider demands of the apartheid state. Likewise this relationship may be made more acute in situations like Northern Ireland where political exigencies are sometimes rendered more important than due process considerations or even the basic issue of whether or not to enforce the law.

This type of tolerated, and indeed sanctioned, behavior on the part of police officers was highlighted by John Stalker in his investigation of "shoot to kill" allegations in 1984. He concluded that officers--in particular officers of the Special Branch (the political police)--had been instrumental in covering up the events surrounding the shootings and in obstructing his own investigations. He describes the role of the Special Branch in his book:

> The Special Branch targeted the suspected terrorists, they briefed the officers, and after the shooting they removed the men, cars and guns for a private debriefing before the CID officers were allowed access to these crucial matters. They provided the cover stories and they decided at what point the CID were to be allowed to commence the official investigation of what occurred. The SB interpreted the information and decided what was, or was not evidence: they attached the labels--whether a man was "wanted" for an offence, for instance, or whether he was an "on the run terrorist." I have never experienced, nor had any of my team such an influence over an entire police force by one small section (Stalker, 1988: 56ff).

Interviews with serving police officers support the contention that the killing of suspects by special police units is tacitly sanctioned at a high level and that there is a complex system in place designed to respond to such killings and protect the officers involved. One officer, himself a member of an undercover squad, had this to say:

> I would say without a shadow of a doubt that, yes there was a decision at a high...probably at government level...that if the intelligence was right and was correct and was good enough....For example, if they knew that there was going to be four gunmen in a car going to shoot a member of the public or a member of the security forces at a given point, then they would kill them....Full stop. There is no doubt about that. You can't hide away from that....It is a fact. It will never be admitted to but it is a fact.[27]

Other police officers interviewed have complained that their normal policing activities are constrained by political considerations such as the need to gain Special Branch authorisation before arresting drug dealers.[28]

## CONCLUSIONS

At the end of August 1994 the IRA declared a halt to its armed operations after protracted negotiations spanning nearly a decade. Sinn Fein, the political wing of the IRA, has stressed its determination to pursue a peace process in the context of achieving an agreed political solution to the problems of Northern Ireland. If a peace process is to proceed and have any chance of success, the reform of the RUC will be high on the agenda and will present many contentious issues. It is clear that nothing less than a reform of the training, structure, operational methods, and religious composition of the force will be acceptable to the minority community. The size of the force--to bring it into line with normal police-citizen ratios--will have to be reduced by at least 50 percent; the Special Branch will have to be divested of its authority over normal policing operations; training will have to stress the democratic role of policing rather than political control; and an efficient and independent system of police complaints must be established.

The RUC has developed into a powerful, semi-autonomous operation designed to fulfil a specific purpose: the suppression of political dissent.    To change this role to one of democratic accountability and policing by consent is the great challenge facing the force.

## NOTES

1. For most of the last two centuries Ireland has been subjected to Emergency Legislation of one sort or another. Between 1800 and 1821 (the year of the Act of Union and Independence), the British government enacted 105 Coercion Acts concerning Ireland. See Farrell, 1986.

2. After a protracted War of Independence, Ireland was partitioned in 1921 to form the Irish Free State and Northern Ireland, which, while remaining part of the UK, had considerable autonomy in local affairs.

3. It should be noted that similar legislation was enacted in the Irish Free State, directed at those who did not accept partition.

4. The Unionist Party, closely allied to the British Conservative Party, had a monopoly of power until the imposition of direct rule from London in 1972. It maintained its large majority by manipulating electoral boundaries to ensure a Unionist victory.

5. These courts are named after the late Lord Diplock, whose *Report of the Commission to Consider Legal Procedures to Deal with Terrorist Activities in Northern Ireland* formed the basis of the non-jury court system.

6. Attorney General for Northern Ireland's Reference (1977) A.C 105.

7. Although the Stevens Report was never published, the conclusions were summarised in the RUC Federation magazine, *Police Beat*, June 1980, 18-19.

8. *Attorney General for Northern Ireland's Reference* (1976) N.I. at 137.

9. Sir Hugh Annesley, *Police Beat,* March 1991.

10. Royal Ulster Constabulary, *Strategy Statement 1992-1995,* January 1992.

11. *Raising the Standard,* Royal Ulster Constabulary Charter. HMSO C.250, January 1993.

12. *Policing in the Community* (1994), Belfast: Northern Ireland Office, 1.

13. Sir John Hermon, "The RUC and the Anglo Irish Agreement," Statement to the RUC, November 29, 1985, *Police Beat,* December 1985.

14. Speech made by Sir Eldon Griffiths, Parliamentary Consultant to Police Federation, reported in *Police Beat*, December 1981: 9.

15. *Report of Her Majesty's Inspector of Constabulary,* Northern Ireland Office, 1993.

16. Independent Commission for Police Complaints for Northern Ireland, *Fifth Annual Report*, 1992.

17. *Report of Her Majesty's Inspector of Constabulary*, ibid., pp. 50, 52.

18. Interview with senior RUC officer in the RUC Complaints and Discipline Branch. March 1992.

19. Sir Hugh Annesley, *The Irish News,* Monday, March 11, 1991.

20. This figure is probably realistic since the percentage of Catholic officers in the RUC Reserve (a part- and full-time force who act in support of the Regular RUC), which does not have a rank structure (all RUCR have the rank of constable), is approximately 3 percent (Mapstone, 1992).

21. Interview with Senior RUC Officers. March 1992, October 1992.

22. *Policing in the Community,* Ibid., p.7.

23. Statement by Sir John Hermon, November 29, 1985, reported in *Police Beat*, December 1985.

24. Semi-structured interviews were conducted with fifty officers from all ranks and from a variety of departments. These interviews were tape recorded and lasted between one and three hours. A number of officers were approached for a second interview. These interviews were conducted by Graham Ellison.

25. It is not possible to generalise here about the extent or prevalence of sectarian attitudes within the force except to note that sectarian remarks were made on a number of occasions. However, the majority of officers interviewed did express essentially Unionist attitudes--a feature which was also manifest in the attitudes of Catholic officers interviewed. (See Mapstone, 1992 for similar evidence.)

26. Sir John Hermon, "The RUC and the Anglo Irish Agreement," ibid.

27. Interview with RUC Sergeant, January 1993.

28. One drug squad officer commented "...Some of these boys are dealing right under our noses and there is not a thing we can do about it. There are certain individuals we are told to leave alone. Other times we would have to get authorisation from the Branch before we could make a move because the chances are they're touts (informers) or something like that." Interview with RUC officer, November 1992.

# SOURCES

Amnesty International (1994), *Political Killings in Northern Ireland*, London: Amnesty International.

Boyce, D. (1979), "Normal Policing: Public Order in Northern Ireland since Partition," *Eire-Ireland*, 14, 35-52.

Brewer, J.D. (1990), "Talking about Danger: The RUC and the Paramilitary Threat," *Sociology*, 24, 4, 657-674.

------ (1991), "Policing in Divided Societies: Theorising a Type of Policing," *Policing and Society*, 1, 179-191.

------ (1993a), "The History and Development of Policing in Northern Ireland," in M.L. Mathews, P.B. Heymann, and A.S. Mathews (eds.), *Policing the Conflict in South Africa*, Tallahassee: University of Florida Press.

------ (1993b), "Re-educating the South African Police: Comparative Lessons," in M.L. Mathews, P.B. Heymann, and A.S. Mathews (eds.), *Policing the Conflict in South Africa*, Tallahassee: University of Florida Press.

------ (1994), "The Ethnographic Critique of Ethnography: Sectarianism in the RUC," *Sociology*, 28, 1, 231-244.

Brewer, J.D. and K. Magee (1990), *Inside the RUC*, Oxford: Clarendon Press.

Brogden, M. (1987), "An Act to Colonise the Internal Lands of the Island: Empire and Origins of the Professional Police," *International Journal of the Sociology of Law*, 15, 179-208.

Brogden, M., T. Jefferson & S. Walklate (1988), *Introducing Policework*, London: Unwin Hyman.

Brogden, M. & C. Shearing (1993), *Policing for a New South Africa*, London & New York: Routledge.

Cain, M. (1979), "Trends in the Sociology of Policework," *International Journal of the Sociology of Law*, 7, 2, 143-167.

Committee for the Administration of Justice (CAJ) (1992a), *Inquests and Disputed Killings in Northern Ireland*, CAJ Pamphlet No. 18, Belfast: Shanway Press.

------ (1992b), *The Casement Trials: A Case Study on the Right to a Fair Trial in Northern Ireland*, CAJ Pamphlet No. 19, Belfast: Shanway Press.

------ (1993a), *Allegations of Harassment and the Use of Lethal Force by the Security Forces in Northern Ireland*, Belfast: Shanway Press.

------ (1993b), *A Fresh Look at Complaints Against the Police*, Belfast: Shanway Press.

Crank, J.P. (1990), "Police: Professionals or Craftsmen? An Empirical Assessment of Professionalism and Craftsmanship among Eight Municipal Police Agencies," *Journal of Criminal Justice*, 18, 333-349.

Dicey, A.V. (1973), *England's Case Against Home Rule*, Richmond: Richmond Publishing.

Ericson, R.V. (1981), "Rules for Police Deviance," in Clifford D. Shearing (ed.), *Organizational Police Deviance*, Toronto: Buttersworth and Co.

Farrell, M. (1986), *The Apparatus of Repression*, Derry: Field Day Theatre Company.

Foster, R.E. (1988), *Modern Ireland 1600-1972*, Allen Lane: The Penguin Press.

Foucault, M. (1977), *Discipline and Punish*, Allen Lane: Penguin.

Gordon, P. (1987), "Community Policing: Towards the Local Police State?" in Phil Scraton (ed.), *Law, Order and the Authoritarian State*, Milton Keynes: Open University Press.

Grimshaw, R. and T. Jefferson (1987), *Interpreting Policework*, London: Allen & Unwin.

Hermon, Sir John (1985), "The RUC and the Anglo Irish Agreement," Statement to the RUC, *Police Beat*, November 29.

Hillyard, P. (1987), "The Normalisation of Special Powers: From Northern Ireland to Britain," in Phil Scraton (ed.), *Law, Order and the Authoritarian State*, Milton Keynes: Open University Press.

------ (1988), "Political and Social Dimensions of Emergency Law in Northern Ireland," in P. Jennings (ed.), *Justice Under Fire: The Abuse of Civil Liberties in Northern Ireland*, London: Pluto Press.

Holdaway, S. (1977), "Changes in Urban Policing," *British Journal of Sociology*, 28, 2, 119-37.

------, (ed.), (1979), *The British Police*, London: Edward Arnold.

*Irish Times*, July 5, 1994.

Jefferson, T. (1990), *The Case Against Paramilitary Policing*, Milton Keynes: Open University Press.

Jennings, A., (ed.), (1988a), *Justice Under Fire: The Abuse of Civil Liberties in Northern Ireland*, London: Pluto Press.

------- (1988b), "Shoot to Kill: The Final Courts of Justice," in A. Jennings (ed.), *Justice Under Fire: The Abuse of Civil Liberties in Northern Ireland*, London: Pluto Press.

Johnson, T. (1972), *Professions and Power*, London: Macmillan Press.

------ (1977), "The Professions in the Class Structure," in R. Scase (ed.), *Industrial Society: Class, Cleavage and Control*, London: George Allen & Unwin.

Kitson, F. (1971), *Low Intensity Operations*, London: Faber & Faber.

Lee, J.A. (1981), "Some Structural Aspects of Police Deviance in Relations with Minority Groups,"in Clifford Shearing (ed.), *Organisational Police Deviance*, Toronto: Buttersworth & Co.

Liberty (National Council for Civil Liberties) (1993), *Broken Covenants: Violations of International Law in Northern Ireland*, Report of the Northern Ireland Human Rights Assembly, 6-8 April 1992, London: National Council for Civil Liberties.

Lustgarten, L. (1986), *The Governance of the Police*, London: Sweet & Maxwell.

------ (1987), "The Police and the Substantive Criminal Law," *British Journal of Criminology*, 27, 1, 23-30.

Maguire, M., and C. Corbett (1989), "Patterns and Profiles of Complaints against the Police," in Rod Morgan & David J. Smith (eds.), *Coming to Terms with Policing*, London: Routledge.

Mapstone, R. (1992), "The Attitudes of Police in a Divided Society," *British Journal of Criminology*, 32, 2, 183-192.

------ (1994), *Policing a Divided Society*, London: Avebury Publishing.

Mark, R. (1977), *Policing a Perplexed Society*, London: Allen & Unwin.

McBarnet, D.J. (1979), "Arrest: the Legal Context of Policing," in S. Holdaway (ed.), *The British Police*, London: Edward Arnold.

------ (1983), *Conviction*, London: Macmillan.

McConville, M. and D. Shepherd (1993), *Watching Police, Watching Communities,* London: Routledge.

Merquior, J.G. (1991), *Foucault,* London: Fontana Press.

Moloney, E. (1991), "Inside the Mind of the RUC," *Sunday Tribune,* 24 February.

Newark, F.H. (1955), "The Law and the Constitution," in Thomas Wilson, (ed.), *Ulster Under Home Rule,* Oxford University Press.

O'Connor, F. (1993), *In Search of a State: Catholics in Northern Ireland,* Belfast: The Blackstaff Press.

Palmer, S.H. (1988), *Police and Protest in England and Ireland 1780-1850,* Cambridge University Press.

Regoli, R.M., J.P. Crank, R.G. Culbertson, and E.D. Poole (1988), "Linkages Between Professionalization and Professionalism among Police Chiefs," *Journal of Criminal Justice,* 16, 89-98.

Reiner, R. (1985), *The Politics of Police,* Sussex: Wheatsheaf Books.

Reuss-Ianni, E. and J. Ianni (1983), "Street Cops and Management Cops: The Two Cultures of Policing," in M. Punch (ed.), *Control in the Police Organization,* Cambridge: MIT Press.

Ryder, C. (1989), *The Royal Ulster Constabulary: A Force Under Fire,* London: Methuen.

Shearing, C.D., (ed.), (1981), *Organisational Police Deviance,* Toronto: Butterworth & Co.

------ (1990), *Post Complaint Management: The Impact of Police Complaints Procedures on Police Discipline,* Discussion Paper: Royal Canadian Mounted Police (RCMP) External Review Cte., Ottawa: Minister of Supply and Services.

Skolnick, J. (1975), *Justice Without Trial,* 2nd Edition, New York: Wiley.

Stalker, J. (1988), *The Stalker Affair,* London: Viking Penguin Group.

Stringer, P. and G. Robinson (eds.), (1992), *Northern Ireland Social Attitudes Survey,* Belfast: Blackstaff Press.

Tomlinson, M. (1980), "Reforming Repression," in Liam O'Dowd, Bill Rolston, & Mike Tomlinson (eds.), *Northern Ireland: Between Civil Rights and Civil War,* London: C.S.E. Books.

Townshend, C. (1983), *Political Violence in Ireland,* Oxford: Clarendon Press.

Uildriks, N. and H. van Mastrigt (1991), *Policing Police Violence,* Aberdeen: Aberdeen University Press.

Walker, C. (1990), "Police and Community in Northern Ireland," *Northern Ireland Legal Quarterly,* 41, 105-142.

Walsh, D. (1988), "Arrest and Interrogation," in A. Jennings, (ed.), *Justice Under Fire: The Abuse of Civil Liberties in Northern Ireland,* London: Pluto Press.

Weitzer, R. (1985), "Policing a Divided Society: Obstacles to Normalisation in Northern Ireland," *Social Problems,* 33, 1, 41-55.

------ (1987), "Contested Order: The Struggle Over British Security Policy in Northern Ireland," *Comparative Politics,* 19, 3, 281-298.

------ (1990), *Transforming Settler States,* Berkeley: University of California Press.

## Official Publications

*Attorney General for Northern Ireland's Reference* (1976), A.C. 105.

*Fifth Annual Report* (1992), Independent Commission for Police Complaints for Northern Ireland, London: HMSO, DD 302526.

*Policing the Community--Policing Structures in Northern Ireland* (1994), London: HMSO. DD. 0302528, C.15.

*Raising the Standard* (1993), Royal Ulster Constabulary Charter, Belfast: HMSO, C.250.

*Report of Her Majesty's Inspector of the Constabulary* (1993), Belfast: Northern Ireland Office.

*Report of the Commission to Consider Legal Procedures to Deal with Terrorist Activities in Northern Ireland* (1972), London: HMSO, Cmnd 5185 ("Diplock Report").

*Strategy Statement 1992-1995* (1992), Belfast: Royal Ulster Constabulary.

# POST-SOVIET POLICING:
# AN HISTORICAL PERSPECTIVE

## Louise I. Shelley

The disintegration of the militia apparatus during *perestroika* facilitated the end of the Soviet state far earlier than acute observers, either inside or outside the Soviet Union, had anticipated. Understanding the role the militia played in the Soviet regime is thus crucial to understanding the collapse of the Soviet state in 1991. Moreover, the nature of Soviet policing is critically important to understanding the authoritarian legacy of the Soviet state in the newly independent states of the former USSR and the formerly communist nations of Eastern Europe.

## SOVIET POLICING: FUNCTIONS AND IMPACT

Western scholars have yet to fully analyze the role of the Soviet militia in the formation and perpetuation, much less the collapse, of the Soviet state. In the highly controlled society of the USSR, the militia represented the most immediate level of Communist Party and state control over the citizen, a control far more visible to the population than that exercised by the more frequently studied security police and military. If one accepts Otwin Marenin's (1985) maxim that examination of the nature of a state requires an analysis of the police and policing, the role of the everyday police in the Soviet Union has as much, or more, to tell us about the Soviet regime as do the functions of the KGB and the Soviet Army.

The evolution and operations of the militia made Soviet police practice a distinctive form of authoritarian policing. Backed by the power of the Communist Party, the Soviet militia not only suppressed individual rights, but imposed a specific state ideology on the population for seven decades. As a tool of state ideology, the Soviet militia had more in common with the police of fascist states than those of nations without proclaimed ideologies, but the analogy with fascist policing cannot go too far, as communist ideology assigned the regular police different functions than those awarded to the police by fascist governments. The consolidation of the state and the economy in the USSR, for example, required police regulation of more aspects of everyday life than was the case in fascist states.

Studies of twentieth-century policing have generally examined police in democratic societies, focusing either on police-state relations or police-citizen relationships. Such analytical paradigms are possible because citizens enjoy an autonomy from the state in democratic societies which permits scholars to distinguish between these two relationships. In an authoritarian society like the USSR, by contrast, the citizen did not enjoy autonomy from the state. Citizen autonomy from the state is only beginning to occur in Russia and some of the successor states, but this change in the relationship between the individual and police power is causing a crisis in law enforcement in the democratizing regions of the former USSR. In order to explain the nature of post-Soviet policing in the newly independent countries, one must examine both the relationship between the militia and the state and the ways in which militia operations directly affect citizens in their everyday lives.

The natural temptation of scholars to overestimate the importance of their subjects is not an exaggeration in the case of the Soviet militia. Therefore, the crisis in post-Soviet policing creates a crisis in these once highly controlled societies.

In the Soviet period, the militia did not just control crime. It policed the entire society by means of far-reaching functions that touched the life of every citizen. In addition to shaping police practice throughout the expanse of the Soviet Union, the militia served as the prototype for the police forces of the socialist countries of Eastern Europe. All police forces in the Soviet bloc were structured along the model of the militia in the USSR. Significant variations did, however, exist among the police forces of socialist countries depending on a country's ethnic composition, the extent of permissible private economic activity and ownership, and the degree of political control exercised over civil society. Therefore, the struggle to change law enforcement is not one just of the Soviet successor states but also of the countries of Eastern Europe (Vigh and Katona, 1993).

Intricately tied to national politics, each General Secretary of the Communist Party of the Soviet Union established a different tone to policing. The militia were totalitarian in the Stalinist period (inspiring many of theories of the twentieth-century police state), became authoritarian in the post-Stalinist period of Khrushchev, and attempted to democratize under Gorbachev. Although the USSR was far less of a police state under Brezhnev than under Stalin, the level of social and political control enforced by the Soviet police was nevertheless greater than in most other industrialized societies during the Brezhnev era. Soviet citizens were simultaneously subordinated to a centralized, one-Party state, a state-owned and state-directed economy, and an official ideology that sanctioned a higher degree of control over everyday life than is possible in most authoritarian regimes. This control has not disappeared with the demise of the Soviet state.

While the highly controlled Soviet state has now passed into history, the ultimate failure of the state's control apparatus--including the militia--to sustain the state does not diminish the influence and power wielded by the militia for the seventy-odd years of that state's existence. Under this apparatus--with its sensitivity to the wishes of the Party--a heterogeneous society acquired a veneer of uniformity.

The citizenry was well controlled by a law enforcement apparatus that combined overt techniques with undercover operations that coopted or compromised the majority of the population. This vulnerable status enhanced state control over the citizenry. It helped ensure a high degree of political control and social conformity. Crime rates were lower and many overt acts of political resistance against the state were deterred by means of the state's penetration of private life.

State intervention in individual life quashed civil society. There was no area of cultural, personal, or economic life that was outside the surveillance of the state. Increasing technology did not result in the substitution of technical means for human ones. Instead, it merely enhanced the surveillance capacities of the state. Corruption and inefficiency, in the absence of legal guarantees for the citizenry, remained the only protections for the citizenry from the intervention of the state.

The Soviet state denied its subjects the concept of autonomous citizenship which was at the basis of the Enlightenment tradition in Europe. While the concept of citizen rights developed throughout western Europe and many parts of the Anglo-Saxon world, in the socialist states individuals remained tools of the state. The USSR never developed a legal framework to control or regulate its law enforcement. Furthermore, civil liberties were not alive nor were they allowed to develop because law enforcement techniques hindered citizen initiative and individual rights. As the disillusioned Trotsky commented, the state "takes the form of the dictatorship of the proletariat, that is, of the most pitiless state, which coercively controls the lives of its citizens in all aspects" (cited in Nove, 1993: 20).

The militia changed dramatically with the development of the Soviet state. While they always remained executors of the will of the Party, the Party's demands changed as Bolshevik policy was institutionalized and the state ceased to fear for its survival. At the end of the Soviet period, the Party again feared challenges to its power, and the militia once again returned to the political front lines. The militia during the seventy-four years of Soviet rule was transformed from a militarized body suppressing political opposition to a law enforcement body responsible primarily for the maintenance of social and economic order. Before the USSR dissolved, the militia was once again an institution attempting to maintain social, political, and economic order in an often hostile environment.

## SOVIET LAW ENFORCEMENT AND PERESTROIKA

During *perestroika*, the society changed quickly. The forces which had been suppressed with such force for many decades emerged with an unprecedented rapidity. The militia could not keep pace with the changes that were occurring around them. They remained a highly static institution in a society in flux.

During *perestroika*, the artificial order quickly broke down-- workers struck, crime rates escalated, and ethnic conflicts occurred daily. The long sought conformity crumbled rapidly because individuals no longer feared the state's authority nor accepted the legitimacy of the ruling Communist Party. The once seemingly invincible militia, demoralized by corruption and personnel purges, could not stabilize the society. The state diverted its resources to control the escalating political disturbances and commandeered the militia to control demonstrations and political unrest. Citizens were left without the most fundamental law enforcement services needed to protect them from the increasing crime problems and the ever expanding organized crime. The republics' resentment of the national policy of militia allocation fueled the demands for greater republic sovereignty (RFE/RL, 1990).

Militia prestige declined (Utitsin, 1988), a consequence both of its ever more frequent deployment in political policing and its role in the execution of unpopular state policies. *Glasnost* made the population ever more aware of the militia's shortcomings--its corruption, disrespect for human rights, and lack of accountability to the citizenry.

During *perestroika*, Gorbachev sought to reverse the relationship between the state and the citizen. Instead of the arbitrary exercise of police power, a socialist law-based state was to be established in which institutions and individuals were subordinate to the law. Citizen access to the courts was expanded. For the first time, citizens were able to contest militia denials of registration permits which governed the residence of all in the USSR.

The idea of a socialist rule of law state arrived too late, though. The Party had lost its legitimacy among the citizenry and could not spearhead a campaign for the renewal of its law enforcement organs or its justice system. Increasingly, citizens took policing into their own hands through the establishment of private police or citizen militias independent of the Party. Although these movements reduced the state's monopoly on law enforcement, they never became major movements. The USSR left a legacy of centrally controlled and state-dominated policing for the successor states.

The emergence of these new forms of law enforcement were part of a general trend away from centralized control to greater republic and regional sovereignty. The shift was, however, occurring without the development of a legal consciousness or a framework of legal norms, which are prerequisites for a police in a democratic society (Reiss, 1971: 220). Many of these new private police were individuals expelled from state law enforcement for misconduct. The private law enforcement increasingly came under the ownership and direction of organized crime.

Militia members became executors of policies of a weak state which could no longer protect its personnel. Law enforcers became vulnerable to the increasing hostility of the populace. Record numbers of militia personnel were attacked and killed by their fellow citizens, while the law enforcers combatted interethnic violence and pursued increasingly vicious criminals. After the killing of a fellow militiaman, militia officers in Leningrad staged a public protest over their work conditions and the lack of state and community support.[1] But this was just the most visible indicator of a serious morale problem resulting in the voluntary departure of numerous militia personnel. More than ever the militia lacked the qualified, experienced personnel it needed to perform its ever more difficult duties. This problem has only intensified in the post-Soviet period.

The militia lost its credibility not only among those policed but among those charged with executing orders. Central authority and direction no longer prevailed at the cost of the interests of the republics. In many republics, non-Slavic militia officers sided with their fellow citizens against the central state. In the words of a leading Soviet militia officer, law enforcers "manifested national priorities to the detriment of nation-wide state priorities" (BBC, 1988). The dissolution of the Soviet state became more likely because it could not rely on its law enforcers to protect its social stability.

Examining the militia in historical perspective, it is apparent that the Soviet militia underwent a transformation similar to that observed in other industrialized societies. Over time, a greater distance was established between the police and the political structure. Yet relationships between the militia and the political structure remained closer in the USSR than in democratic societies because the militia remained tools of the ruling party.

### THE FINAL SOVIET PERIOD

In the dramatic year of 1989, citizens in Eastern Europe asserted their rights as individuals. The existing political systems were toppled, often symbolized by the storming of their security police. Subsequently, many existing law enforcement apparatuses were destroyed or reshaped to accommodate more democratic societies.

An acute examination of past policing techniques has occurred in Hungary, Germany, Poland, and Czechoslovakia because many believe that a close scrutiny of existing police practices is necessary to democratize society (Vigh and Katona, 1993). Many existing methods of police work were deemed incompatible with a democratic society. The first lines of attack in these societies have been on covert policing techniques, citizen collaboration with law enforcement, and the system of planned administration of justice. Some former socialist states have tried to limit police intrusion into daily life by diverse means.

Different reform approaches have been tried in the former socialist states of Eastern Europe. Poland has replaced many of its regular police. It prefers to recruit new personnel and make them sensitive to legal norms rather than retain experienced but corrupted individuals. West Germany had forced the former East German police to follow West German police techniques. In Berlin, police from the East and West are paired on their patrols. Hungarians abolished the network of informants that was the basis of undercover work. In many of these countries, much thought has been given to the conditions necessary to create a more democratic police force.

The political revolution of Eastern Europe had its repercussions in the former Soviet Union. But the destruction of the Communist system was not as thorough. The Russian state and many of the other newly independent states failed to exploit the impetus for change that followed the unsuccessful coup attempt or the break-up of the Soviet Union. Part of the reason may be that elements of the militia and the crack Alpha division of the KGB sided with Yeltsin against the coup perpetrators in August 1991. The pro-democracy stance of these troops may have shielded some of their co-workers from harsh reprisals. The statue of Dzerzhinsky, the founder of the security police, was removed from its pedestal in front of KGB headquarters. The reformers were more successful at removing the symbol of state coercion than in attacking the institutions of state control. While the superstructure of the Soviet state collapsed, the institutions of the Soviet period remained very much intact. Members of the Russian Ministry of Internal Affairs attacked the parliament on October 1993 at Yeltsin's orders. Furthermore, according to the Russian human rights commission, individuals surviving the attack were beaten by law enforcement personnel. Following this event, the law enforcers' service to the president was recognized by increased power and pay for police personnel. Moreover, with the exception of the nascent ombudsman's office, their misconduct has failed to obtain the scrutiny that their conduct often merits.

These problems endure because a commitment to democratization and political change among some in the law enforcement apparatus was not matched by institutional changes that would lead to a more open or accountable police. The society changed faster than the highly bureaucratized militia could respond. Even now, there is no institutional oversight by law enforcement personnel or civilian oversight by members of the community.

In the final years of the Soviet period, the growth of civil society and of mass nationalist and labor movements placed parts of life outside of state control. Individuals, more than ever, resented the authority of the central state and its most immediate representatives, the militia. Citizens could resist the authority of the militia because they now had their own sources of power. The forced volunteerism that characterized the socialist state diminished along with the collapsing Soviet Union.

## THE SOURCES OF POLICING

The militia retained the three central elements of its policing history--continental, colonial, and communist--until the end of the Soviet state. Of the three sources of Soviet policing, the continental tradition was the most important, providing the basis for the structure, mandate, and operational procedures of the Soviet militia as well as its relationship to state authority. Communist policing shared many attributes of the police tradition of western European empires, in which colonial police imposed imperial rule by force on foreign populations, often in regions less economically developed than the imperial center.

Rooted in both the continental and colonial traditions, communist policing nevertheless represented a unique type of policing whose scope and authority far exceeded that of earlier historical models. In contrast to these police models, the Soviet militia represented and enforced conformity with a state ideology that proscribed a wide range of human activity and justified a single party's monopoly of power. The ideological imperatives of state intervention in everyday life, as well as state ownership of the means of production, made the Soviet militia the defender of a broader range of state interests than existed in absolutist European states or empires.

The Soviet Union inherited the absolutist police tradition of eighteenth- and nineteenth-century western Europe; unlike western European states, however, it failed to democratize its policing in the face of industrialization and urbanization. The police in the USSR was not simply a body responsible for crime control but was a vital component of the apparatus of the state.

Despite its final efforts to democratize, the Soviet militia remained an authoritarian police force. These elements remain in the transitional police forces of the emergent state even in the absence of Marxist ideology, the Communist Party, or the Soviet state. Their legacy is present because there has been little effort to confront, outside of the Baltic states, the legacy of Soviet law enforcement.

## POST-SOVIET POLICING

The communist element of policing should eventually disappear with the deligitimation of the basic ideology. But the property relations of the socialist system still exist, particularly in the area of land ownership. In most of the new countries of the former Soviet Union, state and publicly owned property is only gradually being privatized. State paternalism can, therefore, prevail even in the absence of the government structures responsible for delivering these services.

The continental police model remains in the functions, the structure, and the operations of the police forces. The range of functions of the law enforcers, unlike in several Eastern European countries, has not contracted since the collapse of the USSR. The new statutes on the police, adopted by many of the new countries, retain the same functions as in the Soviet period.

### *INTERNAL PASSPORT AND REGISTRATION SYSTEM*

Despite the acknowledgement that the passport and registration system is a violation of human rights, most post-Soviet states have retained this significant militia control over the populace. The Russian Human Rights Commission reporting to President Yeltsin in spring 1994 noted significant abuses in connection with the passport system. For example, in June 1994, even after the passage of the new Russian Constitution that provides for citizen equality, there is differential access to the residential permits provided by the militia. For example, a Russian citizen from another locale must pay 500 times the minimal hourly wage to receive a permanent residence permit in the city while that figure is 1,000 times for a citizen of the former Soviet Union who does not have a Russian passport. This control was exploited to great advantage after the October 1993 storming of the Supreme Soviet. In the subsequent days when emergency measures were introduced, according to the press service of the Ministry of Internal Affairs, nearly 10,000 individuals were expelled from Moscow for violations of the registration rules.[2]

### *LEGISLATIVE FRAMEWORK*

The enhanced powers of the police were evident not only under these special circumstances. The previous Russian parliament's Committee on Defense and Security, disbanded by the October attack on the legislature, was dominated by security, interior ministry, and military industrial personnel only a few of whom were inclined to reform (Waller, 1993a: 5). In the new Russian Law on Security passed in March of 1992, the organs of internal affairs were identified as part of the security organs (Waller, 1993b: 111).

The new law on operational work gives the law enforcers much latitude and the legal safeguards instituted are weak, particularly in a society without a real division of powers or a well-developed legal consciousness. Militia members have the right to engage in surveillance activity, to monitor mail, to eavesdrop on telephone conversations and other forms of communication. Technical devices that are not life threatening can also be used to monitor citizen behavior. Such methods cannot, however, be employed without the sanction of the courts or the procuracy.[3] Yet the procuracy is a limited protection because it works closely with the militia in its investigative work.

### POLITICAL FUNCTIONS

The political functions associated with policing in countries operating under a continental model still continue. In many of the newly independent states of the USSR, militia members are involved in suppressing ethnic disorders, dealing with political protests and monitoring members of the opposition. For example, Interpol (under the Ministry of Internal Affairs) in certain Central Asian countries has been used to locate dissenters from Uzbekistan who have taken refuge in Kazakhstan.[4]   These dissidents have then been detained and returned to Uzbekistan where they have been subject to political repression. This problem indicates that even though the Communist Party is no longer the determining force in the state's monitoring of political life, several of the new independent states have not recognized the individual's rights to exercise political expression without state intervention.

### CONTINUITY OF SOVIET POLICING

The collapse of the Soviet Union did not lead to the collapse of the existing law enforcement structures. Although a unified Ministry of Internal Affairs no longer controls all policing from Moscow in the entire territory of the former USSR, the republic ministries of internal affairs remained and most of these bodies, hardly changed from the Soviet period, continue to control law enforcement in their newly independent countries. They function with the same personnel, the same mandate, and many of the same laws which existed in Soviet times.

The porous borders among the new countries have been exploited by organized criminal groups to their advantage. Coordination of law enforcement among the emergent countries of the former USSR has been justified in terms of the criminal threat. Some of this helps reestablish the ties which existed at the national ministerial level during the Soviet period.

The operations of the law enforcers remain close to those of the continental model. There is still widespread use of informants and undercover techniques to pursue criminals and penetrate the society in most of the newly independent states of the former USSR. Without the incorporation of the concept of civil liberties into law enforcement, the operations of the law enforcers still emphasize the supremacy of the state over the individual.

The law enforcement bureaucracy has the power to perpetuate existing police traditions even in the absence of a Communist Party structure and commands. Infiltration of the state into the lives of the citizens by both the security and militia apparatuses remains a fact in most of the post-Soviet states. For example, the Tadzik legislature, in its new law on the militia requires that state bodies, labor collectives, official, and public associations must assist the militia. This continues socialist practice in the absence of socialist ideology (FBIS, 1992: 113). Cooperation between the law enforcers and the military remains close. Recently, in Russia armed forces personnel have been directed to police work. By combining the forces of the state control apparatus, the new state is perpetuating the traditions of the continental system.

Soviet policing had similar consequences to British colonial policing in much of its empire. It served to "delegitimise indigenous customs, impose centralized social control, and to incorporate local society as a branch of imperial society" (Brogden, 1987: 10). With such a strong impact on the different national groups throughout the former Soviet Union, the legacy of colonial policing will remain for many decades.

The most concrete legacies of this colonialism are the structure and compositions of the post-Soviet police institutions. The Slavs enjoyed a visible presence in the militia forces of all the former republics of the USSR, a staffing pattern needed to enforce the authority of the central state. While some of the new countries have forced Slavic or Russified personnel to depart from their militia, in other countries the newly independent states lack qualified replacements (Beckelhimer, 1993: 6). Slavic personnel continue to operate in the security police of Central Asia, and the situation is not dissimilar in the militia. While some of these new countries have tried to intensify the national element of their police forces, many republics as a result of years of colonial rule are left with the administrative staff of the Soviet period.

With the collapse of the Soviet state, the republics which were part of the USSR acquired their independence. But as in other parts of the world, colonial relationships continued in the aftermath of the empire because many of the former republics did not acquire full autonomy with independence. The independence of many of the former republics of the USSR was not planned for nor anticipated. Unlike the Baltic states or the Ukraine which had sought and worked for independence, many of these new societies did not seek their new status as sovereign countries. Rather their new found status was a consequence of the collapse of an empire.

The Russian assertion that it has responsibility for the twenty-five million Russians living outside its border means that a colonial relationship endures between Moscow and the successor states. Russia continues to assert that it has a legitimate reason to intervene in the politics of these now-sovereign countries.

The collapse of the Soviet empire has not resulted in homogeneous successor states. Several of the newly independent countries, in particular Russia, are still multinational states with significant internal tensions among different ethnic groups. In Russia, the refusal of Tatarstan and Chechnya to sign the treaty of confederation reveals that these regions still feel that they are in a colonial relationship with Russia. Further support for this impression were the military threats made and the war waged against Chechnya since late 1994. The militia practices of the central Russian government in many ways confirm these regions' perceptions. The militia and the judicial system attempt to maintain control over the law enforcement and criminal activity in these regions without relying on the capabilities of the local legal bodies.

The sources of policing remain those which existed in the Soviet period because the newly independent countries have not been able to reconceptualize policing. While it may be premature to expect a major restructuring of law enforcement, this failure to address one of the more important authoritarian legacies of the Soviet period inhibits these countries' ability to democratize.

The post-Soviet police forces of the successor states have also inherited many law enforcement problems of the Soviet period. Independence has not eliminated the problems of endemic corruption, the lack of legal consciousness among the law enforcers, or the limited technological capabilities of the police. In fact many of these problems have been increased by the collapse of the central state.

## CORRUPTION AND THE LACK OF LEGAL CONSCIOUSNESS

The increasing problems of state corruption and organized crime in the successor states have had major repercussions in law enforcement. Police officials suggest that 13,000 law enforcers are in direct collaboration with organized crime and many more are accepting bribes from the so-called "mafia" (*Der Spiegel*, 1993: 105). The corruption problems are exacerbated by the poor pay of the law enforcers, the endemic corruption among the top leadership, and the difficulties of surviving in an economy suffering from hyperinflation. Corruption is as severe if not a more severe problem than in the final days of the Soviet state. Numerous personnel are leaving for the private sector. The head of the Duma Committee on Security, V. Ilyukhin, estimates that there are now approximately 100,000 individuals in the private security forces controlled by organized crime and these bodies exist without any legal norms to regulate their conduct (Interview, 1994).

The lack of legal consciousness among law enforcement personnel was a significant problem throughout the Soviet period. The major effort to introduce a rule-of-law-state in the final Soviet years had major repercussions throughout the law enforcement apparatus. Significant measures were taken to enhance the legal awareness of militia officials and to ensure compliance with the law. But most of the newly independent states are in a situation of economic and political crisis. Almost half of them are facing severe interethnic conflict or even civil war. Under these conditions, observance of legal norms is subordinated to the survival of the state and its citizens.

The police function best in societies where there is strong consensus between the law enforcers and community members. In areas of the former Soviet Union where there is ethnic strife, there is such polarization of the population that law enforcers have difficulty performing their duties. During the Soviet period there was much forced cooperation between the citizens and the law enforcers. Now that citizens can no longer be forced to comply, many refuse any form of cooperation with the law enforcers. As a result, the percentage of crimes reported to the militia have dropped in many former socialist states despite sharp rises in criminality in most of these countries.

Rapid economic decline preceded the dissolution of the USSR. Severe financial hardship has followed the collapse of the USSR because the highly interconnected economic relations no longer function. The absence of militia cars, typewriters, telecommunications equipment, and even gasoline that was noted in the final days of the USSR are even more severe problems for the ministries of interior of the successor states. The underequipped police forces are a poor match for the increasingly sophisticated and well-equipped organized crime groups.

Organized crime, having such extensive resources, is able to pay its personnel far more than what the state can provide. The state is a poor competitor with organized crime for individuals with law enforcement experience. Consequently, the police forces of most of the successor states are severely understaffed and cannot find replacements for departing personnel. This situation should endure in the future.

## FUTURE DEVELOPMENTS

The future development of the police forces in the successor states depends on the types of societies which will develop in the newly independent countries. The police are major actors in these changes, especially in societies in which the law enforcers had such an interventionist role in daily life. The police are never the determining force in the process of democratization, but their actions can impede political and economic transition. Therefore, the role they are assuming in the Soviet successor countries is important in determining the extent to which citizens will enjoy autonomy from the state.

It is unlikely that the fifteen countries which have emerged from the USSR will share similar police forces twenty years from now. The more western parts of the former Soviet Union may strive to achieve a more European model of policing. Many of the emergent Islamic states may choose to eschew western legal models and instead may choose to follow a law enforcement path that has more in common with the Turkish or Iranian experience. The course that these countries will choose to follow will be influenced also by the types of foreign police assistance that they will receive. European and American law enforcement are trying to provide assistance to the Russian police, an assistance that is not always welcomed by their Russian counterparts, while some of the Asian countries are looking to neighboring countries for assistance.

Whatever course these countries choose to follow, they will not achieve a purely European or Islamic model because the socialist legacy will remain. Furthermore, for many states the legacy of colonialism will affect law enforcement for many decades to come.

The domestic political situation as well as their courses of economic development will also influence the path that law enforcement will assume. The support that the Russian militia provided for Yeltsin during the August 1991 coup and again in October 1993 during Yeltsin's showdown with the increasingly hardline legislature reveals that the law enforcers have a concept of democracy. Yet a significant gap remains between the commitment of many law enforcement personnel to a more accountable and democratic police and their actual practices.

Many of the newly independent states have traded one form of violence for another. Once state repression was high and civilian violence relatively low. Now half of the former Soviet republics can no longer control their domestic ethnic and nationalist violence. If these newly independent countries are in a constant state of war, they may follow the Hobbesian alternative and create an authoritarian government, with an authoritarian police, just to avoid constant conflict. Under this scenario, the continental police tradition will be further perpetuated.

If the states create individual property which is distributed with some equity within society, they will create a bulwark against state authority. Then it will be possible to develop a civil society and civil liberties. This may gradually lead to police operating under the rule of law. With a movement away from a socialist concept of property, the state may accept the idea that certain areas of human conduct are outside the purview of government and of state regulation. This would ultimately mean a reduction in the interventionist policing which characterized the socialist states for so long.

While the implementation of either of these two scenarios is premature, it is clear that the present state of law enforcement in most of the former states of the USSR is in a precarious position. The morale of the law enforcement institutions collapsed along with the Soviet state. They are incapable of controlling an escalating crime problem and an increasingly international organized crime complex that is a threat not only to their own societies but to many other nations in the world as well. Therefore, the current state of police activity in the successor states is a cause for concern not only within the boundaries of the former Soviet Union but for many other countries as well.

## NOTES

1. "Leningrad Militiamen Put Forward Demands," *Moscow News* No. 17, 1989, p.2; Zhanna Braun and Il'ia Kaplun, "*Chrezvychannoe proisshestvie na Dvortsovoi ploshadi,*" *Literaturnaia Gazeta,* May 10, 1989, p.13.

2. "*Doklad o sobliudenii prav cheloveka i grazhdanina v Rossiiskoi Federatsii za 1993 god.*" The report was approved at a meeting of the Commission on Human Rights under the President of the Russian Federation, June 14, 1994, pp.15, 30.

3. Law of Russian Federation No.892 "*Ob operativno-rozysknoi deiatel'nosti v Rossiiskoi Federatsii,*" *Vedemosti S''Ezda Narodnykh Deputatov Rossiiskoi Federatsii I Verkhovnogo Soveta Rossiiskoi Federatsii,* No. 17, April 23, 1992, pp.1222-23.

4. Interview with Uzbek dissident, Summer 1994.

## SOURCES

BBC Broadcast Service (1988), "Restructuring in the MVD to Strengthen the Fight Against Crime," SU/0143 B/1, May 5.

Beckelhimer, Michael J. (1993), "Estonia's Men in Blue," *The Baltic Observer*, No.15/59, April 16-22.

Brogden, Mike (1987), "The Emergence of the Police--The Colonial Dimension," *British Journal of Criminology*, 27, 1.

*FBIS Report. Central Eurasia Laws* (1992), "Law on Militia," September 1.

Marenin, Otwin (1985), "Review Essay: Police Performance and State Rule: Control and Autonomy in the Exercise of Coercion," *Comparative Politics*, 18, 1, 101-122

Nove, Alec (1993), "The Soviet System in Retrospect: An Obituary Notice," New York: Harriman Institute, Columbia University, paper.

Reiss, Albert J., Jr. (1971), *The Police and the Public*, New Haven: Yale University Press.

*RFE/RL Daily Report* (1990), "Byelorussia Calls for Return of Militia Troops," No. 114, June 18.

*Der Spiegel* (1993), "'Alarm, jetzt kommen die Russen'," No.25

Utitsin, O. (1988), "*Prestizh militseiskikh pogon*," *Leninskoe Znamie*, September 8.

Vigh, Jozsef, and Geza Katona (eds.) (1993), *Social Changes, Crime and Police*, Budapest: Eotvos Lorand University.

Waller, J. Michael (1993a), "Russia's Security and Intelligence Services Today," *ABA National Security Law Report*, 15, 6, June.

Waller, J. Michael (1993b), "Russia's Legal Foundations for Civil Repression," *Demokratizatsiya*, I, 3.

# THE INDIGENISATION OF POLICING
# IN SOUTH AFRICA

## Mike Brogden

## INTRODUCTION

The crime writer James McClure, in a series of low-key South African crime novels[1], has fictionalized the symbiotic relationship between white and indigenous policing in South Africa. Zondi, the Zulu constable, and the Afrikaner Lieutenant Kramer play dual roles. In front of superiors and the white public, a clear domination-subordination role structure is portrayed. When by themselves, in a crime investigation, Zondi's broken English is transformed into the considered tones of his mission school education, and the two police officers work as colleagues rather than as racially-defined unequals. Such an organic relationship between white and black policing was at the core of the South African condition prior to the election of the Government of National Unity in April 1984. There was both a public face and a private face. The racist public face was far more prevalent than that of private practice in the Zondi and Kramer case. But the critical point about the McClure novels is that in any case involving black members of the old South African Police (SAP), Zondi is an investigator and detective who acts within the designs and trappings of white authority and who can take little public credit for any successes.

It is this institutional inequality of the white and black police that sits at the core of the debate over the reformation of the South African state police. How feasible is it to envisage a South African society where non-racism is the police norm as opposed to the exception? In a society with very divergent population groups, a multiculturalism sharpened by apartheid, should not the accommodation of social differences also recognize the relativity of the policing or social ordering process--that what is unacceptable in one community may be acceptable within the social ordering process of another community? And if such legal dualism (Santos, 1984) is adopted, is it likely to fall prey to the failings of other structures? Many crusades for "popular" law and policing have concluded with such legal processes being incorporated as institutionally inferior to the formal law and agents of the state. In this paper, I examine the possibilities of the development in the New South Africa of a pluralistic policing structure which has none of the inferiority/superiority connotations of apartheid and within which popular--black--legal processes may enjoy legitimacy in their own terms and help construct a society where policing is conducted as an empowering strategy on behalf of indigenous peoples.

The first section of the paper locates the problem historically. It illustrates the "detribalisation" process by which both indigenous groups and legal structures have been incorporated within the dominant white structures. It also documents a "retribalisation" process within which traditional practices have been "reinvented" by the white state as a control device for the indigenous people. The final section counterpoises alternative futures for indigenous ordering structures through affirmative action processes in the new South African Police Service (SAPS) as opposed to the potential for developing popular, local policing structures.

## HISTORICAL PROCESS--DETRIBALISATION TO RETRIBALISATION

While social control in racist South Africa was characterized throughout by diversity, its central objective was one of subordinating the majority to the rule of the minority. While the historical South African state and its colonial predecessors utilized many other means of social control--most visibly the precise spatial divisions formulated under the Group Areas Act and the "homelands" policy--the state police was throughout the most manifest means of social control. In that policing practice, state policy has oscillated between two extremes. Commonly, a "strangers policing strangers" policy was followed. On other occasions, token members of the majority have been incorporated on an apparently "local" policing basis. At other times, a mix of the two systems was followed.

At the outset, native levies were attached to the early white state police. Later a process of "detribalisation" was attempted which posited the white state police as a model for their "racial inferiors."

This was followed by a process of retribalisation in which the state attempted to incorporate traditional African modes of policing and judicial decision-making as the inferior base of a white pyramid of law and policing. In the last two decades, at the height of the apartheid state's domination, the South African Police (SAP) attempted to incorporate members of the majority to police the majority. Finally, in the political transitional process prior to the April 1994 election, there were twin, competing tracks with regard to the indigenisation of policing and social control. The SAP and certain radical interest groups promoted affirmative action-type strategies (incorporating members of the majority within the SAP) within an institutional structure that would remain largely unmodified. Alternatively, there was pressure to reconstruct the institutional problematic of social control to devolve power back to local black communities.

## COLONIALISM AND "STRANGERS POLICING STRANGERS"

The conjunctural crises in Eastern Europe and in Southern Africa have had a major impact on all social institutions. Central to those changes has been the crisis in law and in forms of law enforcement. Policing, social ordering activity, is in a state of flux in both contexts. A new form of colonialism is being undertaken with the export of Western models to many of those countries.

One newly dominant view is that the reconstruction of state policing is the central imperative in that institutional rebuilding process. Bayley (1991) has suggested that in the former Soviet countries policing represents a keystone in the social transformation process. In an adaptation of the orthodox "thin blue line" thesis, he has portrayed policing as cornerstone of the democratic order--construct a democratic police force to give other institutions the breathing space to develop their own legitimacy. In the United Kingdom, for example, a reshuffling of the priorities of overseas aid has made the instructional establishment of police reforms a priority. From Pretoria to Palestine to St. Petersburg, British missions, like those of several other European Union countries, are heavily engaged in the transformation of state police work.

In the British case, these advisory missions accommodate a major irony. The late imperial tradition had perfected a policy by which it could use one indigenous group to police another on behalf of the imperial state. From policing to tax collection, from the civil service to shopkeeping, the British tradition ensured that a local barrier was constructed to mediate the relationship between the ruled and the rulers (Brogden, 1987). In over a hundred nascent nations and dependent territories, the British constructed policing in their own image through the medium of "middlemen."

For example, under the Palestinian mandate, the British organized policing in what later became the State of Israel, primarily through the use of Jewish and Arab levies. With an elite of British (and Irish) police, the British pursued a policy of "strangers policing strangers." Similarly, a century earlier in the Sind, Lord Napier utilized outside "Hindustanis and Purdustanis, men of stout physique but not much in the way of brains" (quoted in Brogden, 1987). The British policy of strangers policing strangers, of using "aliens" to police indigenous communities, is a continuous thread throughout the imperial tradition.

### SOUTH AFRICA—STRANGERS AND LOCALS POLICING

In South Africa, this practice of "strangers policing strangers" has a long tradition. There were varied manifestations of this practice at different historical periods. A few examples make the point.

In the early colonization of the Cape, policing, a low-status function, was conducted by "non-white... 'g e w e l d i g e r s' o r 'geregsdienaars' assisted by 'Caffres' who were in fact bandits from the East given a chance to rehabilitate themselves" (quoted in Brogden, 1987) to exercise control over the two local black populations as well as over the new white settlements. In the early part of the nineteenth century, British expansionism from the Cape relied heavily upon native Khoi-Khoi to police the bands of both the pejoratively labelled Hottentots and itinerant Boers. This tried and trusted policy relied on assumed outcast minorities to police other inhabitants of the Cape, indigenous and colonial.

But it was a complex policy. At the menial level, locals could be recruited to conduct the disciplinary task of whipping an indigenous labor force into imperial line. When Indian and Chinese indentured laborers were imported into Natal in the 1880s, the colonial state found it expedient to appoint Chinese police officers with a limited mandate and without the title of "policeman," since that might lead them to suppose that they had legal authority and powers.

While imperial exigency required a "locals policing locals" strategy at the grass-roots, such an ordering function was coupled with a limited ethnic, spatial, and legal mandate (Brogden, 1989).

Indigenous police, like the parish constable of medieval England, were not to get ideas above their stations in life. Consequently, "local" police were always superintended by "strangers" of the imperial state and of its surrogates.

The first major institutional South African Police, organized by one Robert Baden Powell[2], included a heterogeneous collection of English, Canadians, and Irish to police both Boers and the majority black population. By the time of the development of the Dominion state, policing had come to mean primarily the social control of the indigenous population by white expatriates. Apart from police action against the strikers on the Rand, in the immediate post-war period, the primary function of the white police institution was to discipline farm labor on the veldt and to enforce an early pass system of varying legality in the burgeoning towns and cities. While the policing process itself, was a hybrid of British (or rather Irish Constabulary) and Boer commando (*landdrost*) systems, as adapted according to local exigencies, its essential ingredient was that of white police policing black people. Stranger policing was the dominant mode of social control up to and beyond the outbreak of World War II.

## INCORPORATION STRATEGIES

However, stranger policing was a qualified one. Underneath the dominant stranger policing existed a recurring readiness to fall back on indigenous people to police themselves on behalf of the settler state. Two strategies were important in the process of consolidating what was apparently "local" policing in South Africa in that period. Increasingly the state utilized black officers in a subordinate role to police the majority population. On the other hand, there was an attempt to downgrade the nature of "native" justice through the Bantu Commissioners Courts and related law enforcement practice. In the hackneyed phrase from the informal justice debate "poor justice was to be created for poor people."

### Strategies of Black Police within the SAP

There have always been black police within the SAP and its predecessor organizations, despite their primary role as agents of white supremacy. As early as 1910, there were some seven hundred black police in the Transkei alone. Local police stations used powers of varying legality to recruit local black people as auxiliaries--often without the formal title of police--to extend social control in their districts. But these were, ad hoc, improvised measures of short duration. By the 1930s, the SAP nationally was regularly using black assistants to white police in the control of the majority population. No training was provided for them until the late 1930s--police knowledge was "acquired experience mainly while on duty" (Sachs, 1973: 227). The authority of those black police officers (a term with which they were occasionally dignified) was severely limited and could not be used in relation to members of a different racial group. They were not expected to be literate, which demeaned the policing function of black people, ensured that it was an unskilled activity largely bereft of legal knowledge, and prevented potential career aspirations--once a black police constable, always a black constable. Only during the war-time years did minimal training develop, with increasing differentiation in that training for "coloured" and Asian officers.

Until 1953, there were only two career rungs for "non-whites"--the ranks of first and second class Sergeant--with the first Asian station officers being appointed in the 1960s (a status only achieved by black officers in 1980). Only in the last fifteen years have black police been allowed to wear the same uniforms as white. Not until 1980 was the first black officer given the power to command white officers and to deal with cases involving white suspects on his or her own. Pay was also similarly differentiated--only in the last decade have black officers received the same rights and powers as their white peers (Brogden and Shearing, 1993).

The major boost to the indigenisation of social control occurred after the Soweto uprising of the mid-1970s. State police apologists were sensitive to the worldwide broadcasts of white security officers shooting unarmed black children. Black police could play an important ideological role. They could be used to counteract that stark "strangers policing strangers" image, hence play a critical ideological role in the perception internationally of the South African state. They could counteract criticism of police methods by allowing part of the policing of apartheid to be conducted by the victims themselves (Grundy, 1983).

But as always, it was a cynical tactic. Black police appeared on the television screen to be of the same ethnic group as the policed. In practice, the vast majority of the new black recruits into the SAP were from rural areas, often divided by ethnicity, culture, and language from the township residents. It was stranger policing in another garb.

The crudest aspect of this indigenisation strategy was the formation of a police reserve--Police Specials, *kitzconstables*--in the mid-1980s at the instigation of the then Commissioner, Johan Coetzee. These new appointees, accounting for some 15 percent of SAP numbers by the time they were formally absorbed into the SAP in 1991, were characterized in a variety of documentation as grossly underpaid (and hence susceptible to extortionate practices), often illiterate and versed in a language alien to many townships (communications with residents were more likely to be accompanied by brutality than civility), and largely untrained--six weeks in law and shotgun use (Fine, 1989). The *kitzconstables*, together with the misnamed municipal constables (appointed to serve the quisling township councils by the white administration), and groups of vigilantes (most emotively figured at the Crossroads slaughter of 1986 but far more common than that episode suggested) became in effect *the* police for the majority population. While the state had been for many years reticent about employing members from the majority population for fear of creating a Trojan Horse in its own ranks, those fears, in the event, were largely unjustified (Frankel, 1980).[3]

Although units such as the riot police (and their transitional appearance as Internal Stability Units) might conduct occasional townships forays, policing in South Africa for the majority population came to symbolize, in international media imagery, a manifestation of black-on-black violence. Stranger policing was disguised as *local* policing by mere changes in skin pigmentation.

By the time of transformation into the South African Police Service, under the new democratic government, 60 percent of the SAP was "non-white." That the vast majority of those officers were located at the base of the steep SAP pyramid needs little detailing. Different races were subject to different policing experiences. For example, of the three hundred police officers killed in 1993, the vast majority were black, reflecting black police exposure to the most hazardous situations.[4] Separate training establishments for black, "coloured," Indian, and white officers had formally been abolished although in practice there remained de facto segregation. There had been marginal changes in the "General Staff" with the complement of one Indian General (as opposed to 47 white generals) being altered to include a further Indian, two "coloured," and one black. Of those "non-whites," only General Manuel was regarded by representatives of the majority of the population to have retained committed links with that majority.[5]

## Strategies of Retribalisation—Social Control through the Bantu Commissioners Courts

The second major manifestation of black incorporation into the structure of social control was through a process of "retribalisation." Indigenisation of control could occur through institutional incorporation as well as through changes in the composition of the state police. The essential thesis behind this retribalisation strategy was that a "lower race" was more content with a legal process--assumed to be more primitive--to which it was traditionally accustomed. Retribalisation meant recasting the subject majority population to a more natural relationship with a primitive legal past.

Whereas in the nineteenth century, the colonial state and missionary and educational agencies had inspired a process of detribalisation--encouraging the "native" population up the evolutionary ladder of English and Dutch legal process--retribalisation meant a policy of accommodatory tutelage.

In 1856, for example, Lord Grey attempted to diminish autonomous chiefly authority by requiring them to accept remuneration through salaries rather than from tribal court fines, simultaneously appointing headmen sworn to the imperial state to serve as the local police force. Incrementally, in the late nineteenth and early twentieth century, the colonial state sought to accommodate and incorporate indigenous practice and reconstruct indigenous judicial and policing authority within the suzerainty of Westminster. Similarly, in the early Dominion years, the state assimilated local tribal groups in the rural areas within the white legal process through allocating to the paid headmen policing duties. Bundy (1990: 210) for example notes the function of the latter as both "detectives and as administrative functionaries." Policing, like the judicial function, was part of the expanding web of imperial administration. In the Transkei, in the interwar years, the headmen serve as a "non-uniformed police force, and especially through the subheadmen, as a sensitive and ubiquitous intelligence network" (Bundy, 1990: 209) on behalf of the magistracy. Bundy quotes the evidence of a magistrate to the South African Native Affairs Commission on the headman's contribution to social order:

> ...he is regarded also as a constable. He is supposed
> to keep peace, report the presence of strangers,
> prevent assaults, and generally discharge the duties of
> a police constable (p.209).

Throughout South African history, the state could manage in part with a relatively small white police force by utilizing the chiefs and headmen, exercising tribal discipline through traditional institutions (Beinart and Bundy, 1990: 47).

Between the wars, the dominant detribalisation strategy of the colonial period went partly into reverse--social control could best be ensured by manipulating tribal structures and the practices of customary rules to provide for more insidious control of the majority population. It was a form of social control promoted by local magistrates but also encouraged by more traditional elements in black society. Cooptation meant the retention of largely unfettered power in both civil and criminal cases by conservative, authoritarian chiefs.

> The criminal law and its operatives were matters that
> could temporarily be left in the hands of the native
> population. A process of incorporation of native
> justice was practised (Brogden, 1989: 11).

The development of the Chiefs and Commissioners Courts and the institutionalization of Native law in 1927, by the Native Administration Act, was the logical outcome of this process of retribalisation. Although primarily concerned with civil law cases, Native law, as enacted by this dual court system, sought to provide a uniform system of law for all black people irrespective of their background, education, or urban-rural location. Apart from civil cases, the Chief Courts were limited in their scope to relatively minor offenses. Their criminal jurisdiction included all offenses punishable in Native law, but the chiefs were instructed that all serious crime known to both legal systems must not be tried by them but must be reported to the state police. In practice, the recognition of the juridical function of the chiefs was also a recognition of their policing function and of their headmen roles in those duties.

Above these courts, in a supervisory function, were the Commissioners Courts staffed by white magistrates, civil servants who had gravitated upwards from the Native Affairs Department and to whom the policing and judicial practices of the majority population were simply a technical function of administration which required no specific legal training. These two tiers of courts and the resurrection of traditional tribal policing systems served several functions for the state.

It furnished a cheap, unpaid form of policing--responsibility for the headmen and the subheadmen in their policing function was a matter for the chief not for the state. In resurrecting tribal customs, the state did so in a way that reinforced the conservative authoritarian features of those systems--all power to the chiefs (under the supervision of the white Commissioner) ensured that a degree of vertical control extended from the Pretoria Native Affairs Department to the grassroots of rural society. As the tribal officers were de facto officers of the state, it dispensed a unique system of indigenous surveillance and social control. It also demeaned the majority population by elevating the more serious offenses to the courts controlled and staffed by whites, ensuring that any dispute between white and black was settled according to state (white) law rather than through traditional law. In effect, the relative informalism of tribal law was simply a feeder system for the legitimate (white) law of the state. It was also (deliberately) humiliating. A black person growing up in urban society, educated according to his or her ability, socialized to the dominant legal code and policing structure, was still to be subject to a form of customary law to which he or she had no form of affiliation.

Intra-black disputes became the accepted area for local intra-black resolution through the use of traditional powers, reconstructed in a form that prevented it from infringing on the legitimacy of the wider state. Around the boundaries of that incorporated justice patrolled the SAP. Where indigenous practices in some way appeared to violate those of white interests (in entry to space, in competition for work--as in the case of the Asian shopkeepers banned early from the Orange Free state--or in terms of simple inter-race criminality), only then did the South African Police become involved.

This incipient tradition of allowing a degree of autonomy for black justice and policing served several functions. It saved manpower--"real" policing resources were primarily at the disposal of the white population. It contributed to the debasement process of black people--only whites got "real" policing and justice. It ensured the maintenance of non-challenging structures of authority with the incorporation of the traditional chief's authority as a paid office of the state.

The stated object was to provide an inexpensive and familiar legal procedure for black people, one free from Western technicalities and within easy reach of the communities it was to serve (Van Niekerk, 1986). A generous appraisal of the legislation of the 1927 Native Administration Act was that it hoped to create a simple and inexpensive apparatus--"located on the boundary between state law and indigenous or local law" (Merry, 1991: 183)--for settling disputes between black people with their cases tried by experts in indigenous law and customs (Hund and Kotu-Rammopo, 1983). But fundamentally, the Commissioners Courts and the ancillary policing apparatus created "poor law for poor people."

This institutionalized indigenisation process provided a primary strategy by which the white state could maintain legal, if indirect, control of black people. Its procedures were grotesquely weighted against the majority population who suffered from this extension of legal practice. "The formal law model of adjudication gave way to a process of justice moulded to the requirements of bureaucratic efficiency" (Hund and Kotu-Rammopo, 1983). Until the abolition of the tribal structures (outside the "homelands") in the mid-1970s, this apparently indigenous legal process "...came to be seen by the black community as an instrument in the hands of the apartheid regime" (Van Niekerk, 1986).

## COMPETING STRATEGIES DURING
## THE TRANSITIONAL PERIOD

In the early 1990s, state policing in South Africa was thrown into chaos. With the formal declaration of the end of apartheid in President De Klerk's speech, the indigenisation of social control in South Africa entered a new phase. Like other state agencies, in the SAP hierarchy self-interest overlapped with a desperate attempt to maintain the structures of apartheid by other means. For those senior officers prepared to accept some form of change, one resolution to the crisis was to encourage a process of indigenisation of the SAP while leaving its larger structural characteristics unchanged. However, the rise of a popular justice movement during the struggle against apartheid suggested a different agenda for transforming policing.

### *TRANSFORMING THE SAP--AFFIRMATIVE ACTION PROGRAMMES*
Given the uncertainty, confusion, miasma, and lack of commitment of the SAP General Staff at the official levels to the

transformation process, the primary characteristics of the proposed indigenisation were those of shifting the goal posts without altering the rules of the game. Affirmative action programmes were proposed in which the criteria for what constituted a South African police officer remained substantially the same. Policing in South Africa was to remain fundamentally one of policing through the institutions and structures of the central state. More black (and Indian and "coloured") recruits would furnish an appropriate demographic transition.[6]

The key device to obtain a degree of indigenisation throughout the SAP organization was through a version of affirmative action. In that process, SAP self-interest overlapped in part with those groups committed to more substantive change. The primary characteristics of the SAP scheme was to increase the representation of black, "coloured," and Indian members throughout the ranks of the SAP. Such policies had several strands, all emphasizing some version of an affirmative action approach. Critically, all these mechanisms left the very nature of state control and policing untrammelled while changing the components of the overall machine.[7]

The state police affirmative action programme was initiated by a major SAP conference at the police Staff College at Graaff Reinet in October 1991. As a programme it fitted neatly within the "scientistic" characteristics of the SAP, an institution long committed to the notion that if you cannot psychometrically test something it cannot be viable. Thus the keynote paper, although presented as a document designed to increase entry to the SAP by the majority population, embodied the central principle of determining that a "better calibre" of recruit entered the SAP. Racism and police violence were a function of aberrational factors (not the structure of apartheid itself) in recruiting incompetent officers. Assuming that this police deviance was a consequence of the narrow pool of recruits from which the SAP drew--on the white side, the traditional stereotyped provincial Afrikaner, and on the black, the impoverished rural conservative desperate for any kind of job who had figured so numerically within the *kitzconstables*--the affirmative action programme could solve two problems. A larger reservoir of recruits would mean better quality and therefore, potentially, less police deviance. It also meant by definition, increasing the number of members of the black, "coloured," and Indian population within the SAP. Over time, those members could be expected to climb the rank structure. Within a couple of decades, the General Staff of the South

African Police would be proportionately representative of the whole South African population.

As a strategy, it was principally--if unintended on behalf of its principal progenitors--a strategy of incorporation. The criteria to be used in testing potential recruits were to be widened. More psychologists--or rather psychometrists--were to be employed to ensure, for example, that police officers facing a situation of latent conflict did not overreact. At that level of assumption there could be little debate. But its principal problem was that it left the very definition of what constituted the police task, one hewn out of South Africa's white history, totally unchallenged. The problem was reduced to the simply scientific one of testing a broader range of recruits so that they could conduct the given objectives of the South African Police more effectively. Fundamentally, the process of the proposed affirmative action programme left the nature of the police task and the police relationship to the state and to the community unquestioned.

In that debate, there was some overlap with opposing groups with quite different objectives for change. A second approach--primarily associated with the Management School at the University of the Witwatersrand--represented a more progressive path but also failed to raise the fundamental questions. These educational proposals and several other related initiatives at other South African universities drew heavily upon non-South African financial state resources (especially upon the largesse of the Danish and Dutch governments) and were to that extent committed to a more radical vision of the future.

The Wits staff and their associated network recognized a different problematic and different human resources than did the Graaff Reinet initiative. They appreciated that the latter, in its assumption of a slow indigenous progression up the SAP pyramid, left three problems unchecked. It would, in effect, be generations before the SAPS reflected the population base through the traditional affirmative action construction. Secondly, they rejected the narrow scientistic base of the SAP's selection and promotional policy and the acculturation of the new officers to the traditional rank-and-file and management cultures of the existing SAP. Finally, in their police educational designs, they implicitly re-defined the police task. Through an emphasis on accountability and on community policing,[8] they conceptualized the state police as problem-solvers on behalf of the community rather than as order-maintainers on behalf of a central state.

But what primarily distinguished the Wits approach--and also that of the third approach associated with the University of the Western Cape (UWC)--was its recognition of a major alternative resource in the indigenisation of policing structures. The "struggle" period in South Africa had produced many individuals whose experiences ranged from membership of the ANC's guerrilla army of Umkonto Sisziwele (including infiltration of the SAP's Security Branch) to "legal" involvement in social ordering processes in the black townships, under the general rubric of the Peoples Courts. These latter activities constituted a novel form of non-state policing and voluntary street ordering functions ranging from the closure of noisy *shebeens*, to supporting battered wives, to arresting and sanctioning young thieves, to activities as varied as rubbish collection in the context of the breakdown of all municipal services. Such participants constituted a majority of the students attending the Wits policing course. To that group was added a minority of talented black rank-and-file officers.

In a wide-ranging course of study, these mature committed individuals undertake a policing education that covers topics much wider than that provided by the scientistic and legalist SAP academies. The unwritten intention within such educational design was that these students would provide the core of a "new" state police. However, at the time of writing, the course organizers have not negotiated a conduit by which the non-police students can enter the new SAPS. Two proposals remain on the drawing board. One consists of recruit entry with the possibility of a fast promotion scheme. The other proposal is for a lateral entry into officer rank. Each proposal contains inherent difficulties independently of the present unwillingness (or inertia) of the SAP. Each involves, especially, the problems of career isolation from peers in a state policing agency that is still committed to a theocratic rank-and-file police culture (Brogden, 1994).

The major problem however facing the Wits and related initiatives is that it seeks to integrate members of the majority population into a state police whose problematic, raison d'etre, and monopoly of "legitimate" ordering practices remains largely unchanged. While formally there have been changes in the requirement to downgrade the security orientation that has always dominated the SAP to an SAPS crime-control orientation, the culture and the personnel in the Crime Combatting Division remain almost identical. It is the state policing problematic to which the third, the UWC initiatives address themselves.

The primary assumption of the UWC approach that is that most policing is a non-state practice. The conception of policing as *ordering work* was derived from that body of literature (see the discussion in Brogden and Shearing, 1993) which acknowledges the extent of policing activities in civil society. It recognizes that there are, conceptually, three different kinds of policing personnel: the *state police* for whom the major resources are law and force and whose primary commitment is to the social order determined by that state. Second, there are, as documented in a literature of varying quality (for example, Shearing and Stenning, 1987), the *private police* whose commitment is to the order defined by the paymaster and where the key determinant of ordering practice is the profit motive. But critically, there remains largely unexplored (Johnston, 1992; Marenin, 1993) a whole area of *civil policing*, largely voluntary in character, that characterizes the normative ordering in civil society.

It is to this third context that the UWC courses are oriented. Consequently, they represent a major break from the recognized state provision of policing in South Africa. At this preliminary stage, they have a primary focus on the development of ordering skills in the context of mass demonstrations--to provide for self-ordering and marshalling independently of the state police and to enhance the ability to mediate with the latter in situations of potential confrontation with the state police.[9]

Remarkably, what could have been a fourth approach to the indigenisation of policing in South Africa has not yet materialized in terms of practical assistance. In most other post-colonial contexts and also in situations where nation states such as those of Eastern Europe are developing new police structures, the former colonial states and the Western powers have invested considerable resources in training the new policing personnel. The dominant practice has been to export a version of Anglo-American policing, an evolutionary ladder up which the "developing" state institutions and personnel can gradually climb.[10]

In the South African context, although there have been a number of initiatives sponsored by the European Union and the North American countries in seconding personnel to South Africa (primarily for conflict monitoring purposes), the rigidity of the historical past and practices have prevented, to date, any direct import of SAP personnel for training purposes. Principal, in that regard, were the European

Union sanctions against the training of South African security staff. The forms of police colonialism that have characterized other parts of the world have not permeated the South African situation to anything like the same extent despite the proclaimed commitment of senior SAP staff to follow the Anglo-American path (Coetzee, 1993).

What all these approaches have in common (although to a much lesser extent with the UWC initiatives) is that they take state policing as the given institutional source of order. In a quasi-functionalism, policing is taken to be whatever state police officers happen to be doing. Where there are clear differences between those practices--between, for example, the security consciousness of the SAP, the new SAPS efforts in community policing, and the rhetorical commitment of Western police forces to crime fighting (or bandit catching)--the implicit explanation is an evolutionary one. All police forces are transformed, in a military-crime-community ascension, through a gradual process (Brogden, 1993). In that failure to recognize the key, the ordering functions of policing, the indigenisation process is assumed to be accommodated by the simple absorption, through affirmative action programmes of varying complexity, of recruits from the policed populations. The military model of policing is to be transformed gradually into a crime control model through graduated training of local personnel.

## TRANSFORMING POLICING THROUGH RECONSTRUCTION WITHIN CIVIL SOCIETY

The central problem with the transformation of the SAP to a new South African Police Service is its failure to conceptually analyze the constitution of police work. The expansion of indigenous entry to the SAP leaves the central mission of that institution, as sanctified by its past, largely undisturbed. A rather different approach to indigenisation is one that recognizes the existence of those three distinct forms of policing--state, private, and civil--and pursues through the last a reconstruction of South African policing as a whole.

One key starting point is through the appreciation of the fashionable problem-solving, goal-oriented policing in the West (Goldstein, 1990). Such concepts, with an orthodox pedigree in North America, are in practice little different from historical assumptions of police work as "shit-work"--sorting out the medley of problems on the streets of the Victorian city, whether they be human or vegetable. Problem-oriented policing as currently popular in state police theorizing is, in practice, little more than old wine in new bottles.

But apart from the lack of recognition of history in those several texts, there is a major problem in all those formalistic accounts of the community policing style to which the problem orienteers subscribe. They assume fundamentally, that problem-oriented policing is *state* policing. In doing so, they attempt to achieve the best of both worlds under the same uniform hat--the bearer of armed force as riot-police may be the same individual who, as a problem-solver, constructs an alternative recreational venue for street kids. Specifically, it fails to recognize the alternative form of *civil* policing.[11] Problem-solving policing may be the primary domain not of state police--and certainly not of private police--but rather of *civil* agencies. Indeed, the discovery of problem-solving policing by state police theorists can be represented as an incursion into civil society where such functions may already be conducted by an alternative, civil agency. Problem-solving policing has a civil, not a state, history of legitimation.

In South Africa, indigenous civil policing institutions have a long and legitimate tradition. Indeed, a major factor in the overthrow of the apartheid regime has been the remarkable strength and resilience of civil society institutions in South Africa. In the absence of a state police committed to deal with problems of public order (or rather in the presence of an SAP committed to criminalise those black people whose conception of rights infringed upon those of the white population), local, voluntary policing emerged. As Goodhew (1991) has documented, between the 1930s and the 1950s, the absence of or oppression by the state police gave rise to a variety of self-policing experiments. Order was constructed in the Rand townships despite, not because of, the SAP. Local people fabricated their own social order.

In the last two decades, this process of informal or civil policing emerged as the dominant township mode of forging social order. Civil policing emerged formidably as the alternative indigenous structure to that of the state police during the repression of the 1970s and 1980s. Such indigenous policing structures tended to have several key characteristics. They were voluntary in character. They were intertwined with judicial functions--judicial and policing practices were often part of a seamless web. The whole medley of street problems fell to the lot of the voluntary street patrol. Problem-solving civil policing in these stark contexts ranged from the usual assortment of street complexities to the more serious ones of providing transport in the context of the boycott of state facilities and "dealing with informers" who betrayed local civic and ANC leaders to the state police. In the midst of all these myriad, complex functions and acting under potential charges of treason, the voluntary township policing structures and ancillary Peoples Courts represented to the South African state an embryo of an alternative, oppositional state. This indigenous policing was a dramatic symbol of the potential of civil policing.

Although these structures have suffered, in more recent years, major depredations from assaults by the state police and by the forms of criminalisation which have been an indirect consequence of apartheid ghettoisation policies, they represent a relative triumph for informalism in constituting an alternative process for the indigenisation of social control. The key question that arises, in the South African context, is the extent to which indigenisation in civil society can compete in the new South Africa with indigenisation through affirmative action programs into the state South African Police Service.

## THE PROBLEMS OF INFORMALISM AND CIVIL POLICING
Many of the arguments relating to the development of non-state policing have been discussed in the much wider debate about informal justice and the possibilities of legal pluralism. South Africa faces two crude policing scenarios.

Firstly, the state police stays in form and functions much as at the present time. Through affirmative programmes, the force will slowly be indigenised so that over a couple of decades, other structural factors permitting, the force will become, at all ranks, much more representative of the national population. Such a development clearly contains major flaws. Firstly, the strength of existing police culture should not be forgotten. While SAPS officers may lose their commitment to the defence of the *volk* and white supremacy, the other embedded forms of police culture (and evident corruption) are likely to remain implanted--the commitment to physical force as the major problem-solving device, the paranoid isolation from the community to be policed, the sexism that is prevalent to a large extent in both white state police and black townships cultures, and the prioritization of macho excitement over the relative mundanity of street problem solving.

Simply expanding the black (including "coloured" and Indian) intake into the SAPS and merging the latter with the black "homeland forces" will not solve the South African policing problem. Indigenisation may well have been accomplished, but the functions, practices, and priorities of the SAP are unlikely to have changed a great deal. Whatever the developments in important areas like accountability, in community relations, in demilitarization, in problem-solving training, the SAPS will remain a fundamentally--if indigenised--flawed force. Principally, it will have failed to recognize the vitality of other forms of policing. The private policing of the white suburbs is one such element. But more important is the extent to which the major part of civil society--mainly the black townships--have developed a legitimate tradition of self-policing. The indigenisation of civil policing despite the battering that its structures received in the Emergency period, is an accomplished fact. Simply placing a trained black officer in the uniform of the SAPS is hardly likely to vastly increase the legitimacy of the state police.[12]

This civil policing, historically sanctified through struggle, must be recognized. Its structure of accountability, of community relations, of skill development in problem solving requires new formalized structures. Yet the evident problems in the construction of *local* policing will not be resolved by some overly romantic view of its virtues. However, the future for South African policing is through the development of a *dual* policing structure, a combination of state and civil police, with the ancillary *private* police a particular market commodity.

A more realistic blueprint for the new SAPS must rest on the commitment of three parties--the re-named Ministry of Safety and Security,[13] the arising segment of black police officers, and local communities (racked as they are by a major crime problem)--to demand state policing that empowers those communities. A structure that would take account of the strength of civil policing while at the same time acknowledging the importance of the indigenisation process would look something like the following.

A reconstituted SAPS would operate as a semi-Federal Police force (something like the Royal Canadian Mounted Police). Its primary functions would be to deal with what Brodeur (1983) has called "high policing," the security of the social order of the state. Its mandate would cover--as at present--border security and cross-national forms of crime. With regard to internal crime, its responsibility would be limited to the more serious offence categories from homicide to forcible rape to the more serious drug and property offenses. It would also be responsible--like the FBI--for crime that crosses regional and communal boundaries. Assuming appropriate construction of democratic accountability procedures under the forthcoming Police Act, it would be encouraged to emphasize the crime control features of police culture.[14] With an appropriate level of indigenisation, the SAPS could for the most part represent an institution that no longer oppressed the black townships.

Secondly, the development of local policing structures is critical. Communities should have the right to choose the nature of their local police--state, private, or civil. If the (white) community was content with SAP history and practice, it could use the federal force in a local communal role to deal with both high and low crime. It could, in effect, buy in the new SAPS as the local policing agency. Also, given that in practice many of the white suburbs of the major cities are policed by private security rather than the SAPS, such communities would have the right to continue and formalize such private policing to deal with "low" crime. The major proviso here is that such agencies would be constituted under national legislation that prevented them becoming the private armies committed to the defence of "turf" rather than of individual rights and property and be subject to specific local measures of accountability in law.

Finally, the townships, spatially confined urban structures, should also choose their mode of policing. Where indigenous structures of self-policing have obtained historical legitimacy and where popular justice has deep roots, such civil policing institutions should be recognized as legitimate--again subject to legal and political measures of accountability. *Local,* indigenous, civil policing could reach its zenith in those townships. Police practices as before would draw on the problem solving ideology--whether developed from African history or from North American police scholars. Indigenous policing would be given a quite different meaning to that of the absorption of more black recruits into the SAPS.

This tripartite structure of state police, of private police, and of civil police clearly raises many questions about viability. The central problem relates to the relationship between civil policing and the state police.

*PROBLEMS OF CIVIL POLICING IN THE TOWNSHIPS*

The proposal for this reconstruction of indigenous policing in South Africa draws heavily on the literature on informalism. The popularity of that area of legal study and experimentation in the 1970s largely succumbed to an avalanche of criticism in the 1980s. There were many criticisms both in theory and in terms of observed practice.

In the latter context, civil or popular policing schemes were seen to be a product of a period of intense political struggle and, consequently, very limited in time and space. Spence's (1982) example of self-policing in Chile has been criticized as representing a particular period in that struggle by the working class of that country. Similarly, West's (1987) defence of civil policing in Nicaragua seems lost in the history of more recent events. Civil, indigenous, local policing experiments have been stranded (theoretically) within a particular historical time zone of political struggle.

Secondly, a more general criticism of such informal approaches is that they have often ended representing a lower level of policing and justice than the established state structures (e.g., Abel, 1982). They might act as "feeder systems" to the state system, criminalising through a net-widening process those whose infractions would rarely have come to the notice of the state agency. In various ways, the lack of formal legal safeguards might affect the level of justice--it might, in effect, be "poor justice (or poor policing) for poor people." It could further be colonized by functionaries from the state system whether they be state police officers in search of information or lawyers in search of an expanded territory.

There are several answers to these problems.

In the first place, the informal system of policing and justice that has developed, spasmodically, in the South African townships has long-term legitimacy. Its history is not simply that of short-term squatter camp policing institutions arising against a local tyranny, making the barrios temporarily no-go areas for the state police. Informal civil policing in South Africa, while born out of struggle, has gone through a long-term gestation period that seems to ensure its future continuity, subject to the development of more locally accountable and financial structures.

The second area of criticism derives largely from observation of the development of informal structures in Western countries. There, many informal structures--especially those concerned with mediation practices--have had a transient existence as an alternative to the formal legal structures. Further, where self-policing has been accomplished by agents of civil society, it has degenerated into little more than vigilantism.

The critical rejoinder here is to recognize that the history of indigenous township policing in South Africa has not been that--as in the West and in the notorious Commissioners Courts--as the second rung in a two-tier system. Other schemes failed because in part their legitimacy drew not from the community but from the central state's willingness to accommodate or promote informalism. The South African situation is different. The township self-policing structures' legitimacy derives from the historical struggle not from the state's imprimatur. The long experiential memory of that struggle, in the same way that it denies any legitimacy to even a re-formed and indigenously re-constituted SAP, conversely gives legitimacy to local popular structures, subject to measures of democratic accountability.

Those structures do not operate at a lower level from the policing and judicial practices of the state but exist as parallels on a horizontal plane. There is no necessary reason therefore why they should operate as, for example, net-widening devices and feeder systems for the state legal process. Yet contact between the two processes--the formal SAPS of the state and the informal self-policing of the townships--is inevitable. For example, more serious criminal suspects may be handed over by the latter to the federalized SAPS for trial and potential punishment. Where intercommunal crime occurs, the SAPS as the primary source of police weaponry must have some limited rights of access. Whatever the outcome of the national political process, there cannot be a total cantonisation of policing.

But critically, the SAPS and the local indigenous policing structure must be involved into a continuous process of *negotiation between equals*. Rights of townships entry for the SAP must be subject to local resolution. In this process of negotiation, the existing Local Dispute Resolution Committees provide a base from which such a negotiative role between the two structures could be constructed.

In developing these structures, and especially in the construction of indigenous policing through the existing and latent township struggle structures, there are major problems, both large and small. Amongst other major problems are the relations between the civil policing structures and the local townships' judicial practices and between the latter and the state law: law cannot be reduced to a multitude of local legal processes. There are problems of schisms in local communities, especially where there exist Inkatha-dominated hostels within settled townships[15]. Townships are not necessarily homogeneous communities with agreed perceptions of policing and of local order. In particular, violent inter- and intra-race crime is a major potentially cataclysmic South African phenomenon--the legacy of apartheid's social and economic depredations will not disappear easily. But despite these and many related problems, the indigenisation of social control in South Africa, as a process, need not be an incorporation process into the state's definition of what constitutes policing, the police function, and the nature of the social order to be policed. Developing the township agencies offers a far more democratic path than greater recruitment through affirmative action processes of members of the majority population into the state police.

## NOTES

1. For example, *The Song Dog*, London: Faber, 1991.

2. Colonial policing strategies contain some peculiar apparitions. A key figure in Baden Powell's South African Constabulary had been one Sam Steele. The latter had joined the newly created--and Ulster Orange Order-influenced--North West Mounted Police (NWMP) prior to the Battle of Batoche and the subsequent suppression of the indigenous Canadian French Metis (who had been supported by Irish Fenians). Steele, as a NWMP Captain, pioneered the colonization of the prairies on behalf of the Ottawa government and guarded the 15,000-foot Chilcott Pass at the time of the Klondike gold rush. After his South African policing exploits, he was the first commander of the Canadian Expeditionary Force in World War I but died in disgrace in 1915 after the slaughter of these new colonial levies.

3. Only in the newly created "homelands" or Bantustans were black people allowed to police themselves. This latter policy had diverse consequences in the 1990s. The "tamer" homelands such as Lebowa and KwaZulu were often commanded by white Generals newly retired from the SAP. KwaZulu, under the leadership of the extraordinary Jac

Buchner, developed its own killer squads to deal with ANC opposition. Transkei was a rare exception in constructing autonomy from the SAP. The Boputhatswana Police salvaged an unfortunate reputation by playing a major part in the overthrow of the puppet President Mangope immediately prior to the democratic election.

4. There are numerous examples of continuing and dangerous discrimination. When four black constables were killed in Diepkloof in mid-1993, a black sergeant preached open mutiny at a demonstration of colleagues at the subsequent funeral because of the lack of protection. When the SAP raided the Pan African Congress headquarters in Johannesburg in late 1993, a shortage of bulletproof vests meant that safeguard was only available to white officers.

5. The incorporation of the "homelands" police into the SAPS in 1994 opened up opportunities for creating a more heterogeneous command. But to date, the SAPS has not been characterized by the anything like the degree of openness to the liberation movements as is evidently the case with the reformed South African National Defence Force.

6. The educational process has been essentially one of providing a semblance of equality of opportunity in the SAP while maintaining essential inequality in terms of race. To obtain promotion from the lower ranks, all officers must undertake courses from the Technikon SA in Roodiport. Formally, black and white officers have an equal chance to obtain promotion through these courses. However, the 75 percent failure rate in the course (and consequently the closure of promotion opportunities) is mainly of black police officers because of the cultural and linguistic biases built into the teaching by a predominantly Afrikaner institution. Until recently (September 1994), most promotion aspirants were expected to undertake an *Ethnology* course by the Technikon. The study guide for the course is an extraordinarily crude manifestation of "scientific" racism--it concludes, for example, by noting the different occupations at which different races excel ("Indians make good waiters"). On the corruption at the heart of traditional SAP training, see M. Brogden (1994).

7. SAP policy (insofar as anything a coherent as a policy could be recognized) initially had the field to itself. Despite the priority of the SAP in maintaining the apartheid state, not until late in 1993 did the ANC develop any visible strategy.

8. Community policing, of course, is a rubric under which lie some remarkable practices. The model which I drew up for the SAP and which was accepted as policy by the transitional government drew not upon the work of North Americans such as Hermann Goldstein but upon the work of the Bolshevik jurist Pashukanis and on the approach to legal inequality of the late American scholar, Isaac Balbus. Conversely, on the ground and in the limited study material, there is an enormous commitment to simply implanting North American and British conceptions to the alien contexts of the black townships. In that process, many key figures in Community Policing design are former senior figures in the SAP's Security Police.

9. There are many problems with the UWC initiatives (which are largely funded by the British Government), especially given the attachment to the courses of British entrepreneurial policing advisers, some of whom seem to have an agenda markedly different from the original sponsors of the scheme.

10. That form of late imperialism is evident in many inter-state relationships. Thus in the U.K., for example, the Universities of Exeter and Leicester provide courses for police officers from the United Arab Emirates and Pakistan and Cyprus. Western neo-colonial police structures are supported through the training of senior policing personnel. The indigenisation of social control, in a long imperial tradition (Brogden, 1987) with its Anglo-American roots in the original Irish Constabulary, is constructed through the definition of the policing problematic and policing practices within the parameters of Western policing ideologies.

11. The most recent exegesis on the potential of civil policing structures is in the compendious volume edited by Findlay and Zvekić (1993).

12. This lack of legitimacy of the new state police is evidenced by the 150 SAP/SAPS police officers killed in the January-July 1994 period.

13. The present ANC Minister, Sydney Mufamedi, is generally credited with making an impressive start to a near-impossible task. He is however suffering a major handicap by the lack of administrative staff untarnished by apartheid. Under the Peace Accord, the old guard of Afrikaner civil servants are guaranteed their posts, their (often grotesquely inflated) salaries, and their power to vet new appointments. Yet there are only a few civil servants in his Ministry. The administrative function there traditionally has been conducted not by the Civil Service but by serving police officers who have little reason to damage their self-interest by supporting change. Further handicaps include, to this and to several other observers, Mandela's failure to immediately replace the existing Commissioner, General van der Merwe, with an officer committed to social change; to appoint black advisers who would enjoy legitimacy with the rank and file and to pursue more ruthlessly (within the parameters of the Peace Accord) those former Security Police who still enjoy considerable power within the new SAPS.

14. Not surprisingly, the South African media has not yet produced the kind of cop films that dominate Western television. There is a financial bonanza for any producer who adapts the work of a writer like McClure for a South African television series, sardonically revelling in the racism of the old SAP while giving a new legitimacy to the human frailties of ordinary police officers and thus contributing to a new legitimacy for South African state policing.

15. However, as was evidenced during the election, the peacefulness of that process owed much to the ability by local committees of township and hostel residents to construct and maintain their own peace structures and not to actions of the SAP, which claimed the credit.

# SOURCES

Abel, R. L. (ed.) (1982), *The Politics of Informal Justice*, Volumes One and Two, London: Academic Press.

Bayley, D. (1991), "Policing Democracy," New Brunswick, New Jersey, mimeo.

Beinart, W., and C. Bundy (eds.) (1990), *Hidden Struggles in South Africa*, London: James Currey.

Brodeur, J. (1983), "High Policing and Low Policing," *Social Forces*, 30, 5, June, 507-520.

Brogden, M.E. (1987), "An Act to Colonise the Internal Lands of the Island," *International Journal of the Sociology of Law*, 15, 2.

------ (1989), "The Origins of the South African Police: Institutionalist Versus Structuralist Perspectives," *Acta Juridica*, Cape Town: Juta & Co.

------ (1993), "Community Police Training in South Africa," Silverton, Pretoria: South African Police International Training Commission.

------ (1994), "Report on the Policing Programme to the Council of Technikon SA," Florida, Roodeport.

------ (1995), "The Discourse of the South African Police," in L. Nocks, M. Levi, and M. Maguire (eds.), *Contemporary Issues in Criminology*, Cardiff: University of Wales Press.

Brogden, M.E., and C.D. Shearing (1993), *Policing for a New South Africa*, London: Routledge.

Bundy, C. (1990), "'We don't want your rain, we won't dip.' Popular Opposition, Collaboration, and Social Control in the Anti-Dipping Movement, 1908-16" in S. Bubow (ed.), *Racial Segregation and the Origins of Apartheid in South Africa, 1919-36*, Oxford: Macmillan.

Coetzee, J. (1993) "Memorandum on the Reform of the South African Police to the International Training Committee," Silverton: SAP.

Findlay, M., and U. Zvekić (eds.) (1993), *Alternative Policing Styles*, Boston: Kluwer Law and Taxation Publishers.

Fine, D. (1989) "Kitskonstabels: A Case Study in Black on Black Policing," *Acta Juridica*, Cape Town: Juta & Co.

Fitzpatrick, P. (1992), "The Impossibility of Popular Justice," *Social and Legal Studies*, 1: 199-215.

Frankel, P.H. (1980), "South Africa and the Politics of Police Control," *Comparative Politics*, 12, 4: 481-9.

Goldstein, H. (1990), *Problem-oriented Policing*, New York: McGraw Hill.

Goodhew, D. (1991), "Between the Devil and the Deep-Blue Sea: Crime and Policing in the Western Areas of Johannesburg c. 1930-1962," University of Witwatersrand, History Workshop "Structure and Experience in the Making of Apartheid."

Grundy, K.W. (1983), *Soldiers Without Politics: Blacks in the South African Armed Forces*, Berkeley: University of California Press.

Hund, J., and M. Kotu-Rammopo (1983), "Justice in a South African Township and the Politics of Makgotla," *Journal of Comparative Justice in International Law in South Africa*, XVI, July.

Johnston, L. (1992), *The Rebirth of Private Policing*, London: Routledge.

Marenin, O. (1993), "Policing the Last Frontier," *Policing and Society*, 2, 273-291.

McClure, R. (1991), *The Song Dog*, London: Faber.

Merry, S.E. (1991), "Law and Colonialism," *Law and Society Review*, 25, 4.

Sachs, A. (1973), *Justice in South Africa*, London: Heinemann.

Santos, B. (1984), "From Customary Law to Popular Justice," *Journal of African Law*, 28, 1/2.

Shearing, C.D., and P. Stenning (eds.) (1987), *Private Policing*, Beverly Hills: Sage.

Spence, J. (1982), "Institutionalizing Neighbourhood Courts: Two Chilean Experiences," in R. Abel, op. cit., Volume One, 215-249.

Van Niekerk, G.J. (1986), *A Comparative Study of Indigenous Law in the Administration of Justice in Southern Africa*, Ll.b. thesis, Pretoria: University of South Africa.

West, W.G. (1987), "*Vigilancia Revolucianca*: A Nicagaruan Resolution to Public and Private Policing," in Shearing and Stenning, op. cit., 147-171.

# POLICING THE EUROPEAN UNION:
# THE POLITICS OF TRANSITION

## Neil C. Walker

## INTRODUCTION

Over the past decade, the international organization known until recently as the European Community (EC) and now called the European Union (EU) has undergone a massive transformation (Hoffman, 1993). As a social, economic, and political entity, it has expanded its remit, deepened its authority, and claimed a measure of sovereign power to rival that of its constituent member states. It has also begun to develop a formal role in the sphere of policing far beyond that of any other international organization. This essay examines the relationship between these two sets of developments. It asks in what manner and to what extent has the development of a new policing capacity been informed by the wider political and socio-economic changes within the EU. More briefly, it also investigates the possible avenues of development of policing within the EU. Given current political trends, what will a mature set of policing institutions for the EU look like?

In addressing these questions, the essay will seek to throw light on two broader issues central to the concerns of this book. First, how should we conceptualize the relationship between policing and the political sphere more generally? Policing is obviously influenced by political ideas and interests, but how does this influence tend to be expressed? In what sense, if at all, does the sphere of policing retain a degree of independence from wider political forms and developments?

Secondly, and relatedly, what is the relationship between police and state in the rapidly changing international order of the 1990s? Generations of scholars have operated with the explicit or implicit assumption that policing activities are located within, and inseperable from, the broader matrix of the state. This premise may never have been entirely justified (Johnston, 1992: ch.l), but today it is particularly strongly challenged by two trends: first, the increased prominence of private modes of policing; and secondly, the growth of non-state forms of political organization, whether at the supra-state level, as with the emergence of a policing capacity within the institutions of the EU, or at the sub-state level, as with the increased prominence of popular policing initiatives in the townships of South Africa (Brogden and Shearing, 1993: ch.6; Brogden, this volume). But are there limits to the developmental potential of non-state forms of policing? Must they continue to operate in the shadow of the state,  constrained by state interests and subordinate to the state's own law enforcement capacity? Alternatively, in so far as they succeed in developing  a level of authority to rival that of the state police, how are such new forms of non-state policing likely to be legitimated and with what implications for their mature character?

## DEVELOPMENTS IN THE POLITICS AND POLICING
## OF THE EUROPEAN UNION

Since the signing of the European Economic Community (EEC) Treaty at Rome in 1957, the fortunes of the EU have waxed and waned. From the outset, its development has involved the pursuit of a double agenda.   First and foremost, the EU has pursued a powerful economic agenda. This has focused upon  the creation of a  common market, dedicated to the elimination of trade restrictions such as customs duties and quantitative controls, and the abolition of obstacles to the free movement of persons, services, and capital between member states. Its wider agenda, however, has always included more fundamental political concerns. The EU emerged in the period after 1945 when the major European powers were searching for the means to ensure against further military conflict. It is no accident that the early precursor of the EU, the European Coal and Steel Community (ECSC) instituted at Paris in 1951, focused on the war-making industries. Its aim was to place these industries under a degree of common control sufficient to ensure that no member state retained an independent capacity to prepare for armed conflict (Weatherill and Beaumont, 1993:3).

Each successive period has witnessed changes in the economic and the wider political agenda and in their interrelationship, with uneven consequences for the overall process of integration. After initial success, the institutional transformation of the EU slowed down enormously. Dating roughly from Charles de Gaulle's insistence on a veto on matters affecting vital national interests (The Luxembourg compromise) in 1966 to the negotiation of the Single European Act in the mid 1980s, the new Europe progressed in a series of fits and starts. The expansion of the EU from six to twelve provided one obvious dimension of growth but served to underline the potential for decision-making gridlock. Economic recession across the EU following the 1973 oil crisis also led to a narrowing of perspectives, a concentration on the vital margins of national economic interest at the expense of the wider Union interest. Nevertheless, the Union survived the period of stagnation, confounding the forecasts of "Eurosclerosis" prevalent in the early 1980s. The constitutional authority of its institutions--the Commission, the European Council, the Parliament, and the Court of Justice--was incrementally strengthened as the political and economic costs of disengagement from a Union now entering its second generation came to seem increasingly unpalatable to mainstream political opinion in the member states. The signing of the Single European Act in February 1986 signalled a decisive shift towards qualified majority voting and away from the national veto on many key issues and also announced a renewal of the commitment to a single European market, but this time with a firm deadline of 1992 and a detailed timetable to match (Keohane and Hoffman, 1991).

With the single market substantially complete, the Treaty on European Union (TEU), signed at Maastricht in February 1992, marked a new watershed in European affairs. That the political debate surrounding the negotiation of the Treaty focused on issues of monetary union and constitutional federalism bore witness to the spectacular progress towards both economic and political integration made since the 1950s. The ambitious scope of the new agenda, however, also served to reawaken concerns over the loss of national sovereignty. The final text of the Treaty may have represented another modest victory for the integrationists but, as demonstrated by the intense domestic difficulties surrounding ratification of the Treaty not only by traditionally "awkward partners" (George, 1990) such as the United Kingdom and Denmark, but also in the pivotal pro-European states of France and Germany, the "Eurosceptics" were now more effectively mobilized than at any time since the early 1980s (Hoffman, 1993).

On the policing front, the development of a European dimension came rather later and, as with the wider political development, has followed a somewhat uneven trajectory (Benyon et al., 1993: chs. 4-6). The Trevi organization provided the first major initiative. From 1975 it served as an intergovernmental forum for member states to develop common measures, first in respect to counterterrorism and latterly in drugs, organized crime, police training and technology, and a range of other policing matters. In its mature form, Trevi comprised an elaborate multitier structure, including a ministerial level, a senior administrative level, and a working-group level staffed by civil servants, police, and related professionals.

The Schengen system provided a second important step towards a European law enforcement capacity. The initial Schengen Agreement of 1985 paving the way for the abolition of border controls between five member states was closely influenced by the decision of the 1984 Fontainebleau European Council to move towards internal market liberalization within the EC, a decision which did much to establish the necessary political momentum for the launching of the "1992" initiative. A more detailed Implementation Agreement in 1990 established a number of related law enforcement measures, including the Schengen Information System and operational co-operation in matters such as "hot pursuit," cross-border observation, and controlled delivery. The Schengen blueprint now embraces all EU signatories except the United Kingdom, Ireland, and Denmark, with the latter taking the first steps towards membership in 1994 by requesting observer status (Statewatch, 1994b: 11).

The recent development of the institution of a European Police Office, to be known as Europol, represents the most ambitious plan yet conceived for an independent policing capacity at EU level. Following a German proposal to the Luxembourg European Council in June 1991, Europol was recognized in the Justice and Home Affairs (JHA) Chapter of the TEU as a new, pan-Union policing capability more comprehensively integrated within the legal and political structures of the EU than any of its predecessors. Its foundation provision envisages a system of information exchange for the purposes of preventing and combating terrorism, drug trafficking, and other serious crimes within the EU, while broader forms of co-operation to aid criminal investigation and analysis are also anticipated. A Ministerial Agreement establishing a Europol Drugs Unit (EDU) as the first stage in the new organization, with jurisdiction to address "associated money-laundering activities," was signed in June 1993. Its headquarters were opened at the Hague in January 1994 with a view to its becoming fully operational by the end of the year.

As suggested, Europol, unlike its forerunners, is properly embedded within the constitutional structure of the EU (Muller-Graff, 1994). While Trevi had no formal status and was merely parasitic upon the legal framework of the EC and Schengen, although recognized in international law, was constituted as a quite separate legal entity from the EU, Europol, to use the architectural metaphor popularized in recent debate over the changing Europe, is built into the masonry of the Third Pillar of Justice and Home Affairs policy, which, alongside the First Pillar of the original EEC and the Second Pillar of a common foreign and security policy, supports the entire legal edifice of the EU. The JHA Chapter, which has provided an institutional successor to Trevi, also covers complementary matters such as immigration, asylum, EU external frontiers policy, fraud and drug prevention strategies, customs cooperation, and judicial cooperation in civil and criminal matters.

In all of these matters, the main political institutions of the EU, for the first time, have a significant role to play. A general policy-making brief is allocated to the Council of Ministers (the political executive) aided by a new Co-ordinating Committee of permanent representatives (K4 Committee). The K4 Committee is assisted by three steering groups covering immigration and asylum, police and customs co-operation, and judicial co-operation respectively, and these three groups will be supported by a plethora of monitoring bodies and working parties, including groups covering Europol, terrorism, organized crime and drugs, and police operational and technical co-operation generally. Two other central EU institutions have an important, if somewhat more modest role. The Commission (permanent Civil Service) is "fully associated" with the policy process (Art.K.4), although it has no power of initiative in policing matters. The European Parliament has a very general entitlement to be informed and consulted about developments and can ask questions of and make recommendations to the Council (K.6) but has no power of veto over the decisions of the Council (Walker, 1993a).

Despite these advances, the development of a comprehensive

policing agency at EU-level--a police organization which has operational powers of arrest and search to supplement its specialist capacity in matters such as information exchange and crime analysis-- remains a somewhat remote prospect. It was a prospect which was explicitly raised at the Luxembourg summit in 1991 but which was marginalised in the Maastricht Treaty itself, which commits the member states no further than a promise to look at possible avenues for expansion of Europol's limited remit before the end of 1994. In institutional terms, too, the Third Pillar has weaknesses as well as strengths. In particular, the continuing absence of direct law-making competence on the part of the EU in respect to police powers and the criminal law acts as a brake on progress. Under Art.K.3 of the TEU, conventions may be drawn up between member states on matters falling within the JHA area, but the unanimity requirement entails that institution-building and common policy-making can only proceed at the pace of the most reluctant member state.

These formal restrictions have assumed a real significance in the post-Maastricht period when the uneven pace of progress on police cooperation has closely mirrored that in the wider political arena (Walker, 1994a). The EDU agreement was originally intended to be completed by the end of 1992, and after it was eventually signed in June 1993, it took another five months until the location of the headquarters of the new unit, the very issue which had caused the initial delay, was resolved. More importantly, it was not until the Lisbon European Council of June 1992 that the decision was taken to draft a convention under Art.K.3 which would provide the legal basis for a fully-fledged Europol. October 1994 was projected as the completion date for this convention, but continuing disagreement amongst member states over matters as significant as the range of crimes to be covered by the new organization and the role of the European Court of Justice--the Supreme Court of the EU--in the adjudication of disputes involving Europol and of the European Parliament in its supervision made it impossible to honor this deadline.[1] Meanwhile, a series of complementary conventions under K.3, covering matters such as the regulation of the external borders of the EU, the introduction of simplified extradition arrangements between member states, and the establishment of the European information system and the customs information system--two data exchange systems aimed at enhancing internal security within the EU--

have been plagued by similar delays.[2]

Difficulties have also attended the launching of the Schengen system. When the Executive Committee of the Schengen Agreement announced at their June 1994 meeting that border controls between the Schengen states would be abolished by October 1994, it was their fifth attempt to set such a deadline (Statewatch, 1994b: 11). So far as the overall trend towards European cooperation is concerned, however, just as problematical as the difficulties besetting Schengen is its resilience and also that of other organizations such as Interpol and the Council of Europe, which plan to operate alongside Europol in the policing and criminal justice field. So fragmented are the roots of international police cooperation that a variety of different bodies have been primed to exploit the new demands and opportunities for European regional cooperation in the 1980s and 90s. Each has its peculiar strengths, which it can use to expose and exploit the relative weaknesses of Europol (Anderson et al., forthcoming: ch 2).

Schengen is more cohesive, limited to a more manageable core of committed continental member states. Interpol has longstanding expertise in information exchange and a global network, whereas Europol provides too restricted a perspective but also a concentration of resources and expertise on the vital European region as reflected in a spate of recent initiatives culminating in the establishment of a European Liaison Bureau in May 1993. The Council of Europe is the traditional source of international criminal law and human rights law in Europe and already covers the states who may become members of an enlarged EU and an expanded Europol. It is clear, therefore, that Europol and the Third Pillar generally do not yet enjoy unchallenged regional hegemony, nor can they expect to in the near future. The prospects for policing at the EU level, therefore, may depend not only upon the internal dynamics of the EU and its fluctuating relationship with member states but also upon the continuing vigor and strategic sophistication of rival organizations.

## *EURO-POLICING AND EURO-CRIME*

How, then, are we to account for developments in transnational policing within the EU? A number of reasons have been put forward. These have concentrated on the demands of law enforcement and public security and have certainly provided some of the more prominent official rationales for new law enforcement initiatives (den Boer and Walker, 1993: 8-9). The most commonly articulated argument of this type has proposed that the abolition of frontier controls between member states will remove the traditional filter function of borders and so remove a key disincentive to international crime. This is a specific variant of an older and more general theme, which speaks to a general increase in the mobility of the individual criminal and in the international dimension of criminal transactions and enterprise, particularly as regards high-profile activities such as terrorism, drug trafficking, and money-laundering (Home Affairs Committee, 1990: v-vi). A third line of analysis is less concerned with new trends in transnational deviance and more with how certain international movements affect the domestic security context. This focuses on the migratory flow from economically disadvantaged and politically destabilized regions in the South and East of the EU, and emphasizes the importance of limiting and policing that flow in order that new problems of crime and public security are not "imported" (den Boer, 1993; 1994).

How convincing are these arguments? Do they suggest that policing developments in the EU can be explained and justified primarily by reference to law enforcement imperatives without regard to wider political considerations? While there may be a rational core to some of the arguments adduced, it would be naive to assume that policing solutions can simply be "read off" from problems in the social environment. Just as in the domestic domain, in the international domain a policing initiative can never be viewed as the objectively justified answer to a self-evident problem but instead represents merely one alternative response to a socially constructed issue of concern (crime).

There are a number of dimensions to this argument (Walker, 1993b: 126-128). To begin with, the *absolute level* of European crime or the European crime threat is obscure. Attempts even to identify the conceptual range of European crime, and to differentiate it from domestic crime, are thin on the ground, and those which have been made have failed to provide criteria which are both clear and convincing (Anderson et al., forthcoming: ch.1).[3] Relatedly, there have been no systematic efforts to develop statistical analyses of European crime. Moreover, the task of quantification would encounter formidable obstacles. Drug trafficking, money-laundering, and other crimes perpetrated by criminal networks and syndicates typically take place in low-visibility zones where the "dark figure" of crime remains deep in the shadows. Other recent growth areas which have been deemed to be of sufficient concern to figure in the provisional remit of Europol, such as auto theft, computer crime, and trafficking in arms, nuclear substances, and dangerous waste (Statewatch, 1994a: 16), suffer from the same measurement problem. By its nature, terrorism is a more visible phenomenon. However, one ironic consequence of the large-scale investment in preemptive strategies is that it is unclear what the potential scale of the problem is and what, therefore, is required by way of policing to contain it within certain levels.

A second argument points to the *relative gravity* with which many international crimes are viewed. Any purely quantifiable analysis of crime can be no more than a crude and superficial form of "painting by numbers" (Maguire, 1994: 236). To the extent that it purports to compare incommensurables, it is bound to provide a flat and distorted picture. This is particularly so when crimes such as terrorism, trafficking in nuclear substances, and drug trafficking are at issue. Arguably, they pose such a profound threat to the state or to civil society that they defy meaningful comparison with most "ordinary crimes."

Thirdly, there is the question of criminogenic conditions and their effect on the *overall trend* of international crime. In particular, it remains highly controversial just what impact the removal of border controls as part of the 1992 programme will have on the incidence of international crime. Some, including the British Government and police, would argue that borders, in particular sea borders, provide "the first opportunity for prevention and the last chance of detection" (Home Affairs Committee, 1992: 95), the effective removal of which eradicates significant physical and psychological barriers to international crime. Others are more skeptical. They argue that much of the detective work presently carried out at borders could be done just as effectively elsewhere (Latter, 1991) and that many of the theoretical benefits of border controls have, in any case, been unavailable over much of mainland Europe over the past decade, as their enforcement has become increasingly lax (Van Duyne, 1993: 101). They also argue that in so far as border controls retain some significance, this is only true in certain settings and even here their influence is subordinate to other considerations. Where borders cut across "European crime regions," that is, established trading routes and communities involving a busy--and often interfluent--commerce in drugs, toxic waste, luxury consumer items susceptible to VAT-fraud, etc. (Van Duyne, 1993: 102-03), they are likely to retain a strategic significance. However, their capacity to deter may be overshadowed by the powerful economic forces of supply and demand which shape these trading communities, including changing fashions amongst users and clients and shifts in wider international trade routes and patterns (Van Duyne, 1993: 101).

As both arguments tend to rely upon counterfactuals and upon evidence open to competing interpretations, the debate remains unresolved. Indeed, the issue is further clouded by the fact that, partly because of continuing disagreement between the United Kingdom and Ireland and the continental member states, border controls throughout the EU have not yet been fully removed, with no guarantee that they will be in the foreseeable future.[4]

Finally, there is a fundamental issue of *policy perspective*. Just how appropriate is it to view these matters primarily through the conceptual prism of policing and law enforcement? Drug abuse, terrorism, and migration patterns--open and clandestine--have deep social, economic, and political roots. Given the requisite political will, they may be more or less amenable to treatment at their source. The dominance of a law and order discourse, therefore, does not flow inexorably from developments in international crime but is invariably a matter of normative preference and political choice.

## THE POLITICS OF EUROPEAN POLICE COOPERATION

Clearly, therefore, an analysis which attempts to understand the emergence of European policing in narrow terms, as a technical matter of criminal justice policy divorced from the wider political canvas, is inadequate. But what does this wider political canvas reveal? In the first place and in the foreground, there is a series of public political discourses or ideologies in terms of which the argument for enhanced police co-operation has been advanced. Secondly and in the background, there is a set of underlying factors whose true motivation may not be revealed in political debate but which are influential nonetheless. As argued below, the significance of these public political discourses and underlying influences is not exhausted by their contribution to the emergence of the new European policing initiatives.

These factors also hold the key to the future development of European policing.

### Public political discourses

The broadest and most important discourse affecting the course of European police cooperation is the discourse of *European integration* itself. Within this perspective, the EU is seen as qualitatively different from all other international organizations. It is conceived of as a "novel form of political domination" (Bryant, 1991: 204; see also Weiler, 1991; Streeck and Schmitter, 1991; MacCormick, 1993), an institution which transcends the state and which promises to provide a form of political authority to rival the state. When Chancellor Kohl announced his proposal for Europol in 1991, although he took some member states by surprise, "he was not suddenly pulling a rabbit out of a hat" (Cullen, 1992: 78). His proposal was in sympathy with thinking on police cooperation within German political circles generally in the latter part of the 1980s. It also fitted the profile and typified the ambitions of the increasingly dominant EU member state at a point when political confidence in the integration process had reached new heights generally across Europe. It was intended, and succeeded, as a potent symbol of European union precisely because it was so audacious, promising to transfer authority in an area which was one of the traditional and most jealously guarded preserves of the state. Of course, as we shall see, the conservative emphasis upon state sovereignty is the other side of the macro-political coin, representing a major obstacle in the path of significant additional policing competence at EU level. Nevertheless, this should not be allowed to shroud the fact that the Europol idea was launched, not in spite of, but in part *because of* its integrationist implications and that for enthusiasts of European union the development of an ambitious European policing agenda continues to be ideologically attractive.[5]

A second public political discourse contributing to the development of European policing is the discourse of *functional spillover*. Since the inception of the EC, a key argument associated with its expansion has been that intervention in one policy sector requires consequential adjustments in other policy sectors (Weatherill and Beaumont, 1993: 5). In particular, for the primary objective of economic integration to be pursued, interventions are required in a wide array of cognate areas of social policy (Lindberg, 1963; Pentland,

1973; Hix, 1994: 4-6, Moravcsik, 1993: 474-480). These range from measures of antidiscrimination law to ensure a level economic playing-field between employees of both sexes throughout the EU, to a common level of social welfare provision across member states in order to stop the "social dumping" of enterprises in low-tax states and thus encourage equal competition across states. The argument, rehearsed above, about the need to compensate for the security deficit consequential upon the removal of border controls is merely an instance of the functionalist theme as are more general claims that the growth of crime connections across the new Europe require a proportionate policing response (Anderson, 1994). For present purposes, their truth value is of less significance than their political efficacy. Functionalist argument appeals to a technocratic image of public policy as the performance of a range of necessary and politically neutral tasks. Its success has rested on its capacity to present the process of integration as insulated from and as "ideologically transcendent over the normal debates on the left-right spectrum" (Weiler, 1991: 2476-2477). The language of functional spillover, therefore, is much more than a theoretical hypothesis purporting to *explain* change. It is also a powerful ideological currency which taps deep reserves of pro-European thinking, and which, when invoked, as in the Euro-policing debate, may actually help to *bring about* change.

The relationship between the master discourse of European integration and the discourse of functional spillover is a complex one. At one level, they represent the tension, built into the foundations of the EU, between the wide political vision of the new Europe and the narrow economic conception. One discourse makes a virtue out of integration as a new kind of political project, while the other flourishes through its denial of grand politics. Nevertheless, each is sufficiently open ended and flexible that they are capable of being harnessed together by means of skilful "discursive manoeuvre" (Garland, 1985: 172). As was demonstrated by the manner in which the European Commission, and in particular its president Jacques Delors, used the technocratic vehicle of the 1992 programme to develop a new expansionist political culture (Weiler, 1991; Peters, 1992), the logic of functional spillover can, with only a subtle variation in emphasis, be presented as contributing to the uniqueness of the European political vision rather than as a denial of the political character of the EU. On the other hand, as intimated above, the grand narrative of European integration is an altogether more risky ideological enterprise, which continually threatens to run aground against the entrenched interests of member states. As we shall see, therefore, in the policing domain the functional argument often has to proceed against the wider current of opinion in the integration debate.

A third public political discourse supporting enhanced European police cooperation is the discourse of *internal security* (Bunyan, 1993; Bigo, 1994; den Boer, 1993, 1994). As it involves a more negative and conservative imagery than the assertive and innovative discourse of European integration and as it is more explicitly politically committed than the discourse of functional spillover, the discourse of internal security also lies in a somewhat ambivalent relationship with the first two. We have already encountered one aspect of the third approach in the argument about the police implications of mass immigration, but this can only be understood as part of a wider political project which focuses on the security of the EU as fundamental to its political well-being.

There are two issues underpinning this political project. First, there is the search for European cultural identity, an inquiry which has undergone a strong revival in the context of the pro-European surge of the late 1980s and the subsequent controversy surrounding the Treaty of Maastricht (Federal Trust, 1991; Smith, 1991, ch.7). It is frequently contended, often in reaction to the narrow technocratic vision of the functionalists, that the cultural sphere is lagging behind the political and economic ones in the process of European integration. This is unsurprising, given the historical roots of the concept of Europe. As Waever and Kelstrup argue, "[it] is, not some eternal core idea which we find far back in history and whose development we then trace through the ages" (1993: 65). Relatedly, Europe as a single entity lacks the popular mythology and symbolism out of which a common historical memory and tradition is forged. As Smith (1992: 83-84) argues, "[w]hen it comes to the ritual and ceremony of collective identification, there is no European equivalent of national or religious community." The development of a European cultural identity, therefore, is a precarious enterprise, a weaving together of a number of distinct "conceptual fragments," including Europe as a territorial community, as the fount of liberty, as the hub of civilization, and as Christendom (Waever and Kelstrup, 1993: 65). The thinness of this vision, together with its strong undertones of cultural imperialism, means that the new European cultural politics tends to accentuate a theme present in all identity politics, namely the idea of exclusion (Cable, 1994). Put simply, it is easier to define what Europe is not, rather than what it is. "Europe" is not central and Eastern Europe; it is not Islam; it does not include its former colonies; it does not embrace any political vision which deemphasizes the individual and her/his liberties in favor of a strong collectivism. The new status of European citizenship, introduced by the Treaty of Maastricht, emphasizes this exclusionary logic by narrowly confining citizenship to those who qualify as citizens of the constituent member states and thus consigning those who do not to a process of double marginalisation (Closa, 1992; Martiniello, 1993).

There is also an important economic agenda at work in the reinforcement of Europe as a security community. The material success of the EU stands in stark contrast to the poverty and insecurity of the post-Warsaw Pact states to the East and to the economies of Northern Africa ravaged by war and climactic changes. The end of the Cold War and of the ideological bipolarity of East and West has recast the West in the image of the promised land. In these circumstances, exclusion and resistance to strong migratory pressures come to seem necessary to maintain the relative prosperity of the West (den Boer, 1993, 1994; Waever et al., 1993; Anderson et al., forthcoming, ch.5).

In this view, therefore, Western Europe is an idea, and a place, which must be protected against cultural and economic threats from alien forces situated within or beyond its borders. There is a growing tendency for these issues to be condensed and treated as a single, multifaceted problem of internal security demanding a similarly one-dimensional response. As Bigo (1994:164) has argued, this perspective has been achieved through the elaboration of a broadly inclusive "internal security ideology," in terms of which a wide range of social concerns, from terrorism to immigration, and from organized crime to asylum, are located along a mutually reinforcing "security continuum." A range of police practices, from reinforcing the hard outer shell of the EU's external frontiers to conducting systematic internal checks, both contributes to and is encouraged by the new internal security ideology.

### Underlying Influences

Alongside the public political discourses, two sets of underlying influences stand out as of particular significance. In the first place, there is the development of a dense structure of transnational bureaucratic interests (Den Boer and Walker, 1993: 10-11; Bigo, 1994; Walker, 1993a: 40-41). One important consequence of the tendency to view police cooperation in functional terms is to allow the functionaries--the administrators and police professionals--a key role in developing frameworks of cooperation. Bureaucratic proliferation has been compounded by the peculiar pattern of police institution-building in the new Europe. The mixture of recent exponential growth in European regional organizations (Laffan, 1992) and continuing uncertainty over Europe's broader political future has led to a hedging of bets, with Schengen, Europol, the Council of Europe, and Interpol each sustained by a particular vision of the Europe of the next millennium (Walker, 1994b: 26). Further, not only are there police bureaucracies competing in the same "crowded policy space" (Raab, 1994), but the location of international policing initiatives within increasingly ambitious designs for political integration, together with the success of the "internal security ideology" in linking policing and disparate other issues along a single chain of signification, has meant that bureaucracies have tended to grow ever more extensive--hence the elaborate matrix structure of the Third Pillar, with its multiple layers of authority and its vertical division into a range of specialist functions. The upshot of this bureaucratic growth is the development of a new network of administrative and professional elites with vested interests in the maintenance and expansion of European policing.

Domestic policing concerns provide a second underlying factor supporting developments in European policing. The existence of a European policing agenda and policing institutions serves national policing interests in a number of ways, quite apart from any direct assistance provided in the pursuit of narrow law enforcement objectives (Walker, 1992, 1994b: 27-30). In particular, the existence of a European dimension creates certain structural pressures towards the intensification or consolidation of central control at the national level, a trend which may independently attract considerable support from domestic police and politicians. For example, the Trevi meeting at the Hague in December 1991 determined that national satellite units were prerequisite to the establishment of Europol, a position reinforced by the draft Europol convention; this has precipitated the institution of new national criminal intelligence capacities across Europe and has strengthened the authority of existing agencies. In other cases, the existence of a European dimension need not require centralizing reforms but may be instrumental in encouraging and justifying them. The need to provide representation and to articulate a national point of view on the labyrinthine committee networks of Interpol, Schengen and the Third Pillar may stimulate greater coordination within domestic policy elites. The growing demand for knowledge and skills training associated with new patterns of European policing may precipitate an increasingly centralized and homogenized provision of training and work pre-socialization (Benyon et al., 1993: ch.3).

Alongside the structural pressures which it generates, the development of a European dimension might also serve to provide ideological support for domestic police practices and initiatives. Unlike local trends and events, in the occurrence of which domestic agencies may be seen as already heavily implicated, developments in European policing and crime may be appealed to as objective circumstances which are beyond the control and outside the responsibility of domestic agencies but whose local ramifications they have no option but to respond to. The existence of a separate European agenda on terrorism, drug trafficking, money-laundering, or organized crime, an agenda whose profile is enhanced by mass media representations (Schlesinger and Tumber, 1994), may thus be usefully invoked to justify the allocation of new resources or the design of new initiatives towards these crimes at the domestic level (Walker, 1993a: 42-44; 1994b: 30).

## PROSPECTS FOR EUROPEAN POLICING

The emergence of European policing, therefore, has been overdetermined by a range of wider political factors from the broad narratives of integration, functional spillover, and internal security, to the narrower interests of new European bureaucracies and old domestic police and political elites. In this final section in which, for convenience of exposition, the above order of analysis is reversed, an attempt is made to explore the implications of these factors for the future development of European policing. In particular, we ask whether these factors will in general retain their capacity to promote European policing, and what fundamental constraints, if any, may be imposed by the master discourse of European integration within which the debate between the irreconcilable themes of political union and state sovereignty is played out. The answer we arrive at will, in turn, help to illuminate the wider question as to whether the scope and direction of European policing is bound to reflect not only the substantive *content* of macro-political debate and the strategic *goals* of political actors, as the above analysis seems to suggest, but also the limitations imposed by the traditional *forms* of political authority.

## CURRENT TRENDS

It would seem that all the political factors set out above, with the exception of the master discourse of European integration, are likely, at worst, not to impede the further development of police cooperation and, at best, to continue to support its extension. International policing structures and agendas may remain an attractive reference point for domestic actors seeking to justify greater coordination of national policing and the deployment of resources towards high profile international crimes although this approach may become susceptible to the law of diminishing returns. As the idea of European policing becomes embedded in popular consciousness and extends to more mundane activities, it may gradually become demystified. Like domestic policing in an earlier era, European policing may have to come to terms with a more skeptical external audience, one more likely to demand that European policing institutions be made fully accountable and one less prone to uncritical acceptance that European imperatives be permitted to shape domestic policing (Walker, 1993a: 47). On balance, however, international policing is likely to continue to provide an attractive imagery for domestic policing to draw upon for some time. As domestic police institutions are increasingly seen as ineffective vehicles for reducing crime substantially and instead come to be viewed "primarily as managers of crime and keepers of the peace" (Reiner, 1994: 75), then any association with the international agenda, with its accent on those crimes offering the most profound threat to social and political order, tends to reflect favorably on the domestic agencies, offering a reminder that policing can speak to more fundamental problems and make deeper claims to legitimacy.[6] As for the bureaucratic interests at the heart of European policing, these, too, appear secure in the medium-term future. For so long as uncertainty remains over the wider political agenda, a plurality of organizations will continue to vie for ascendancy in the design of Europe's policing future and will be strategically placed to consolidate or expand their position.

As regards the discourse of internal security, there are complex and, to some extent, conflicting processes at work. The economic and cultural politics of exclusion exists alongside a strong tradition of liberal toleration and a public abhorrence of racist politics. For example, the European Council meeting at Corfu in June 1994 approved a plan on the part of the JHA Ministers to combat racism and xenophobia, with concrete measures to be announced at the subsequent summit in Essen in December 1994.[7] Yet, as intimated earlier, the Council of Ministers, in harness with the European Commission, is simultaneously engaged in a project with a quite different undercurrent. It is involved in the drafting of a series of regulations, conventions, and policy measures imposing restrictive common visa requirements for entry to member states, developing a common framework of immigration policy which also seeks the lowest common denominator, expediting procedures for addressing--and dismissing--asylum claims, and developing a framework of controls which sharply differentiates between relaxed internal borders and tight external borders. It is also involved in the creation of general police and intelligence systems and specific anti-crime measures which target many of the same audience as these broader measures, and, indeed, which may be directly drawn upon to aid the implementation of such measures (den Boer, 1993, 1994; Anderson et al., forthcoming, chs. 4-7).

In the final analysis, however, the fact that these measures and the politics of identity and economic advantage which underpin them are in no explicit sense racially motivated or articulated and so can readily co-exist with anti-racist policies is likely to make them more effective and resilient. By focusing on the immediate and urgent question of security as opposed to the wider geo-political conditions which frame this question, they pander to the "respectable fears" (Pearson, 1983) of old Europe about external threats to its way of life. This tends to marginalise other ways of seeing and treating the problems identified and, in particular, to avoid the need to confront more explicit and less palatable questions about the growing inequality between the world's regions.

Functional spillover arguments are also likely to retain their plausibility for the foreseeable future. Recent developments in the EU have opened up new areas where functionalist logic may be persuasively applied. For instance, developments in administrative policing within the EU, including the enforcement of competition law (Lavoie, 1992) and the framing of a draft convention under the Third Pillar to ensure that fraud against the financial interests of the EU is treated as a criminal offence in each member state,[8] reflect the persuasiveness of the argument that the increasingly wide-ranging and sophisticated regulatory framework through which the EU raises and spends money and shapes private economic activity requires penal or quasi-penal sanctions and an effective investigatory capacity. Similarly, the developing social policy profile of the EU increases the likelihood of public order incidents assuming a "a real European character," including EU-wide anti-immigration protests and co-ordinated protests by farming interests against the Common Agricultural Policy (Van Reenen, 1989: 46). The European dimension to the problem may strengthen the case for a European solution as is also the case in the area of terrorism. Incidents such as the attack by the Greek Revolutionary November 17 Group on the local EC offices in December 1990 in protest against austerity measures (Riley, 1991: 23-24) and fears of new external terrorist threats in response to the EU's expanded role in foreign affairs illustrate the ever-increasing range of circumstances in which functionalist arguments can be deployed to justify an increased central policing capacity.

## *POLICING BEYOND THE SOVEREIGN STATE?*

Even if these factors generate increased momentum in favor of police cooperation, it is still arguable that this will remain restricted by the intransigent barriers of state sovereignty. Policing has traditionally been closely bound up with the protection of the sovereign state. As Marenin (1982: 258) argues, policing is invariably concerned with the protection both of the "general order" in which all members of the community have a stake and of the "specific order" which serves the interests of those in a dominant social or political position within the state. The state has an interest in securing both these forms of order (Walker, 1994a: 25-28; Anderson et al., forthcoming, ch. 3). The preservation of general order, through the maintenance of general public security and the prevention and detection of routine types of crime, is prerequisite to the securing of a more specific form of order.

Further, general policing tends to have unequal effects: it benefits disproportionately those groups with most to lose from the breakdown of general order, which tend to be those whose interests are most closely identified with specific order.

By definition, however, it is with the direct protection of specific order that the state is most intimately concerned. It is on account of this linkage that international policing poses such an acute threat to the state and its sovereign interests. This is so because, ironically, many of the areas in which the demand for cooperation is greatest are also those which bear most directly on state-specific interests. Terrorism is the clearest example. From Trevi to Maastricht, its international dimension has placed it on top of the agenda of European co-operation, but, as the protracted dispute over whether to include anti-terrorism within the formal objectives of a developed Europol indicates,[9] states continue to guard jealously the right of operational initiative. Public order problems, which have recently expanded into areas of political protest but which traditionally contributed to the international policing agenda in the form of football and holiday hooliganism, provide another case in point. So too, if less obviously, do money-laundering and drug trafficking. They do not pose such a direct threat to the physical security of the state as do the first two examples, but their social and economic significance is such that their treatment may reflect the priorities and affect the interests of those most closely associated with the specific order of the state (Levi, 1991; Dorn et al., 1992; Gilmore, 1992).

The close link between police and state undoubtedly explains much of the unevenness of the development of European policing institutions. Does this suggest that ultimate authority over policing is bound to remain at the state level, or does the long-term future hold out a more flexible prospect? In answering this question we must consider both sides of the coin: whether there are any social and political developments which may make the state a less appropriate site for transnational policing and whether there are any developments which make the EU a more appropriate site (Anderson et al., forthcoming, ch.3).

As we have seen, the legitimacy of policing within a state has tended to be linked with the basic *raison d'être* of that state. Marenin's analysis is but one variation of a highly influential thesis which argues that the maintenance of order within its borders is one of the core functions of the classical Hobbesian state (Weber, 1948: 78; Giddens, 1987: ch.7; Held, 1989; Jessop, 1990; Poggi, 1990). However persuasive, such an argument must guard against ahistorical generalization. Insofar as the Hobbesian model has evolved, the nexus between state and police may have become less intimate and less exclusive.

In a close analysis of the development of the modern state system, Waever and Kelstrup (1993) argue that the Hobbesian state has indeed undergone internal transformation of a type capable of modifying its relationship to policing. The early state, distinguished by its novel claim to an administrative monopoly over a territory with set boundaries, a claim necessarily underpinned by a capacity to secure against internal and external threats, is a creature of the sixteenth century, predating the nation state by two centuries. Only with the development of the idea of the nation state, which had much to do with the Enlightenment search for a non-religious cosmology (Waever, 1993: 28-30), did the institutions and coercive supports of political authority begin to be supplemented by a conception of cultural identity; this involved the weaving of a sense of "imagined community" (Anderson, 1991) from a myth of nationhood built around a common heritage and the development of a mass public culture. With the emergence of the EU, we enter a third phase in the development of the relationship between cultural identity and political identity, when "the coupling state-nation is weakened without a new synthesis being achieved at the European level" (Waever and Kelstrup, 1993: 69). Unsurprisingly, given the potency of tradition in the construction of identity myths, in this third phase cultural identity remains predominantly at the national or subnational level, while political identity becomes dispersed across a number of levels--national, subnational, and supranational. That is to say, the nation state, having once replaced the Hobbesian conception of the "nationless state," in turn gradually becomes more "nation" and less "state."

In demonstrating the separability of cultural identity from political identity, this perspective views the relationship between the state and policing as contingent. The policing function may be intrinsic to the political authority of the state, but it is not linked to the cultural package of nationhood by the same watertight analytical bonds. This does not, however, mean that there is no longer a powerful symbolic link between policing and the modern Western European nation state, even if its political authority is in long-term decline. Although its sovereignty may no longer be   exclusive, the nation state still retains a significant degree of political authority and so remains a legitimate candidate for a strong policing role. Secondly, while analytically distinct, cultural identity and political identity have become interwoven in the empirical context of the nation state's development. The national idea, although  rooted separately from that of the state, flourished in the protective political environment of the state. Many of the incidents of statehood, including military and policing functions, tended to be drawn upon in the symbolic creation and sustenance of national identity. Indeed, the fact that the development of the nation state, although postdating the emergence of a general policing capacity within the territorial state, in many cases coincided with the development of institutions specializing in policing functions has helped to create an enduring legacy associating police institutions with national unity and order (Reiner, 1994: 755-756).

Nevertheless, it is important to stress that the link, however strong, is a product of concrete circumstances. These circumstances may be variable between different nation states. For example, Emsley (1993: 84) has argued that the continental gendarmeries had a vital role in the "internal colonization" of rural communities  in the nation-building period. Their instrumental policing function was subservient to their symbolic role of showing the flag and securing the authority of the nation state, thereby "turning  peasants into Frenchmen, Italians, Spaniards and Russians" and marking out "national territory" (p.87). By contrast, in a state such as England, where there was no gendarmerie tradition, where the peasantry was less widespread, and where perceptions of national identity developed earlier and more pervasively, the police were less closely involved in the initial project of nation formation, although  they were heavily employed in a second wave of national social integration after the initial dislocations of the Industrial Revolution (Reiner, 1994: 755). And just as circumstances vary across states, they are also changeable over time. In the final analysis, therefore, the connection between policing and nation state is not sacred and constant but stronger or weaker, more or less resilient. It will tend to loosen as political authority *in general* shifts and when, in a reflexive adjustment of perceptions, increasing numbers come to appreciate--as mainstream German political opinion already has--that the location of policing functions at national level is not part of a reified social order but is a question of political choice.[10]

If there appears to be no insurmountable obstacle to the disassociation of the policing function from the nation state, and, indeed, there is some evidence that this is already taking place, much then depends upon the strength of the "pull" attracting policing functions towards the supranational level. As with the Hobbesian state, in order to understand how the "post-Hobbesian state" of the EU might acquire the authority to police its territory, we need to appreciate the conditions under which it arose and sustains itself. Whereas the Hobbesian state emerged out of armed struggle or was at least strongly influenced in its constitution by the particular balance of military power between and within territories (Tilly, 1990: 19), the defining context for the EU has been the rather different imperatives of post-war Western European growth. From limited economic goals the Union has gradually assumed a wider range of social and political objectives against a background of social democratic philosophy.

Unlike the Hobbesian state, therefore, the link between the integrity of the political entity and the policing function is not a direct one. Can sufficient indirect links nevertheless be forged to legitimate a robust policing function at the EU level? Given that each involves a process of extrapolation from a base of common economic interests and activity, the discourses of functional spillover and internal security re-enter the frame as routes, or perhaps as one convergent route, to achieving the link and displacing the already weakening authority of the nation state. Whether, and in what precise circumstances, these projects could deliver such an eventuality remains a matter of speculation, although we can predict with some confidence that an approach dominated by a denial of grand politics in the name of technocracy and by an emphasis upon the marginal political status of many of the clients of the new supranational police would be unlikely to generate a model of policing which incorporated high standards of democratic accountability and widespread respect for individual rights (Walker, 1993a: 37-46).

Other means are available, however, of matching a European policing capacity to the defining attributes of the EU. Meehan (1993: 177) has argued in her discussion of EU citizenship that the legitimacy of the European order is most plausibly and attractively conceived of as resting upon a particular "cluster of meanings." As the new Europe originated as a series of voluntary agreements between states, each of whose political orders was premised upon a framework of individual entitlements and duties, the legitimacy of the EU has also come to depend upon its regulation of the economic, social, and political domains being couched in terms of individual rights and obligations. That is to say, the appeal of the EU depends on its offering an advanced form of citizenship, incorporating Marshall's (1950) classic troika of civil rights (and associated economic freedoms), political rights and, to a more limited extent, social rights of the citizen. Arguably, in so far as such a holistic treatment of citizenship rights is gradually developed and extended--and the new status of European citizenship and the 1989 Social Charter constitute important, if limited, initiatives in the political and social domains--this may in time persuade the citizenry of the legitimacy of accepting a corresponding set of obligations from the same political authority, together with the institutions, *including policing institutions*, required to render such rights and obligations effective (Walker, 1994a: 38-39). Again, it is a matter of some speculation just how likely this affirmative discourse of citizenship is to flourish and to supply the necessary preconditions for a European police force, although we may conclude that, if it were to gain ground, its accent on active membership of the political community would encourage a much higher standard of democratic control and constitutional protection than is the case with the alternative discourses.

## CONCLUDING COMMENTS

Our analysis of developments in European policing reveals a close but complicated relationship between police institutions and the socio-political environment within which they are located. Wider political discourses and power struggles are undoubtedly deeply implicated in developments in the narrower policing domain. However, we must guard against a naive determinism. Like other institutions within the spectrum of crime and criminal justice (Garland, 1990: 280-281), the development of policing is overdetermined by a wide range of factors. In turn, these policing institutions are capable of sustaining a number of diverse meanings and of developing along quite different lines. Indeed, as we move from the traditional state, through the nation state, and, now, gradually, towards the post-Hobbesian political order, the relationship between policing and the wider political context in the present transitional phase becomes less fixed, more open to a diversity of influences, and more amenable to reciprocal cause and effect. The contemporary history of European police cooperation, then, emphatically reinforces our understanding of policing in general as a "semi-autonomous social field" (Falk Moore, 1973: 720; Goldsmith, 1990: 93). More importantly, it also suggests that we have now reached a critical but fluid moment in the development of new institutions and that the options chosen and rhetorics of justification employed over the next few years will be significant both in resolving the long-term future of European policing and as an indicator of the overall political complexion of the EU as it enters the new millennium.

## NOTES

1. This was confirmed after a meeting of JHA ministers at Berlin on September 7, 1994. See *Agence Europe*, No. 6311, September 9, 1994.

2. Mr. Padraig Flynn, European Commissioner with responsibility for Justice and Home Affairs, has expressed public regret about the lack of progress made on the Third Pillar conventions and has sought to attribute this to the need for unanimity. See *European Report*, No. 1967, July 16, 1994.

3. Martin and Romano (1992: 5), for example, seek to define "multinational systemic crimes," which involve criminal organizations operating across national jurisdictions, as the key form of international crime. While an emphasis upon organized crime might be one way of settling conceptual boundaries, in the absence of evidence that non-organized international crime is neither prevalent nor has serious implications for victims and their communities, there seems no compelling reason why only crimes perpetrated by relatively organized entities should interest those concerned with international law enforcement.

4. On July 15, 1993, the European Parliament initiated proceedings against the European Commission under Art. 175 of the EC Treaty, based on the failure of the Commission to ensure that the January 1993

deadline for the removal of internal border controls was met (Statewatch, 1993: 7).

5. The completion of an ambitious version of the Europol convention, establishing Europol as a full-scale criminal intelligence agency capable of developing an operational arm, was the primary objective of the German government during its presidency of the European Union in the second half of 1994. This is not surprising given that the German government was still led by the architect of the Europol idea, Chancellor Kohl, who was narrowly re-elected in the German general election of October 1994 on the basis of a strong pro-EU stance. See, *The Guardian*, October 27, 1994.

6. A recent example from the UK demonstrates well how reference to the international agenda can enhance the public acceptability of domestic proposals. During the week of the introduction in January 1994 of the Police and Magistrates' Courts Bill--a highly controversial piece of Government legislation intended to increase central control over policing--the Commissioner of the London Metropolitan police, Sir Paul Condon, revealed that he believed a national police force to be inevitable and that he welcomed aspects of such a development. The fact that this statement did not generate criticism of the most senior police officer in the UK for compromising his professional impartiality and taking sides with the Government, is, arguably, due to the fact that he explained the inevitability of this development on the grounds of trends in the rest of the world and in European crime in particular. The appeal to an external imperative helped to neutralize and legitimate his statement before a domestic audience (Walker, 1994b: 30).

7. See *Agence Europe*, No. 6269, June 26, 1994, and No.6311, September 9, 1994.

8. The proposal was adopted by the European Commission on June 15, 1994. See *Agence Europe*, No. 6256, June 22, 1994.

9. Throughout the negotiation of the Europol convention, the Spanish Government was alone in arguing strongly that Europol's jurisdiction should include terrorism. At the meeting of JHA ministers in Berlin on September 7, 1994, it was agreed that terrorism should not be explicitly

named within Europol's competences, but that it should be left open for it to be incorporated in the future. See *European Report,* No. 1974, September 10, 1994.

10. See note 5 above. During the second half of 1994, Germany encountered most resistance to its ambitious conception of Europol from France and UK. See *The Guardian,* October 27, 1994.

## SOURCES

Anderson, M. (1994), "The Agenda for Police Cooperation," in M. Anderson and M. den Boer (eds.), *Policing Across National Boundaries*, London: Pinter, 3-21.

Anderson, M., M. den Boer, P. Cullen, W. Gilmore, C. Raab and N. Walter (forthcoming), *Policing the European Union*, Oxford: Clarendon.

Anderson, P. (1991), *Imagined Communities* (2nd ed.), London: Verso.

Benyon, J., L. Turnbull, A. Willis, R. Woodward, and A. Beck, (1993), *Police Co-operation in Europe: An Investigation*, Leicester: Centre for the Study of Public Order, University of Leicester.

Bigo, D. (1994), "The European Internal Security Field; Stakes and Rivalries in the Newly Developing Area of Police Intervention," in M. Anderson and M. den Boer (eds.), *Policing Across National Boundaries*, London: Pinter, 161-173.

Brogden, M., and C. Shearing (1993), *Policing for a New South Africa*, London: Routledge.

Bryant, C. (1991), "Europe and the European Community," *Sociology*, 25, 189-207.

Bunyan, T. (1993), "Trevi, Europol and the New European State," in T. Bunyan (ed.), *Statewatching the New Europe: A Handbook on the European State*, Nottingham: Russell Press, 15-36.

Cable, V. (1994), *The World's New Fissures*, London: Demos.

Closa, C. (1992), "The Concept of Citizenship in the Treaty on European Union," *Common Market Law Review*, 29, 1137-1169.

Cullen, P. (1992), *The German Police and European Co-operation*, Edinburgh, European Police Co-operation Working Paper No. 2.

den Boer, Monica (1993), *Immigration, Internal Security and Policing in Europe*, Edinburgh, European Police Co-operation Working Paper No. 12.

------ (1994), "The Quest for European Policing; Rhetoric and Justification in a Disorderly Debate," in M. Anderson and M. den Boer (eds.), *Policing Across National Boundaries*, London: Pinter, 174-196.

den Boer, M., and N.C. Walker (1993), "European Policing after 1992," *Journal of Common Market Studies*, 31, 3-28.

Dorn, N., S. Murji, and N. South (1992), *Traffickers: Drug Markets and Law Enforcement*, London: Routledge.

Emsley, C. (1993), "Peasants, Gendarmes and State Formation," in M. Fulbrook (ed.), *National Histories and European History*, London: UCL Press, 69-93.

Falk Moore, S. (1973), "Law and Social Change: the Semi-autonomous Social Field as an Appropriate Subject of Study," *Law and Society Review*, 7, 719-746.

Federal Trust (1991), *Europe's Future: Four Scenarios*, London: Federal Trust for Education and Research.

Garland, D. (1985), *Punishment and Welfare: A History of Penal Strategies*, Aldershot: Gower.

------ (1990), *Punishment and Modern Society*, Oxford: Clarendon.

George, S. (1990), *An Awkward Partner: Britain in the EC*, Oxford: Oxford University Press.

Giddens, A. (1987), "Nation-States and Violence," in *Social Theory and Modern Sociology*, Cambridge: Polity Press, 166-182.

Gilmore, W.C. (1992), "Introduction," in W.C. Gilmore (ed.), *International Efforts to Combat Money Laundering*, Cambridge International Documents Series, Vol.4, Cambridge: Grotius.

Goldsmith, A. (1990), "Taking Police Culture Seriously: Police Discretion and the Limits of the Law," *Policing and Society*, 1, 91-114.

Held, D. (1989), "Sovereignty, National Politics and the Global System," in *Political Theory and the Modern State*, Milton Keynes: Oxford University Press, 214-242.

Hix, S. (1994), "The Study of the European Community: The Challenge to Comparative Politics," *West European Politics*, 17, 1-30.

Hoffman, S. (1993), "Goodbye to a United Europe?" *New York Review of Books*, 40, No. 10, May 27, 27-31.

Home Affairs Committee (1990), "Practical Police Co-operation in the European Community, 7th Report 1989-90," HC 363-I, London: HMSO.

Home Affairs Committee (1992), "Migration Controls at External Borders of the European Community: Minutes of Evidence, 1991-92," HC 215, London: HMSO.

Jessop, B. (1990), *State Theory: Putting Capitalist States in Their Place*, Cambridge: Polity.

Johnston, L. (1992), *The Rebirth of Private Policing*, London and New York: Routledge.

Keohane, R.O. and S. Hoffman (1991), "Institutional Change in Europe in the 1980s," in R.0. Keohane and S.Hoffman (eds.), *The New European Community; Decisionmaking and Institutional Change*, Boulder: Westview.

Laffan, B. (1992), *Integration and Co-operation in Europe*, London: Routledge.

Latter, R. (1991), "Crime and the European Community After 1992," Wilton Papers, London: Her Majesty's Stationery Office.

Lavoie, C. (1992), "The Investigative Powers of the Commission with Respect to Business Secrets under Community Competition Rules," *European Law Review*, 12, 20-40.

Levi, M. (1991), "*Pecunia non olet*: Cleansing the Money-lenders from the Temple," *Crime, Law and Social Change*, 16, 217-302.

Lindberg, L.N. (1963), *The Political Dynamics of European Integration*, Stanford: Stanford University Press.

MacCormick, N. (1993), "Beyond the Sovereign State," *The Modern Law Review*, 56, 1-18.

Maguire, M. (1994), "Crime Statistics, Patterns and Trends: Changing Perceptions and Their Implications," in M. Maguire, R. Morgan, and R. Reiner (eds.), *The Oxford Handbook of Criminology*, Oxford: Clarendon.

Marenin, O. (1982), "Parking Tickets and Class Repression: The Concept of Policing in Critical Theories of Criminal Justice," *Contemporary Crises*, 6, 241-266.

Marshall, T.H. (1950), *Citizenship and Social Class and Other Essays*, Cambridge: Cambridge University Press.

Martin, J., and A.T. Romano (1992), *Multinational Crime: Terrorism, Espionage, Drug and Arms Trafficking*, London: Sage.

Martiniello, M. (1993), "European Citizenship, European Identity and Migrants: Towards the Postnational?", Leiden, ECPR Workshops.

Meehan, E. (1993), "Citizenship and the European Community," *The Political Quarterly*, 64, 172-186.

Moravcsik, A. (1993),"Preferences and Power in the European Community: A Liberal Intergovernmentalist Approach," *Journal of Common Market Studies*, 31, 472-524.

Muller-Graf, P.-C. (1994), "The Legal Bases of the Third Pillar and Its Position in the Framework of the Union Treaty," *Common Market Law Review*, 31, 493-510.

Pearson, G. (1983), *Hooligan: A History of Respectable Fears*, London: Macmillan.

Pentland, C. (1973), *International Theory and European Integration*, London: Faber.

Peters, B.G. (1992), "Bureaucratic Politics and the Institutions of the European Community," in A.M. Sbragia (ed.), *Europolitics, Institutions and Policymaking in the 'New' European Community*, Washington DC: The Brookings Institution, 75-122.

Poggi, G. (1990), *The State: Its Nature, Development and Prospects*, Cambridge: Polity.

Raab, C. (1994), "Police Cooperation: the Prospects for Privacy," in M. Anderson and M. den Boer (eds.), *Policing Across National Boundaries*, London: Pinter, 121-136.

Reiner, R. (1994), "Policing and the Police," in M. Maguire, R. Morgan, and R. Reiner (eds.), *The Oxford Handbook of Criminology*, Oxford: Clarendon, 705-772.

Riley, L. (1991), *Counterterrorism in Western Europe: Mechanisms for International Co-operation*, MA Thesis: University of Essex.

Schlesinger, P., and H. Tumber (1994), *Reporting Crime: The Media Politics of Criminal Justice*, Oxford: Clarendon.

Smith, A.D. (1991), *National Identity*, London: Penguin.

------ (1992), "National Identity and the Idea of European Unity," *International Affairs*, 68, 77-102.

Statewatch (1993), "Borders--European Parliament Acts," *Statewatch*, 3, No.4, 7.

Statewatch (1994a), "Europol," *Statewatch*, 4, No.3, 16-17.

Statewatch (1994b), "New Date Set for SIS," *Statewatch*, 4, No.4, 11.

Streeck, W., and P.C. Schmitter (1991), "From National Corporatism to Transnational Pluralism: Organized Interests in the Single European Market," *Politics and Society*, 19, 133-164.

Tilly, C. (1990), *Coercion, Capital and European States*, Cambridge: Polity.

Van Duyne, P. (1993), "Implications of Cross-border Crime Risks in an Open Europe," *Crime, Law and Social Change*, 20, 99-111.

Van Reenen, P. (1989), "Policing Europe after 1992: Cooperation and Competition," *European Affairs*, 3, 2, 45-53.

Waever, O. (1993), "Societal Security: the Concept," in O. Waever, B. Buzan, M. Kelstrup, and P. Lemaitre (eds.), *Identity, Migration and the New Security Agenda in Europe*, London: Pinter, 17-40.

Waever, O., B. Buzan, M. Kelstrup, and P. Lemaitre (eds.) (1993), *Identity, Migration and the New Security Agenda in Europe*, London: Pinter.

Waever, O., and M. Kelstrup (1993), "Europe and Its Nations: Political and Cultural Identities," in O. Waever, B. Buzan, M. Kelstrup, and P. Lemaitre (eds.), *Identity, Migration and the New Security Agenda in Europe*, London: Pinter, 40-92.

Walker, N.C. (1992), "The Dynamics of European Police Co-operation: The UK Perspective," *Commonwealth Law Bulletin*, 18, 1509-1522.

------ (1993a), "The Accountability of European Police Institutions," *European Journal on Criminal Policy and Research*, 1, 4, 34-52.

------ (1993b), "The International Dimension," in R. Reiner and S. Spencer (eds.), *Accountable Policing: Effectiveness, Empowerment and Equity*, London: Institute for Public Policy Research.

------ (1994a), "European Integration and European Policing: A Complex Relationship," in M. Anderson and M. den Boer (eds.), *Policing Across National Boundaries*, London: Pinter, 22-45.

------ (1994b), "Reshaping the British Police: The International Angle," *Strategic Government*, 2, 1, 25-34.

Weatherill, S., and Beaumont, P. (1993), *EC Law*, Harmondsworth: Penguin.

Weber, M. (1948), "Politics as a Vocation," in *Essays from Max Weber*, London: Routledge and Kegan Paul.

Weiler, J.H.H. (1991), "The Transformation of Europe," *Yale Law Journal*, 100, 2403-2483.

# REINVENTING POLICING: POLICING AS GOVERNANCE

## Clifford Shearing

## INTRODUCTION

What I find most interesting and useful about examining the evolution of policing is the extent to which understanding developments in policing contributes to an understanding of the evolution of governance and vice versa.[1] By governance I simply mean the activity or business of governing--that is, attempts to realize a way of doing things (Shearing, 1992a: 399-403), or what Foucault called "the conduct of conduct" (Gordon, 1991). At the heart of the changes that have been and are transforming policing are shifts in the location, strategies, and mentalities of governance[2] that privatization, in its many guises, is promoting. These shifts in governance are creating enormous inequalities with respect to both the availability of governmental goods and control over their provision. This is evident in the case of policing where some people, generally the well-to-do, have benefitted enormously from privatization while others, generally the poor, have become even less secure and less autonomous than they already were.

Nowhere is this more apparent than in South Africa where I have spent a good portion of the last three years seeking to contribute to a reinvention of policing in ways that will lessen this inequality. In doing so, I have sought to mobilize both the discourses and practices of privatization in ways that will enhance the security of poor people and their control over what security means to them and how it is provided. In doing so, I have sought to challenge the translation that has been established, both there and elsewhere, between neoconservative agendas and privatization and deregulation (Rose and Miller, 1992: 199). In doing so, I have explored the extent to which forms of policing that operate through contractual exchanges that provide for "consumer" choice (Johnston, 1992) can be used to give expression to a progressive agenda that seeks to provide people with greater control over their lives.[3]

What I propose to do here is first to review some of the changes in the discourses, strategies, and practices that have transformed and are transforming policing within the English speaking world. Here my focus will be on the manner in which state and non-state resources are networked. I will begin with recent non-state developments and will move from there to an analysis of these developments by placing them within the context of problems of governance that have been important in shaping the course of policing. Finally, I will then turn to the interventionist work I have been doing in South Africa in which I have sought to respond to and to mobilize contractual features of private policing to enhance poor people's access to security. In my view, the most significant feature of privatization has been the extent to which responsibility and authority for governance has been relocated from the state to private entities as part of a general shift in governance that favors self-regulation.[4] This shift is associated with a growing recognition by those who have relied on the state as a source of order that the eighteenth century hope that the political center could develop technologies that would accomplish effective state rule has not been realized. Nowhere is this more evident than in policing, and it is here that we find some of the clearest evidence of the emergence of new strategies of governance that do not seek to promote control from the political center. In contrast to the established forms of policing, contemporary policing has become and is becoming increasingly fractured, embedded, and decentered. This fracturing applies not simply to the *mechanisms of central rule* but to the *loci of rule* itself. We now have increasingly autonomous governments away from the center. What has occurred is not simply a shift in the way in which rule takes place (that is, self-regulation as a strategy of central rule) but the emergence of multiple centers of rule with considerable autonomy.

## GOVERNANCE AND POLICING

This relocation of governance in general and policing in particular away from the political center has been made possible through the emergence of what might be termed, following Beck (1992), "subpolitical" centers that exist within a legal and political space that is neither purely public nor private. These centers frequently take the form of corporate entities with responsibility for governing sizable populations.[5] These corporate governments are exercising responsibility for and often directly assuming many of the costs of a range of governmental functions, including security. Examples of such subpolitical governing entities, or what Maccauley (1986) has termed "private governments," abound. In the field of policing they range from corporate entities who promote security within commercial, residential, industrial, and recreational complexes to ones that regulate financial markets. These entities interact with the state as part of networks of governance but these networks do not have a simple or a single center of control. Governance takes place through what Rose and Miller (1992: 176) identify as "an elaborate network of relations formed amongst ... complex institutions, organizations and apparatuses." These networks do not provide a basis for state rule. Rather governance takes place through the "forging of alliances" in which the state and non-state authorities seek to manage each other in an attempt to produce effects that they regard as desirable. These alliances and attempts at managing them take place within a terrain of technologies of governance and political mentalities that are drawn upon, invented, and developed as part of this ongoing process of management (Rose and Miller, 1992: 180; Hunt and Wickham, 1994).

In the West, for many centuries, government has meant rule by and from the political center. Within this general strategy a variety of formulas have been developed to make rule from the center possible. In Britain, for instance, prior to the eighteenth century rule from the center was accomplished in large part via a formula in which the center delegated responsibility for governance to the sub-political centers of feudalism. What this meant was that the sovereign delegated responsibility for such matters as policing to local structures under a system of central supervision. Rule was essentially contracted out under the supervision of an audit process. During the heyday of this arrangement in Britain, under a system known as "frankpledge," populations who did not succeed in maintaining the order of the center were required to pay a financial penalty to the Crown for not doing so (Critchley, 1979).

Transparency of populations based on intelligence gathering was a critical feature of this strategy. The knowledge that made this possible was, however, neither collected by nor lodged at the political center. The sovereign did not, and did not need to, receive and process intelligence reports on the state of populations being policed. This was left to local structures. All that concerned the sovereign was that such intelligence existed and that it was being utilized to "keep the peace." This was "action at a distance" (Rose and Miller, 1992), but it was not rule that required or depended on a single panopticon gaze. The gaze was local, fractured and unintegrated. The labor on which this system of policing depended, both with respect to the collection of intelligence and the activities that followed from its use, was essentially private and unpaid, although it took place under the supervision of the center. Citizens were expected, as part of their responsibility as citizens, to patrol at night, stand guard at the gates of walled towns, engage in the "hue and cry" and so on. In response to the breakdown of this system various private initiatives developed as well as public sphere initiatives, in particular, magistrates (Radzinowicz, 1948: 2).

For a variety of reasons to do with the breakdown of feudalism, this strategy of "rule at a distance" collapsed. After a long period of thinking and experimentation in response to this failure, a new strategy of de-privatized policing emerged in which the capacity for policing was located directly within the apparatus of the state itself. The emblematic case of this development within the English-speaking world is the series of reforms championed by Sir Robert Peel that reshaped policing in Ireland and Britain during the nineteenth century. These reforms were intended both to reestablish control over order maintenance by the center and to shift the character of policing from a past-oriented, bandit-catching enterprise to a preventative, future-focused one. The "new police" Peel established were to be judged not by the number of criminals they caught and brought to court but by the absence of crime. An often-cited passage from the General Instructions issued in 1829 outlines this shift.

> It should be understood, at the outset, that the principal object to be attained is *"prevention of crime."* To this great end every effort of the Police is to be directed. The security of persons and property, and all the other objects of a Police Establishment, will thus be better effected than by the detection and punishment of the offender after he has succeeded in committing the crime....When in any Division offences are frequently committed, there must be

reason to suspect that the Police is not in that
Division properly conducted. The absence of crime
will be considered the best proof of complete
efficiency of the Police (cited in Radzinowicz, 1968:
163).

This risk-focused approach to policing was to be achieved
through a new strategy for accomplishing transparency in which
knowledge about the populations being governed was to be made
directly available to the center. To realize this, Peel proposed the
establishment of a body of "constantly watchful" police within the state
who would, by virtue of their distribution across the whole of territory
to be controlled, be able to realize an "unremitting watch" that would
establish a central panopticon gaze (Foucault, 1979) over the
populations to be controlled (Radzinowicz, 1968: 164).[6] Persons who
knew that there was no chance that they could breach the peace without
being caught would keep the peace. The threat that would maintain the
peace under these conditions was certain capture and punishment.
While Peel clearly recognized the necessity of a supportive public, the
move to establish a specialized state police and to organize them so that
they, as state agents, would maintain a constant watchfulness reflects
a disenchantment with a reliance on citizens as a source of policing.
Policing was to become a specialized state enterprise and would no
longer be primarily a civil one.[7] Public participation was to be
encouraged as a complement to police surveillance and not as a
substitute for it.

This attempt to shift the focus of policing from remedying
what had happened to preventing what might happen, through the
creation of a panopticon watch from the center, was immediately
frustrated by the "institutions of privacy" (Stinchcombe, 1963) that
restricted police access to private places. These legal restrictions made
it difficult for the police, as specialized state agents, to watch over
everyone, yet it was precisely this that they were required to do under
the Peelian strategy.

In responding to these frustrations, the new police have over
the years developed a variety of strategies for circumventing the
constraints of the institutions of privacy. Central among these have
been strategies that have sought to persuade citizens, with access to
private places, to do the watching for the police and report what they
know to them. Indeed the story of post-Peelian policing is a story of

the strategies the police have developed to persuade citizens to take on the job of constant watchfulness for them by becoming police informers. While some of these schemes have involved offers to buy information, the majority have been based on the premise that victims can be persuaded to share their knowledge with the police if they can contact them easily and if the police respond promptly to their calls for help. The most common strategy used for this purpose has been the dial-a-cop formula promoted though 911 numbers (Shearing, 1974). Most recently, the police have devoted considerable energy to developing schemes for persuading populations who are not victims to share information with them. While some of this sharing has been driven by promises of money, in most of the schemes the private labor that the police have relied upon has been unpaid. Recent examples of schemes to persuade citizens to participate in state policing as informers included neighborhood watch, team policing, and crime-stopper programmes.

What is critical in all these schemes to promote an unremitting watch is that the locus of order maintenance remains the center. State-community partnerships are encouraged, but the locus of control remains the state. Those generating intelligence within these strategies or diverting problems away from the center are not involved in making themselves or the populations to which they belong more autonomous. They have very little, if any, power over what security they will or will not get. These developments, while motivated by a desire to realize a strategy of preventative policing through centrally based expert surveillance, have in fact proved fatal to it. This is evident with respect to the two central objectives of this strategy. First, policing has not been *deprivatized*. Instead, it has been *reprivatized*. Some deprivatization occurred as citizens were no longer involved with functions like patrolling and guarding. Instead they have been deployed as the mainstay of a police intelligence system. The net result is that while private involvement in policing has changed, the police have remained as dependent on the unpaid labor of private citizens as they ever were. Second, policing has not become risk focused. The indirect strategy of watching through citizen-informers, and particularly victims, has ensured that policing has remained an essentially past-oriented, bandit-catching enterprise (Shearing, 1974).

This failure has proved to be particularly telling as we have moved increasingly into a risk society in which preventative governance, what O'Malley and Palmer (1994) have termed "prudentialism," has become increasingly important. This risk orientation does not simply arise from the reflective features of modernism that Beck (1992: 104) has identified, in which modern society is required to respond to the dangers that modernity brings in its wake but from the "universalism of the market" that "neo-liberalism" has promoted (O'Malley and Palmer, 1994). As the market comes to rule so it becomes increasingly important to anticipate and respond to whatever it is that threatens the range of interests that operate within the market. These include, but are by no means limited to, profit. One of the consequences of the centrality of profit, however, is that loss reduction, a risk-focused strategy, becomes a central concern to those who operate within markets (Shearing, 1992a).

## THE PRIVATIZATION OF POLICING

Now that I have reached this point in my story, it is time to return to more contemporary developments and the shift to more decentralized forms of governance that the increasingly widespread acceptance of a neo-liberal market discourse which promotes privatization is making possible. This shift is not just a return to older feudal forms of rule at a distance. Rather, it constitutes a new formula in which governance is being accomplished through the operation of "loosely coupled" networks of institutions. In this system it is not simply the mechanisms of rule that are being decentralized but authority itself. This contrasts sharply with earlier strategies of decentralized rule from the center. Now decentralization is rule by subcenters. What integrates these networks of subcenters of governance is not the oversight of an overarching regulator but shared discourses and practices of governance. These discourses and the strategies of governance that they institutionalize provide for common patterns of rule. Particularly important are market-oriented discourses and the "enterprise culture" (Keat and Abercrombie, 1991) that are reshaping conceptions of governance in general and of policing in particular (O'Malley and Palmer, 1994). A critical feature of this rethinking is the constitution of security and the policing that provides it as a commodity that not only can be, but should be, bought and sold within a market (Spitzer, 1987). Within this conception, policing shifts from what the police do and becomes *any* activity that promotes security. Of course, just what security is, is a contested question.

One consequence of this relocation of policing within a network of institutions has been the emergence of what Richard Ericson (1993) has called "communications policing," to draw attention to the exchange of knowledge between centers of governance that networked policing relies upon. The distribution of knowledge between the police, the media, insurance agencies, private security companies, traffic engineers, car manufacturers, hospitals, and the like is now a vital part of policing, and the state police occupy an important role in facilitating this exchange.

The growing legitimacy of the notion of security as a commodity whose meaning is to be defined within the market (Johnston, 1992) is the other side of the coin of the questions that have long been raised about the possibility of a societal "public interest," such as that advanced by postmodern sensibilities. In challenging the idea of "society" as a loci of interest, the commodification of policing also directly confronts the classic British notion of "police independence" that has received acceptance in many parts of the English-speaking world. Within the context of a mentality that sees policing as a commodity, the idea that policing should be undertaken by independent professionals answerable, in the often-quoted words of Lord Denning, to "the law and the law alone" makes little sense. From the standpoint of a market sensibility, it is precisely this culture of independence, and the arrogance it encourages, that lies at the root of the failure of the political center and its police to provide its citizens with the security they require. As will become clearer as I proceed, the issue is that as the concept of the public interest is eroded so too is the idea of the state as the protector of society.[8]

From within this market conception it is partial, not impartial policing, that is required. It is, as Keat (1991: 5) notes, "meeting the demands of the 'sovereign' consumer that becomes the new and overriding institutional imperative." Although definitions of security share a concern with the prudent avoidance of danger, there is no single universal definition of security. What security means, and what practices are required to promote it, varies from situation to situation and from customer to customer. As policing is rethought in terms of this "contractual imagery" (Abercrombie, 1991), its primary purpose is no longer conceived of in terms of "justice being done and being seen to be done" but as the provision of a customer defined product. Within such a conception, accountability is to the market and to customers not to an abstract public interest.

This shift in thinking has had the effect of defining as policing a whole range of activities that often have nothing whatever to do with what the police have traditionally done or are able to do. Policing not only becomes, in the cliche of the private security industry, "everybody's business" but it becomes anything that can and does promote security as this is defined and redefined by customers.

These developments are at odds with the way in which policing has been provided for by law in the post-Peelian period. In Canada, for instance--and the Canadian case is typical of the situation in English-speaking countries--Police Acts require governments to set up police departments. In doing so they provide for such things as standards of recruitment, training, accountability, and so on. These Acts fit well with the Peelian notion that policing should be a state matter that the police and only the police provide. This is reinforced by associated budgetary provisions that give the entire state budget for policing to the police.

These arrangements make little sense in the context of the market mentality I have outlined. Even within a conception of governance that regards the provision of security as quintessentially a state function, for example Nozick's (1974) minimal state, a market mentality of what the state should be providing to its citizens leads not to police but to security. What state legislation should be obligating the state to provide is safe, secure spaces in which people can live and work. As this market mentality invades the state, its logic is beginning to reshape state governance. At the discursive level this is evident in the new market language that is to be found in police departments everywhere and includes the use of terms like "CEO's" instead of police chiefs, "the police industry," "customers," "products," "market share," and so on. In adopting this language, the police are embracing a private-sector mentality that is redefining the way in which they view themselves, their role, and their relationship to citizens (Johnston, 1992: 66-70).

This is affecting state policing in a variety of ways, most of which are evident in the principles that are informing the "progressive" initiatives that are taking place under the rubric of community policing. Most importantly, "public" policing is now being defined in the same way as "private" policing is, namely, as a customer-driven, risk-reduction enterprise that requires the mobilization of a wide range of resources that may or may not include the classic police resource of physical coercion. These developments, along with the challenge to the notion that governance is by definition a "public" matter, have eroded the distinction between public and private policing.

This "private" approach to state policing is being promoted through the risk-focused strategy of problem-solving policing that private security pioneered (Brogden and Shearing, 1993). However, and this is important, within the hands of the state police problem-solving policing is less customer oriented and more client oriented than it is when it takes place within the terrains of subpolitical entities. This is so because within state policing the language of the market, for the most part, has been used figuratively to create the appearance of consensual policing rather than to radically transform the relationship between the police and citizens. Citizens who rely on the police for security are not customers within a market relationship even though they may, for political reasons, be presented as if they were. Unlike powerful corporate entities who are able to use the market and their location in it as customers, to call the tune within the realm of private security, this has not been the case within the domain of state policing.

A significant feature of the market developments I have just reviewed is that the shift to risk-focused, problem-solving policing is realizing the Peelian dream of a preventative police. However, this is not being accomplished as a consequence of a panopticon gaze even though within the realm of private governance the institutions of privacy tend to enable rather than limit such surveillance. Intelligence and its gathering remains important, but it is, as it was during the pre-Peelian period, now much more fractured and decentered. It is shared through networks and located within nodes of these networks (Ericson, 1993), but it does not constitute a panopticon gaze. Neither is it a knowledge designed to promote deterrence though the identification of bandits. The knowledge problem-solving policing requires is knowledge about the nature of problems, the distribution of resources, the results of earlier problem-solving attempts, and so on (Eck and Spelman, 1987).

The reshaping of state policing is doing much to build a new structure of policing that includes both public and private agencies whose activities are integrated through the adoption of similar discourses and strategies (Shearing, 1992a; Johnston, 1992; Ericson, 1993). These changes have gone a long way to reshape policing so that it is becoming more and more a providential, risk-focused enterprise that integrates a wide range of resources including, but not limited to, coercion. It is, however, doing very little, if anything, to shift control over policing from the hands of the powerful into the hands of the poor and dispossessed. Indeed, its effect has been to provide a more powerful mechanism of rule, albeit rule that is located as much at political sub-centers as it is at the state level. This is especially true of private policing which has little incentive to respond to the needs and concerns of those whose social and economic location do not provide them with access to safety markets.

As I indicated at the outset, nowhere is this growing inequality clearer than in South Africa where 50 percent of the population is unemployed, where the number of persons employed within the private security sector is 4 to 5 times the number of state police, and where the state police are vigorously pursuing a strategy of "community policing," that is, appropriating market imagery and establishing institutions such as "community police forums" to promote the appearance but not the reality of contractual policing. Neither these state initiatives nor the continuing presence of private governance is shifting control over policing to the victims of apartheid. The rich will continue to ensconce themselves behind the walls of their "gated communities" served by private security. At the same time, the poor will remain where they have always been as targets of policing that serves others. If this happens, South Africa will have taken its place among Western nations where the gulf between rich and poor is widening daily. This brings me to the final part of this chapter, namely, what I and my colleagues in South Africa are doing to respond to these developments.

## POLICING THE NEW SOUTH AFRICA

Before I turn to this analysis let me briefly review the ground I have covered. I have sought to identify three primary strategies of governance: Pre-Peelian, Peelian (which includes what O'Malley and Palmer, 1994, have termed Keynesian policing), and Post-Peelian with its neoliberal shift to contracts and markets. Each of these strategies involves both public and private participation. Both the pre-Peelian and the Peelian strategies seek to accomplish rule by the center. In both strategies, privatization is a vehicle for "the proliferation of state control."

In the pre-Peelian strategy, although rule is from the center, the actual mechanics of governance are effectively contracted out to local structures that are supervised by the center. These sub-centers are instruments of central rule. Organizationally, governance takes a pyramid form with control located at the top, which is public, and implementation at the bottom, which is private. Surveillance is important in this strategy but it is undertaken at the local level and the knowledge it produces remains at this level. Within the confines of this strategy the center is also engaged in surveillance, but the target of its surveillance is the policing structure itself and not the populations to be policed. The center regulates policing; it watches the watchers.

Within the Peelian strategy the locus of rule continues to be the political center. What Peel sought to accomplish was the "state-ification" (Habermas, 1993: 432) of policing. His intention was to retain the pyramid form and to locate the actual machinery of policing within the state in the form of an expert system staffed by professionals.

Peel hoped that this development would shift the focus of policing from remedying the past to colonizing a future. What actually happened was quite different. The police soon found that they could not watch directly and that they had to rely on citizens to do their watching for them. Policing was reprivatized rather than deprivatized. The result, with very few exceptions, was not an unremitting watch but a system for identifying past breaches of the peace. This result was the opposite of what Peel had envisaged. Policing became even more retrospectively focused than ever, and it remained highly dependent on nonexpert and unpaid citizen labor.

The next major change in strategy was more complicated and involved both state and corporate initiatives. In both cases, the neoliberal advocacy of the relocation of governance to civil society through market mechanisms provided both the discursive legitimation as well as the models for practice. With the growth of private security, the machinery of policing and its control has shifted to the level of political sub-centers, while the attempts to mobilize civil resources by the state through a range of police initiatives has led to a "societalization of the state" (Habermas, 1993: 432). In neither case is the autonomy of the poor promoted. The effects of these twin developments are evident in South Africa where the transformation of policing is being accomplished in ways that is leaving those who are able to buy security as a commodity with as much control over policing as they had during the apartheid era, while at the same time doing little to provide the victims of apartheid with a comparable level of control over their security.

## *STRATEGIES FOR POLICING*

Let me now turn to the final section of my presentation. My goal in the work I have been doing in South Africa has been to explore strategies to address the power inequalities inherent in the developments I have reviewed. In particular, I have sought ways of providing black people, especially poor black people, with the same sort of autonomy and control over what security means, and how it is to be provided, as rich people enjoy. Given the theoretical framework outlined here, the question I have asked myself as a person who wants to contribute to social and political change in South Africa, is how can this understanding be used strategically by disempowered South Africans to enhance control and autonomy over their lives. In responding to this question I have accepted that the market mentality is a global phenomena and that it will colonize, and indeed has already colonized, South African sensibilities. This has led me to ask whether and to what extent this mentality presents opportunities for empowerment and how these opportunities can be realized. This objective has brought me face to face with the serious difficulties that confront any attempt to operate within a mentality that has been the source of inequality. Not the least of these is the ability of powerful market players to dominate less powerful ones, for instance, by constructing compliant "customers."[9] The position I have taken is that if the market mentality is to be empowering to blacks some way must be found to create them as powerful customers who can use the market to reshape the inequalities that are continuing to pervade South Africa.

I am fully aware that in an ideal world it might not be appropriate to work within the terms of neoliberal discourses and that a more radical critique might be appropriate. But I am persuaded that working within the dominant discourse is strategically the most useful thing to do at the moment. This does not mean that it may not be possible at some other moment to launch a direct assault on the market mentality as a source of inequality. But this is not the moment.

The strategy I have adopted in the light of these considerations has three related components.

First, engage the state in ways that will provide for a relocation of control over tax revenues in a manner that will provide blacks with purchasing power.

Second, establish blacks as powerful customers with ability to control their security.

Third, do this in a manner that will have currency in the present South Africa political climate.[10]

Over the last year or so, the interventions I have been involved in promoting in South Africa have been located at an institute I played a role in establishing at the University of the Western Cape, called the Community Peace Foundation. This work has been taking place on two principal terrains. On the one, we are seeking to reshape the legislative framework that will govern policing in the new South Africa, while on the second, we are seeking to create new institutional arrangements for policing that will give expression to this legal frame.

Let me begin at the legislative level. Here our work has, to date, focused primarily on the new interim constitution that will provide the framework for governance within a new South Africa from the first to the second election. At this level, our principal concern has been to establish legislative directions that will take the state's security budget out of the direct control of the police.

We successfully persuaded the multiparty forum that drafted the constitution to accept a legal framework that distinguishes between the provision of security and the provision of police. This has resulted in provisions in the constitution that enable the new legislature to establish laws that will give at least part of the budget for security to local levels of government to be used to buy policing resources either from the state police or elsewhere. This is a strategic move designed to enable the placement of state resources in a location where it will be possible to mobilize them to empower blacks as consumers of security. Our objective here has been to place them at the lowest level possible within the state.

The model we have had in mind in proposing this is a modified version of the Canadian arrangement whereby the federal police can be hired by other levels of government on a contractual basis to meet their legal responsibilities to establish police departments. The modification we envisage, and it is a crucial one, is that local governments in South Africa will not be required to set up police departments but will be required instead to fund initiatives that will provide people within their jurisdiction with safe and secure places in which to live and work. These initiatives may or may not involve the national police. Where they do, contracts for specific services will be entered into.

In our view the national police should have as its principal function the application of physical force within the rule of law. Our position here is at odds with developments within community policing that have led to an enormous expansion of the police role and, thereby, enhance rather than reduce police ownership of policing. Our position is that while *policing* should not be conceived in terms of the application of non-negotiable physical force, the *police* role can be conceived in these terms. In taking this stance we are adopting the classic Weberian position and the position of a number of contemporary minimum state theorists (see Johnston, 1992, for a review) that the state should monopolize physical coercion. This position is particularly necessary in South Africa where the widespread use of coercion by private entities has been a major problem. It is a principle that we believe is relevant to any attempt to support and extend networked policing in a manner that will enhance security for all who share a territory.

This legislative work is taking place in conjunction with research designed to discover institutional structures that will permit poor people to access tax revenues in a manner that will enable them to become customers. Our thinking here has been influenced by work within the housing arena where the emphasis is also on finding ways of permitting poor people, and particularly groups who constitute themselves as a "community," to function as customers rather than simply as clients and recipients of professional expertise over which they have no control. With the rich it is the customer who controls the housing budget and decides what will and will not be built. With poor people this is not the case. Poor people are clients of experts and not customers assumed to have the expertise necessary to make informed choices.

Within the security arena the empowerment that market relations can provide can only be accomplished, if the above analysis is correct, if solutions can be found to the following problems.

First, it is necessary to identify communities who share interests.

Second, these groups need to develop the skills and knowledge required to operate as demanding customers of security services.

Third, some scheme needs to be devised to provide them with access to buying power. Within the legislative framework we have devised, this means finding some way of turning the tax revenues available to local government into purchasing power that can be deployed at the level of specific groups.

Fourth, all this needs to be done in a manner that is consistent with the municipal governments' responsibility to facilitate the provision of security that is the backbone of our legislative framework.

Fifth, black people need to be empowered to become powerful customers within a context that recognizes the police responsibility for the exercise of nonnegotiable physical force and their responsibility to preserve the state's monopoly of force.

Sixth, if security is to be provided, blacks must be empowered to engage and reap the benefits of problem-solving, risk-focused policing.

## REINVENTING POLICING

We are still a long way from having models that meet these requirements. We are, however, making progress. At present we are working at developing two institutional arrangements that we hope will provide a core around which we can build. The first concerns the development of institutions whose job it will be to meet municipalities' responsibilities for enabling local communities to lead safe and secure lives. To accomplish this we are developing what we are calling Safety Centers as the institutional sites of these responsibilities. We envisage these Centers as situated at the neighborhood level. Their task will be to locate groups that require security--women's groups, businesses, residential groups, sports groups, youth, and so on--and to create dialogical forums within which they can meet and discuss how their security is to be accomplished.

These forums constitute the second set of arrangements we are exploring. We have conceived of them as "triangles of security" that will always involve three principal parties--interest group representatives, a police representative, and a Safety Center representative. The intention is that these persons will work together within these forums to develop plans for policing that will benefit the group.

In order to avoid the problem of the community component in this triangle being overwhelmed by the other two parties, we are experimenting with two ideas. The one involves ensuring that interest groups meet together in workshops before they participate in such forums to develop plans that they will present at the forums. We are also looking for some mechanism that will establish an onus on the other two groups to accept these plans unless they violate some set of guiding principles and minimum standards of safety. One way of accomplishing this and dealing with disagreements that might arise would be to build in some sort of appeal process. The next step is to find a way of bringing these plans together as part of a larger municipal plan. We have not tackled this issue yet.

We are still very unclear as to how to go about funding the plans developed through these dialogical forums and how to keep operational control at a local level. One idea we are considering would be to establish well-funded corporate entities at the Safety Center level controlled by a local board to manage the budgets, locate and contract for resources, and so on. These corporate entities would have the ability to operate effectively as powerful customers within the security market. They would act on behalf of persons living in the small geographic areas for which Safety Centers are responsible. In holding these corporate entities accountable to the communities they are required to serve, one idea would be to establish regular meetings with people in the area. These meetings would operate in a similar way to shareholder meetings in nonprofit companies.

In developing these plans and ideas we are working very close to the ground in two ways. First, we are examining local initiatives, of which there are many in black South African towns. Second, we are constantly organizing workshops with a whole variety of people and organizations to discuss and respond to our ideas. Once we have established plans that we think might work, we intend to move to the development of pilot projects that will be developed in conjunction with local community groups. Exactly what the final institutional arrangements we are developing will look like will depend on what transpires in these processes. While we are a long way from finality, we are already confident that we are on the right track and that we will make considerable headway in reinventing policing in ways that will give blacks substantial control over their security arrangements.

In summary then our hope is that the process of dialogue on which our work is based will provide us with the ideas needed to develop structures that will:

Define policing in terms of the networking of a range of resources not limited to the actual or potential capacities of the state police.

Establish a system for allocating tax revenues to very local communities that will enable them to participate effectively in a market for security.

Radically decentralize control over policing in ways that will shift control over policing out of the hands of the police and into the hands of the people who require security.

It is with this hope that I come to the end of this chapter.


## NOTES

1. The argument developed in this chapter engages issues being explored in the literature that has developed around Foucault's concepts of "government" and "governmentality." In particular, it is concerned with the way in which contemporary forms of governance are understood and related to earlier forms.

2. I am following Hunt and Wickham (1994) in using the term "governance" to refer to what Foucault terms "government" and "mentalities of governance" to refer to the mentalities or rationalities that shape the way governance is exercised. In talking of mentalities as shaping rather than as determining modes of governance I am following Rose and Miller (1992) who conceive of this relationship as one of "translation."

3. A recent attempt to develop such an agenda for governance more generally is Hirst (1994). The arguments developed by Hirst for an "associative democracy" that will institutionalize "new forms of economic and social governance" resonate with the normative argument developed in this chapter and with an earlier presentation in Brogden and Shearing (1993).

4. In making this claim, and it is one that I will seek to develop as I proceed, I am seeking to distance myself--along with Beck (1992) and more particularly Hirst (1994)--from understandings of privatization that see it in one way or another as simply another stage in the development of "liberal rule at a distance" in which the state and those who rule through it respond to the problematics of governance by encouraging the emergence of multiple "centres of calculation" that promote ways of doing things that the state seeks to guarantee (Miller

and Rose, 1992). This is the position adopted by many of the early commentators (including myself) on the emergence of modern private policing who saw it as widening the net of social control. (For a review of this literature see Shearing, 1992 and Johnston, 1992.) Rose and Miller (1992: 189) express this analysis as follows.

> Self regulatory techniques can be installed in citizens that will align their personal choices with the ends of government. The freedom and subjectivity of citizens can in such ways become an ally, and not a threat, to the orderly government of a polity and a society.

The position I have adopted in this paper, and it is one that is consistent with the Foucaultian notion of the "governmental" as involving more than the "executives and formal organs of state" (Miller and Rose, 1990:1) is that "sub-political" (Beck, 1992) centres of calculation may well be, and often are, not simply sites of calculation that provide for the exercise of rule at a distance but are often sites that frustrate the "ends of government."

5. Sometimes and in some places these are very transitory and shifting populations (as, for example, the populations of shopping complexes and recreational facilities in Europe and North America); at other times and in other places they are more permanent (for example, the huge feudal-like corporate estates that occur throughout much of Zimbabwe).

6. Radzinowicz outlines the strategies (that continue to dominate the organization of state policing) to be used to provide for this panopticon gaze.

> Superintendents were told that potential criminals would be best deterred by "making it evident that they are known and strictly watched, and that certain detection will follow any attempts to commit a crime." To this end the seventeen divisions were subdivided into sections and again into beats, each constantly patrolled by a rota of constables at every hour of the day and night. At the centre of the division was a police station or watch house, at which an inspector was always on duty to keep order,

to hold a reserve party ready to meet emergencies, to record charges, to detain persons or release them on recognizances, and to be responsible for any property brought in. A second inspector went round the division, receiving reports from the sergeants, who accompanied their men on the beats.

This organization was supplemented by an information service. Every constable was expected to get to know his own beat and section thoroughly and to learn to recognise those living in them. Information was issued from time to time about forms of crime that were particularly prevalent, the methods of the criminals, and means that police and public could adopt to frustrate them. Empty houses were specially marked or watched, jewellers were informed of the latest devices for hooking goods out of shop windows, laundresses of the practice of obtaining linen from them on false pretences (Radzinowicz, 1968: 164).

7. This Peelian model of professional police responsible for order has drawn support from and has been shaped by Keynesian conceptions of governance which have also questioned the effectiveness of leaving the provision of public goods like safety and security to private initiative (O'Malley and Palmer, 1994). Within this conception, victims of crime become clients who can turn to a benevolent and paternalistic state for expert support as part of a general umbrella of state provided services. Like the critique of Peel's time, when reliance on the "voluntary associations for the prosecution of felons" that were during the eighteenth century "to be found in almost every part of England and Wales" (Radzinowicz, 1948: 122) was criticized as ineffective, the Keynesian political mentality disputed the effectiveness of institutions of civil society, in this case the market, as a reliable basis for keeping the peace.

8. This change is reflected in the shift identified by O'Malley and Palmer (1994) in their discussion of the shift from the style of policing that a Keynesian rationality promotes to one that a neoliberal mentality fosters. What is involved, however, is more than a partnership between police and the community in which the community is seen as a key

resource that the police must draw upon but rather a shift to a contractual relationship in which the citizens are constituted as customers who require service and who may turn to a host of resources, including the police, for satisfaction (Shearing, 1992a). In the first case what one has is empowerment which equips "individuals to govern themselves" in ways that will promote "rule at a distance" by expert systems (O'Malley and Palmer, 1994:11), while in the second the possibility of a challenge to central rule by persons who can establish themselves as genuine customers exists. Whether this challenge is realized, as I will indicate below, is a function of the manner in which the market relations in which customers operate are constituted (Shearing, 1992b.)

9. Habermas' (1989) concerns about the manner in which the "public sphere" has been and is being transformed and the limitations this places on the possibility of developing more radical forms of democracy through communicative action is relevant here.

10. Before I go on to this analysis one further caveat is in order. The policy my colleagues and I have been developing is grounded both in the Western developments I have reviewed here and in an analysis of indigenous developments within South Africa in the form of popular policing. While these have been addressed in recent work I have done with Mike Brogden (1993), raising them here would take us too far afield.

# SOURCES

Abercrombie, N. (1991), "The Privilege of the Producer," in R. Keat and N. Abercrombie (eds.), *Enterprise Culture*, London: Routledge.

Beck, U. (1992), *The Risk Society: Towards a New Modernity*, Newbury Park: Sage, 1992.

Brogden, M., and C. Shearing (1993), *Policing for a New South Africa*, London: Routledge.

Critchley, T. (1979), *A History of Police in England and Wales* (2nd ed.), London: Constable.

Eck, J., and W. Spelman (1987), "Who ya gonna call? The Police as Problem-busters," *Crime and Delinquency*, 33, 1, 31-52.

Ericson, R. (1993), "Community Policing as Communications Policing," in D. Dölling and T. Felte (eds.), *Community Policing*, Holzkirchen: Felix Verlag.

Foucault, M. (1979), *Discipline and Punish*, Harmondsworth: Penguin.

Gordon, C. (1991), "Governmental Rationality: An Introduction," in G. Burchell, C. Gordon, and P. Miller (eds.), *The Foucault Effect: Studies in Governmentality*, London: Harvester/Wheatsheaf.

Habermas, J. (1989), *The Transformation of the Public Sphere*, Cambridge, Mass: MIT Press.

------ (1993), "Further Reflections on the Public Sphere," in C. Calhoun (ed.), *Habermas and the Public Sphere*, Cambridge, Mass: MIT Press, 421-461.

Hirst, P. (1994), *Associative Democracy: New Forms of Economic and Social Governance*, Amherst: The University of Massachusetts Press.

Hunt, A. and G. Wickham (1994), "Foucault and Law: Towards a Sociology of Law as Governance," mimeo.

Johnston, L. (1992), *The Rebirth of Private Policing*, London: Routledge.

Keat, R. (1991), "Introduction: Starship Britain or Universal Enterprise?" in R. Keat and N. Abercombie (eds.), *Enterprise Culture*, London: Routledge.

Keat, R., and N. Abercrombie, eds., (1991), *Enterprise Culture*, London: Routledge.

Macauley, S. (1986), "Private Government," in L. Lipson and S. Wheeler (eds.), *Law and Social Sciences*, New York: Russell Sage Foundation.

Nozick, R. (1974), *Anarchy, State and Utopia*, Oxford: Blackwell.

O'Malley, P., and D. Palmer (1994), "Post-Keynesian Policing," Mimeo.

Radzinowicz, L. (1948), *A History of English Law and Its Administration from 1750*. Vol 2: *the Clash Between Private and Public Interest in the Enforcement of the Law*, London: Stevens and Sons.

Radzinowicz, L. (1968), *A History of the English Law and Its Administration from 1750*. Vol 4: *Grappling for Control*, London: Stevens and Sons.

Rose, N., and P. Miller (1992), "Political Power Beyond the State: Problematics of Government," *British Journal of Sociology*, 43, 2, 173-205.

Shearing, C. (1974), "Dial-a-Cop: A Study of Police Mobilization," in R. Ackers and E. Sagarin (eds.), *Prevention and Social Defense*, New York: Praeger.

------ (1992a), "The Relationship between Public and Private Policing," in M. Tonry and N. Morris (eds.), *Modern Policing*, Chicago: University of Chicago Press.

------ (1992b), "A Constitutive Conception of Regulation," in J. Braithwaite and P. Grabosky (eds.), *The Future of Regulatory Enforcement*, Canberra: Australian Institute of Criminology.

Spitzer, S. (1987), "Security and Control in Capitalist Societies: The Fetishism of Security and the Secret Thereof," in J. Lowman, R. Menzies, and T. Palys (eds.), *Transcarceration: Essays in the Sociology of Social Control*, Aldershot: Gower.

Stinchcombe, A. (1963), "Institutions of Privacy in the Determination of Police Administrative Practices," *American Journal of Sociology*, 69, 150-160.

# CHANGING POLICE, POLICING CHANGE: TOWARDS MORE QUESTIONS

## Otwin Marenin

### INTRODUCTION

In the introduction I raised this question: to what degree can the police be autonomous in the reconstruction of preferred forms of the state, social orders, and policing? What lessons do the case studies provide? Five can be enumerated.

For one, state policing is only one type of policing. The typical image of the state and society arranged in a triangular and hierarchical order, with the state at the apex guaranteeing, in response to elite or public demands, certain forms of social control and order is misleading. More properly understood, policing is a field of contest among the state, private interest groups (including economic associations), and communities over the division of authority and responsibilities for constructing and protecting secure routines of daily life. In this three-cornered struggle, the police themselves (even when they are agencies and agents of the state) are one of the interest groups contesting the authorization, organizational forms, functions and roles, and locus of accountability of policing. The most interesting theoretical question about policing in general is this: what determines the division of functions and accountability among the three basic types of policing (state, private, communitarian), and how do periods of massive social change alter (or do they) the distribution of types and the determination of specific forms within each type (e.g., private policing)?

The current dominance of state policing in practice and in police theory may be, as Walker and Shearing argue, a historical phase. Walker's discussion of the European Union posits the emergence of a supra-national police force as the state (this historical phenomenon) declines in authority and acceptance. Shearing posits the movement of control over policing away from the state towards sub-centers of control and accountability. Nonstate policing can move toward private forms (when powerful groups and social trends support such change) or communitarian forms (when communities struggle to determine and support forms of securing their routines which do not depend on the state nor are unequally allocated to private interests which can afford to pay for such services). In all these possibilities, the state and policing done by the state in a monopolistic fashion declines and may eventually disappear. Policing is always determined and reproduced but can move toward new centers of political and economic power. In the end, the state becomes merely another contestant and aspirant for acceptance and power and responsibility. The participation of actors and their respective powers in the process of reconstructing policing is an empirical and open question.[1]

The three types of policing which emerge from this process-- state, private, and communitarian or populist--are equally capable of being effective and legitimized, equally capable of emerging in the future in response to other societal trends and the actions of the police themselves. Yet the variety of types can also be hidden. Even when the state remains and the police look like state police, private policing may be the reality, such as Stanley argues existed in El Salvador before the success of the revolutionary groups. Or, as Chevigny shows, police violence and abuse may be simply a form of legitimate and delegated public power.

Second, policing within the three basic types is constructed in a vast variety of forms in different times and places. State policing, the staple of the comparative police literature, appears in many guises (e.g., Bayley, 1985). The question then is, can we suggest or hypothesize under what conditions particular types and forms of policing will emerge?

Shearing suggests that current trends toward privatization and the "market" will lead to the commodization of security services and a consequent shift of policing toward economic groups, but unequally, in social systems which are stable. In unstable or changing systems, ownership of policing may be movable toward community groups. In this process, shifting ideologies of state-society relations provide the background and legitimations for shifts in the locus of policing.

Conditions in changing societies may provide windows of opportunity to redefine the location and control of policing types and forms. But such domestic developments will be affected by their international contexts. As the cases of El Salvador and Russia make clear, international aid and advisors, since both are channelled through state auspices, will tend to maintain the dominance of state policing but in "cleaned up" forms. In El Salvador, the efforts by UN and foreign police advisors are not designed to create communitarian policing (which is one option) but rather seek to eliminate existing hidden private forms of policing and replace the corrupt and inefficient and brutal state police with a more democratic form. In Russia, the struggle for the creation of new states out of the rubble of the collapsed Soviet empire has led to a shift in control of the police from the disappeared center to new state centers, these controlled by nationalistic elites who see the police as an essential element in the new states' legitimation and as a protection for themselves against insurrectionist challenges. International assistance to the CIS states is designed, as it is in El Salvador or Haiti, to reconstruct more democratic forms of policing under new statist power centers.

In more stable social and economic systems (even when political stability is disrupted)--e.g., Hong Kong, Yemen, Saudi Arabia, Kuwait, Italy, or Ireland--changes in policing seek reform and not reconstruction or redistribution of control over policing. Changes occur in the forms but not in the types of policing.

Third, the capacity of the police to be autonomous varies across time and space. What, then, accounts for variations in autonomy or the actor-object status of the police? What factors determine the limits and capacities of the police, as an institution, to influence the construction of themselves and their environments?

Again, the case studies suggest only rough and general answers and avenues to be investigated. Partially, answers depend on the definition of autonomy and what the police are autonomous from or for. If autonomy from the state is the criterion, then the most autonomous police in these studies would be a European Union police (if it emerges), with the police in South Africa (under the proposed indigenized and community-controlled security centers) next, followed by the police in Brazil, El Salvador (before the cease fire) and the CIS states, with the police in Northern Ireland, Hong Kong, Kuwait, Saudi Arabia closely tied to and controlled by a state. Italy is probably the least autonomous state policing form (but the state itself has a tendency to degenerate into a conglomeration of feuding bureaucracies and political fiefdoms).

On the other hand, if autonomy means autonomy from society,

the rankings and judgments will differ. El Salvador (before) and South Africa (after) are closely tied to nonstate control, though that control is located differently, while the police in Northern Ireland (before the recent cease fire), Hong Kong, or Kuwait are clearly responsive to community preferences only when the state accepts those preferences as legitimate.

The consequences of different forms of autonomy for policing are unclear and contested. For example, Brogden and Shearing would argue that autonomy from the state is a prerequisite for democratic policing. The advisors travelling among the new Salvadoran police, though, likely think the exact opposite, namely, that the emergence of a democratic state and of state control of policing is essential for democratic policing.

Fourth, forms of policing are inextricably caught in a tension between stability and breakdown, a dynamic which is normally hidden by the stability of state and society. In times of massive change, conflicts over the preferred conception of the future are obvious and unavoidable, are acted on, and are won and lost by different groups. The creation of a particular form of policing is not automatic nor easy nor will it necessarily result in an equitable contribution of the goals (safety, order, security) achieved by groups and strata in any society. But policing is continuously recreated, not only in times of change. It has no necessary forms, goals, functions or missions--only those decided upon in the process of reconstruction. Even the ascribed social needs for safety and routines and social order are not enough to determine forms of policing, for policing is but one possible response to this need.

Fifth, we may be observing the emergence of universal norms of policing, even as the particular forms of policing become more varied. What is notable in the discussion of countries in this book is the commonality of what is accepted as legitimated actions by the police, and the obverse, what is universally condemned as unacceptable.

A growing complex of regimes promoted by international organizations, international consultants, and advisors, by professional interactions and the emergence of an "international brotherhood of the police" all lead to, in rhetoric and promise, a similar endpoint for changing the police.[2] Do periods of upheaval give greater opportunities to move toward the emerging universalistic standard of good policing? On the face of it the answer would seem to be yes, as all norms and institutions are challenged. But what really happens? Is there a fundamental reevaluation of policing to determine what is necessary or appropriate for the new societal order, or do the police merely follow in the wake of other reforms, cleaning up the debris of revolutionary violence and social disorders? (That seems to be the situation and the reform effort in Haiti now.) Do the police move themselves or are they moved towards "good policing"? In terms of policy and reform, the question is what kind of civil society and what kind of state is necessary for good policing. More precisely, what kind of reproduction process of civil society and of the state is necessary for the reproduction of good policing?

These lessons raise fundamental issues about how to understand and theorize about policing. Below, I wish to sketch elements of a general approach, suggest models of state policing forms which stress the interaction between policing, state and society and which accept the potential of the police to be actors in their own behalf, and also suggest some generalizations about the interconnections of state, society, and policing.

## BASIC ELEMENTS IN A THEORY OF THE POLICE IN CHANGE

### *CONTINGENT REPRODUCTION*

Change is created as much as is order. The idea of reproduction merely stresses the contingent and unresolved nature of all social forms. These have to be and are recreated every day by all the myriad decisions which concretize values and interests in policies and routines, be these coercive, productive, distributive, political, religious, ideological, or social. There is no state, only the process of reproducing the idea and functions of the state each day. There are no police, only the decisions of the police to continue to do their jobs in routine, accepted and habitual ways. The stability of the process, which gives life and credence to the notion of institutionalization, reflects the stability of decision-norms, rules, preferred values, and accepted interests which shape decisions. But each day decisions could, in theory and in practice, be done differently and lead to different results. This notion of contingent reproduction is not an unusual idea, though scholars and practitioners more often stress the other side of the process, the routinizing forces which create stability.[3]

## AGENCY

The police are actors but they act under constraints. To quote Thompson (1978: 153, 164), the police act

> not as autonomous subjects, "free individuals," but as persons experiencing their determinate productive situations and relationships as needs and interests and antagonism, and then "handling" this experience within their consciousness and their cultures in the most complex ways, and then acting upon their determinate situation in their turn.[4]

Experience and history produce both the constraints which limit choice yet also the will to struggle against the constraints. The police in their capacity as subjects will act to reconcile structure and choice by their perceptions of interests and values and will seek to manage their specialized jobs as they see best. Even when the police exist as an apparatus of the state, their relations to their employing state are neither that of unthinking tool nor rampant vigilante.

## AUTONOMY

Autonomy for (the capacity to act and the power to influence decisions) exists potentially at five analytically defined levels of policing: the determination of street decisions, policy selections, organizational structures, roles and functions, and types of policing. (Solutions or answers to the first four sets of choices define the forms of policing within each of the three--state, private, populist--types.) Street decisional autonomy, or individual officer discretion, is a fundamental trait of all policing widely verified by research and experience, and a source of conflict among street officers, organizational managers, publics, and political elites. Second, the selection of policing policies and priorities is also a common activity of police forces everywhere from the development of organizational styles to the selection of particular internal procedures or public contact policies, e.g., a community-oriented policing philosophy and strategy or a stress on drug law enforcement. Third, organizational structures have to be chosen, e.g., whether to have one or multiple forces in one social setting and which kind. The role of the police themselves in such decisions is not well described except as the personal influence and decisions of the leadership (e.g., Stead, 1983). Fourth, the roles and functions, hence the jobs of the police have to be determined. Such choices are made and they aggregate over time and clearly are influenced by the same forces which shape the development of other state and societal institutions and roles. The agency of the police in such decisions is also little studied. Lastly, preferences for types of policing have been little recognized as societal choices which should be studied, hence little theorizing has occurred.

For the police, the struggle for autonomy (or the capacity to influence the contexts and conditions of their own work) is an ongoing process for two main reasons. For one, the police are both agents and objects of change. They have their own reasons and interests and will seek to protect these, yet they are also under continuous pressures to construct policing by the preferences of other social actors. The police themselves contest the definition of policing which is to govern their work and they seek the power and participation to help establish rules on how to hold them accountable, to judge the legitimacy of demands for policing, and to create the criteria for evaluating their performance. The weapons employed by the police are ideology,[5] threat, bluster, political manipulation, service, resistance, and outright use of force (coups). Solutions to such issues are simultaneously the outcome of struggle and constraints on further struggles.

Secondly, their role embodies inherent, unresolvable contradictions which cannot be resolved permanently but must be justified in their specific struggles and resolutions on an on-going basis. Contradictions mean that the police are expected and have to carry out opposing tasks and roles simultaneously, and they seek to help shape the balance and compromises which are necessary.

## THE CORE CONTRADICTIONS OF POLICING

Every reproduction of policing is an attempt to reconcile inherent contradictions into effective and legitimate forms of order maintenance. Such contradictions will continue even during periods of massive social changes. The core contradiction is about the uses made of force, whether for protection or for repression (e.g., Bittner, 1980; Klockars, 1991). Are the police to protect the general order necessary for the routine reproduction of any society or are they to accept and carry out the role of defender of particularistic sets of interests, including their own? The two tasks can mingle and a specific performance or outcome will be judged differently by groups as being either protection, repression, or some balance.

A second contradiction is that between autonomy and consent--the police need autonomy to do the job but also legitimation of their discretion and power (e.g., Brogden, 1982). The police must use force yet their use of force will, if used consistently, excessively, or non-legitimately, create resistance and de-legitimation.

How are such contradictions dealt with and reproduced during change? How, for example, are the core contradictions of policing different during times of change when social anchors which provided the material and ideological foundations for contradictions shift or even disappear?

## MODELS OF STATE POLICE IN CHANGE

### *ELEMENTS OF THE MODEL*

Below, let me focus on one type of policing (state policing) and suggest a framework for thinking about the reproduction of state policing forms.[6] The role and power of the police in reproducing change depends fundamentally on two contextual (to the police) aspects: the nature and dynamics of the state for which they work and the nature and dynamics of society in which they exist and work (as well as the linkages between state and civil society, of which the police are themselves one). Each of these aspects of a social formation has attracted much theoretical interest and analysis, and a variety of models of the state, of society, and of state-society linkages exist. The question is how the police affect the reproduction of both the state and civil society and how they are themselves affected by the actions of others who also seek to reproduce a social formation in a preferred form. The state, civil society, and the police each are shaped by complex and shifting constellations of causative forces and are linked to each other in complex and shifting patterns.

Analytically speaking, one needs to consider at least three distinct processes of reproduction which occur simultaneously and are linked in the real life of societies and are each affected by different constellations of agency and constraints. Each process is described below in the form of a simplified matrix which sketches selected characteristics and dynamics of the state, of civil society, and of the police.

The matrices are conceptualized as interactive or overlaid. Each matrix embodies its own dynamics, yet the matrices also interact or, rather, the forces which produce reproduction in each matrix are affected by forces in the other two matrices. The matrices sketched below are based on observed and theorized overlaps among patterns of reproduction in each society's history.

The police themselves are characterized by the uses made of their coercive capacity (their core characteristic), whether for protection or repression.[7] Figure 1 indicates the possible space for balances of repression and protection and places representative examples of state policing within the matrix.

## Figure 1

### *FORMS OF POLICING*

**Repression**

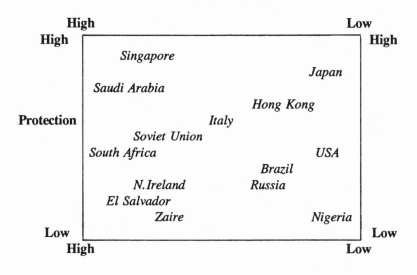

The nature of the state is described by a two-dimensional matrix created by the axes autonomy and managerial capacity.[8] State autonomy can range from high or hegemonic control to low or agent status. Managerial capacity reflects a combination of factors, specifically the "organizational technology" (Therborn's phrase, 1978) employed and the degree of stateness or cohesion, which can rank from high or unified states speaking with one voice to low or "decayed" (Young's phrase, 1984) states in which employees of the state act largely on their own interests. Bureaucratically organized and unified states tend to have higher capacity than states which incorporate patron-client relations and group conflicts into the structures of the state.[9] Figure 2 indicates the possible space created by the two axes and places examples within.

## Figure 2

### *STATE FORMS*

**Managerial Capacity**

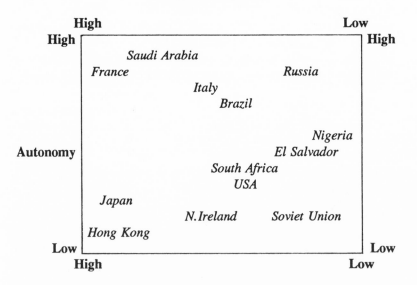

Civil society is described by a matrix created by the axes fluidity of group structures and the intensity of group conflict. "Group"

includes all social groupings, whether based on class, culture (ethnicity, religion) or shared interests. Fluidity is an estimate of the stability of the group structure (or of the vertical and horizontal stratification patterns) of each social formation. Figure 3 indicates the possible space and places some examples within.

## Figure 3

### *GROUP RELATIONS IN CIVIL SOCIETY*

**Group Conflict**

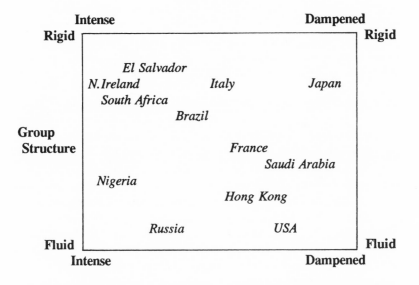

Changes which now are happening in countries experiencing upheaval or massive changes can be represented by tracks through the matrices. None of the tracks spells out in any detail what the specific changes are nor how such changes will be achieved, but the matrices do state the general dynamics of change and the conditions under which such change will happen and the constraints imposed on the police and other agents of change.

Periods of upheaval provide the opportunity to reproduce new configurations, for each existing pattern is under challenge, each has collapsed from its former incarnation, and agency to move toward preferred forms is powerfully at work. Each of the patterns is continuously reproduced; each is process as well as outcome. For example, autonomy is not the temporary removal of external restraint over an organization or agent or an attribute of an organization; it is the shifting result of a continual tug of war between actors, each wishing to create preferred conditions. Autonomy is the continuously reproduced balance of control and resistance.[10]

## HISTORICAL EXAMPLES

Looking specifically at the repression and protection roles of the police, under what conditions can the police move towards a reproduction of themselves which emphasizes the protection role (assuming that this is the preferred and "universal" definition of good policing)? What general state forms and what specific examples, historically, have embodied the four logical combinations of high and low protection and repression; and can analysis of these state forms provide hints and policy guidelines on the process of movement toward preferred policing standards?[11]

Figure 4 locates forms of the state and policing within one matrix.[12] The corners indicate tendencies toward extreme manifestations or ideal types. One can think of historical prototypes for each state category, with the exception of nonephemeral anarchist utopias.

The placement of policing and state forms is not deduced from the characteristics of states, e.g., their ideology, relative autonomy, penetration of or by society, involvement in productive and distributive economic relations, external interactions, or other variables. Rather, placement is based on descriptions of the police and their work, categorized by types of states in which patterns of repression/protection occur. Placement is tentative since many of the relevant variables have not been adequately described, e.g. what work of the police constitutes repression and which protection, nor are many variables easy to conceptualize, e.g., the autonomy of the state.

An example of the modern police state is the Weimar Republic. The police provided both effective repression (of the undesirable) and protection (the streets were safe to walk in), and were tightly controlled by the state (Chapman, 1970; Liang, 1970). The police achieved high levels of intelligence gathering, information control, neutralization and intimidation of opponents--the hallmarks of "political policing" (Turk, 1982: 115-166).

## Figure 4

### *STATE SYSTEMS AND POLICING SYSTEMS*

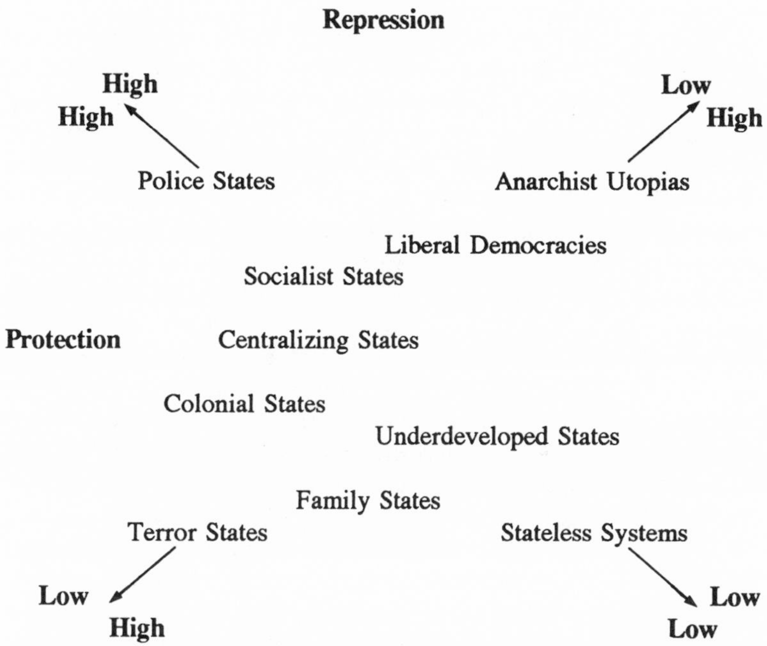

**Repression**

In terror states (Kampuchea is a recent example), policing is unchecked, arbitrary, brutal, and is not interested in protecting people who are left to fend for themselves as best as they can. The police are turned loose on the populace to implement the agenda of a small group (which controls the instruments of coercion) and are allowed to pursue their own vendettas.

Stateless systems lack "institutionalized" police forces. Policing, the reproduction of order and the protection of life, property, statue, power and morality is achieved by sanctioned self-help and informal mechanisms, haphazardly, and by reaction to events (Nader and Todd, 1978).

Anarchist utopias envision a society in which policing is interested only in protection; where the state has yielded to the cooperative efforts of all which promote peaceful interactions and progress. Policing is neither required or, if deviance occurs, its correction is the responsibility of all (Tifft and Sullivan, 1980).

The police in socialist societies have been relatively unexamined, yet certain characteristics seem to hold: the existence of large and secret police forces, in addition to the regular police; the involvement of military and semi-military organizations in the routine maintenance of order; the encouragement of numerous forms of informal but structured order maintenance mechanisms; and the deep penetration of policing, by the regular police and by secret and informal methods, into the lives of people (e.g., Brady, 1983; Conquest, 1968; Dutton, 1992; Salas, 1979; Shelley, 1990).

Policing is one of the mechanisms by which centralizing states gain domination. The police are organized to provide the growing state with the information necessary to detect challenges and obstacles and the powers to crush resistance. In Bayley's (1975: 360) summation, the development of national police systems in continental Europe was most significantly affected by "transformations in the organization of political power, prolonged and violent popular resistance to government and the development of new law and order tasks, as well as the erosion of former bases of community authority as a result of socio-economic change" (also Diamond, 1971; Williams, 1979).

Colonial states were imposed by force and local collaboration. The police were created to promote the colonizers' values and interests and acted primarily as a para-military force to suppress native challenges, "pacify" rebellious areas, and stand as the first line of defense for the colonizers' property and persons (e.g., Ahire, 1991; Brogden, 1987; Jeffries, 1952; Tamuno, 1970).

Family states are state systems in which power is controlled and exploited by a small kin group for personal gains. Zaire over the last 30 years provides the textbook example (Haiti in recent years is another) of greed, corruption, and abuse of power by Mobutu's "family." The police are left alone to ravage people; they are "an occupation force on the 'backs of people' extracting goods, money, sex through robbery, extortion, beating and scavenger raids on local markets and roads" (Callaghy, 1982: 19-20; see also Marenin, 1986:

533-540; Schatzberg, 1988). The "family" cares neither for people nor the police (who frequently go unpaid) and shows an interest in social conditions only when organized challenges to its power and privilege appear on the internal and external horizons.

The police in underdeveloped countries are, generally, insufficiently trained, equipped, organized, or motivated to provide much protection for people, except the powerful. The capacity for repression is equally limited, though that capacity can be effectively utilized when targets can be pinpointed. The exercise of police power is unsystematic, sporadic, particularistic, and often corrupt (e.g., Bayley, 1969; Carter and Marenin, 1981; Danns, 1982; Enloe, 1980).

The police in liberal, democratic regimes tend to be fairly ineffective in providing protection but are much better at reproducing order; they engage sporadically and on a small scale in repression; yet in general reflect in their actions a concern to be responsive to a variety of organized pressures and individual demands and to some notion of order and law which transcends particularistic interests.

These short sketches could be and need to be expanded or be replaced by specific states. The summations gloss over differences in categories. For example, policing in the Soviet Union compared to Cuba was conducted very much differently; the effectiveness and role of the police in Japan compared to those in the United States are as night and day. Policing in developing societies can partake of other forms, e.g., family states or socialist states. Also, policing will change in each society over time.

## MODELS OF POLICING

One can summarize these examples in terms of group structure and conflict, characteristics of the state, and the autonomy of police organizations and of individual officers.

### High Repression/High Protection Policing

Societies at the high repression/high protection corner tend to have entrenched, if not rigid, social structures. Group conflict is dampened and channeled by state control.

States are nonautonomous. They are controlled and take direction from the ruling group. Managerial capacity, the ability to decide on and carry through policies in society, tends to be high.

The police, as organizations and individuals, tend to be nonautonomous.

### High Repression/Low Protection Policing

Societies at the high-repression/low-protection corner tend to have a social structure which is rigid or solidifying, conditions which indicate the emerging victory of one group or class over another (centralizing states) or successful group or class dominance (colonial, socialist, family states).

Group conflict tends to be effectively suppressed as challenging groups and class have been either eliminated or been deprived of political and economic power. The style of politics is heavily ideologized to indicate and justify the correctness and necessity of the dominance of the ruling group; politics is defined as a zero-sum game, as a contest in which only winners count.

States tend to be nonautonomous and under direct group, class or personal control. Managerial capacity is high though distorted toward the implementation and protection of particularistic conceptions of societal welfare.

Police organizations are somewhat autonomous from state control by design, neglect, or assertion by the police themselves. By design the police are given much discretion to translate received and perceived commands into control activities; police agencies, by assertion, claim authority and power over the policing tasks they perform and which are crucial to the survival of the state structure; police force may be autonomous by neglect, e.g., in family states, in which ruling cliques are uninterested in what the police do as long as the police suppress popular discontent and remain incapable of challenging the ruling clique. Lastly, the autonomy of individual officers tends to be either low (in police organizations which are autonomous by design or assertion) or high when organizational autonomy results from malign neglect.

### Low Repression/High Protection Policing

Societies at the low repression/high protection corner tend to have fluid and complex group and class structures. Political life, in turn, is characterized by conflicts among numerous groups all having bases of power which allow them to contest for control of the state. The style of politics is pragmatic with a variety of ideological appeals used to justify the existence and virtue of  interests which are in conflict and the methods for their resolution; and politics is defined, ultimately, as a non-zero sum game though temporarily control over the state and its resources falls into particular hands.

States tend to be relatively autonomous. Managerial capacity is low.

Police organizations tend to be nonautonomous in practice (controlled by local and national political agencies) yet tend to engage in a rhetoric of autonomy which argues the need for professionalized discretion and judgement. Police officers tend to be relatively autonomous--constrained, in the main, by organization and work dynamics yet also subject to external pressures which are disaggregated, noncumulative, and noncoinciding.

### *Low Repression/Low Protection Policing*

Societies at the low repression/low protection corner tend to have relatively fluid group structures and conflict is based as much on personal and family conflicts as on group identities.

The state is weak and often in the very process of being created. It tends to be non-autonomous but also internally divided. State agencies and "state-like" offices (e.g., economic parastatals) retain significant autonomy from their state. The state's managerial capacity is limited.

Policing is limited and supplemented by informal and self-help activities. The police tend to be autonomous from the state and officers autonomous from their organization.

## CONCLUDING COMMENTS

If the argument made is plausible and the definition of good policing accepted, the change toward good policing requires a simultaneous movement of civil society toward fluid group structures engaged in dampened conflict; towards states which are relatively autonomous and whose managerial reach and capacity is limited; and police forces which are granted autonomy and share in the reproduction of their own roles, organizations, policies, and discretion.

## NOTES

1. This is not a universally agreed-upon sentiment. For example, Bayley (1994: 144) argues that "while it might be possible to reduce the police role in policing, it is not possible to remove the state from policing.... The state cannot renounce the responsibility [for crime prevention]. The maintenance of domestic order is as crucial to the legitimacy of government as defense against external enemies."

2. As argued below, the emerging universal goal is high protection and low repression, and the policies which will lead to both. For a discussion of a possible universal definition of good policing see Cottam and Marenin (1989).

3. Of course, the state exists. The argument here is simply that the question of stateness (the degree of state presence) can be approached from two poles: one, that the state is obviously there and powerful (as we know from experience); the other pole is that the state is an idea which is constructed in particular forms, and it can change. Approaching the concept of state, or policing, from the "fluid" pole raises different questions about the nature of the state and the process of its reproduction. Most importantly, the state is not reified or its necessity accepted as given.

4. Thompson talks about people in general, but that includes, of course, the police and their specific situations. The constraints under which they labor are specific to them as coercive organizations, but their agency is universal.

5. In Manning's (1979: 102) words, the police protect their organizational interests by defining themselves and their job as "politically neutral agents of a politically neutral state delivering a uniform product," a "police service."

6. Similar models and arguments could be developed for the other two basic types of policing.

7. For a discussion of the meaning and measurement of protection and repression see Marenin, 1990: 122-125. The distinction overlaps to some degree the categories of low and high policing (e.g., Brodeur, 1983).

8. For discussion of these characteristics see Therborn (1978) and Marenin (1987). Staples (1990) uses a similar conception of the state to examine and explain shifting forms of social control in US history.

9. The placement of examples is a judgment made on the basis of general knowledge, as is true of the placement of examples in the other three matrices. The exact location of each country probably would be contested by specialists, and it will change over time. But, at this time, exact placement is less important than the utility of the matrix as a conceptual framework for analyzing changes in the central characteristics and relationships of policing, the state and civil society.

10. Change toward good policing is the attempt to move or reproduce the police as close to the high protection/low repression point as possible. Success will depend on reproducing the necessary supporting forms of the state and society.

11. The analysis and labelling of repression and protection in different societies examines the activities of the police at the level of roles and functions. One could, and would have to for a complete analysis, examine and explain police agency and autonomy and the constraints under which it is created and reproduced at the other four levels of police autonomy (street, policy, organization, type) as well.

12. This is a very rough categorization of states and their policing. The three earlier matrices are combined to show historical patterns of how state, society and policing forms seem to have developed together. The labels for the state categories are convenience labels, that is labels in current usage. The labels are not analytically distinct categories, that is, built from stated combinations of characteristics of states, societies, and policing.

## SOURCES

Ahire, Philip Terdoo (1991), *Imperial Policing*, Philadelphia: Open Universities Press.

Bayley, David H. (1969), *The Police and Political Development in India*, Princeton: Princeton University Press.

-------- (1975), "The Police and Political Development in Europe," in Charles Tilly, ed., *The Formation of National States in Western Europe*, Princeton: Princeton University Press, 328-379.

-------- (1985), *Patterns of Policing*, New Brunswick: Rutgers University Press.

-------- (1994), *Police for the Future*, New York: Oxford University Press.

Bittner, Egon (1980), *The Functions of the Police in Modern Society*, Cambridge: Oelgeschlager, Gunn and Hain.

Brady, James (1977), "Political Contradictions and Justice Policy in People's China," *Contemporary Crises*, 1, 127-162.

Brodeur, J.-P. (1983), "High Policing and Low Policing: Remarks about the Policing of Political Activities," *Social Problems*, 30, 5, 507-520.

Brogden, Michael (1982), *The Police: Autonomy and Consent*, New York: Academic Press.

-------- (1987), "The Emergence of the Police--The Colonial Dimension," *British Journal of Criminology*, 27, 1, 4-14.

Callaghy, Thomas (1982), "Police in Early Modern States: the Uses of Coercion in Zaire in Comparative Perspective," paper, American Political Science Association Conference, Denver.

Carter, Marshall H., and Otwin Marenin (1981), "Law Enforcement and Political Change in Post Civil War Nigeria," *Journal of Criminal Justice*, 9, 2, 125-149.

Chapman, Brian (1971), *Police State*, London: Macmillan and Co.

Conquest, Robert (1968), *The Soviet Police System*, New York: Praeger.

Cottam, Martha, and Otwin Marenin (1989), "Predicting the Past: Reagan Administration Assistance to Police Forces in Central America," *Justice Quarterly*, 6, 4, 589-618.

Danns, George K. (1982), *Domination and Power in Guyana: A Study of the Police in a Third World Context*, New Brunswick: Transaction Books.

Diamond, Stanley (1971), "The Rule of Law and the Order of Custom," in R.P. Wolff (ed.), *The Rule of Law*, New York: Simon and Schuster, 115-144.

Dutton, Michael (1992), "*Dreaming of Better Times*. Traditions, Utopias and the Chinese Public Security Bureau," paper, American Society of Criminology Conference, New Orleans.

Enloe, Cynthia (1980), *Police, Military and Ethnicity: The Foundations of State Power*, New Brunswick: Transaction Books.

Jeffries, Sir Charles (1952), *The Colonial Police*, London: Max Parrish.

Klockars, Karl B. (1991), "The Rhetoric of Community Policing," in Jack R. Greene and Stephen D. Mastrofski (eds.), *Community Policing: Rhetoric or Reality*, New York: Praeger, 239-258.

Liang, Hsi-huey (1970), *The Berlin Police Force in the Weimar Republic*, Berkeley: University of California Press.

Manning, Peter (1979, 1977), *Police Work*, Cambridge: MIT Press.

Marenin, Otwin (1986), "United States' Aid To African Police Forces: The Experience and Impact of the Public Safety Assistance Program," *African Affairs*, 85, 341, 509-544.

------ (1987), "The Managerial State in Africa: A Conflict Coalition Perspective," in Zaki Ergas (ed.), *The African State in Transition*, New York: St Martin's Press, 61-85.

------ (1990), "The Police and the Coercive Nature of the State," in Edward S. Greenberg and Thomas F. Mayer (eds.), *Changes in the State: Causes and Consequences*, Newbury Park: Sage, 115-130.

Nader, Laura and Harry F.Todd (1978), *The Disputing Process: Law in Ten Societies*, New York: Columbia University Press.

Salas, Luis (1979), *Social Control and Deviance in Cuba*, New York: Praeger.

Schatzberg, Michael (1988), *The Dialectics of Oppression in Zaire*, Bloomington: Indiana University Press.

Shelley, Louise I.(1990), "The Soviet Militsiia: Agents of Political and Social Control," *Policing and Society*, 1, 39-56.

Staples, William G. (1990), *Castles of Our Conscience: Social Control and the American State*, 1800-1985, New Brunswick: Rutgers University Press.

Stead, Philip John (1983), *The Police of France*, New York: Macmillan.

Tamuno, Tekena (1970), *The Police in Modern Nigeria, 1861-1965*, Ibadan: Ibadan University Press.

Therborn, Goran (1978), *What Does the Ruling Class Do When it Rules? State Apparatuses and State Power Under Feudalism, Capitalism and Socialism*, London: NLB.

Thompson, E.P. (1978), "An Orrery of Errors," in E.P.Thompson, *The Poverty of Theory and Other Essays*, New York: Monthly Review Press, 1-210.

Tifft, Larry and Dennis Sullivan (1980), *The Struggle to Be Human*, Sanday: Cienfuegos Press.

Turk, Austin (1982), *Political Criminality: The Defiance and Defense of Authority*, Beverly Hills: Sage.

Williams, Alan (1979), *The Police of Paris, 1718-1789*, Baton Rouge: Louisiana State University Press.

Young, Crawford (1984), "Zaire: Is There a State?" *Canadian Journal of African Studies*, 18, 1, 80-82.

# CONTRIBUTORS

**David H. Bayley** is a professor in the School of Criminal Justice, State University of New York at Albany. He is a specialist in international criminal justice with a particular interest in policing. He has done extensive research on the police in India, Japan, Australia, Canada, Britain, Singapore and the United States. His work has focussed on strategies of policing, the evolution of police organizations, organizational reforms, accountability, and the tactics of patrol officers in discretionary law enforcement situations. He has written, among others, *The Police and Political Development in India* (Princeton University Press, 1969), *Forces of Order: Policing Modern Japan* (University of California Press, 1976, 1991), *Patterns of Policing: A Comparative International Analysis* (Rutgers University Press, 1985), *Singapore: A Model of Community Policing* (National Institute of Justice, 1989), and *Police for the Future* (Oxford University Press, 1994). He is completing a multi-year research project on the future of policing in Australia, Canada, Great Britain, Japan, and the United States which will be published as *Uncertain Guardians: The Future of the Police in Modern Democracies*.

**Mike Brogden** is professor of criminal justice and Director of the new Institute of Criminology and Criminal Justice at The Queen's University of Belfast, Northern Ireland. He is the author of *The Police: Autonomy and Consent* (Academic Press, 1982), *On the Mersey Beat* (Oxford University Press, 1991), and (with Clifford Shearing) *Policing for a New South Africa*, (Routledge, 1993). He has been a member of the International Training Committee of the South African police since 1992 and, during the recent South African election, was seconded by the European Union to act as Security Adviser for that process. He has been writing on and researching police structures and practices for some twenty years.

**Paul Chevigny** is professor of law at New York University Law School. He is the author of several books concerning police in the USA, including *Police Power: Police Abuses in New York* (Random House, 1969). He has investigated police violence in several countries for Human Rights Watch, and is currently at work on a comparative study of violence and accountability in six cities of the Americas.

**Monica den Boer** wrote her Ph.D. dissertation at the European University Institute in Florence, Italy. From January 1991 until December 1993 she was a Research Fellow at the Department of Politics of the University of Edinburgh, Scotland, where she participated in a research project, "A System of European Police Cooperation after 1992." This involvement culminated in a number of publications, including a coedited volume (with Malcolm Anderson) titled *Policing Across National Boundaries* (Pinter Publications, 1994), and a co-authored volume titled *Policing the European Union* (Oxford University Press, forthcoming). She is currently a researcher at the Netherlands Institute for the Study of Criminality and Law Enforcement in Leiden.

**Graham Ellison** studied at The Queen's University, Belfast, and is now completing his Ph.D. at the University of Ulster. His dissertation deals with policing in Northern Ireland.

**Otwin Marenin** is a professor in the Political Science Department and Director of the Criminal Justice Program at Washington State University. He has taught at Ahmadu Bello University and University of Benin (Nigeria) and the Universities of Baltimore, Colorado, and Alaska-Fairbanks. His research and publications have focussed on international police assistance programs, on police community relations in small communities in the United States, and on the origins and practices of policing in Africa, in Nigeria and, most recently, in Alaskan Native communities.

**Jeffrey Ian Ross**, Ph.D., is a Social Science Analyst at the National Institute of Justice, U.S. Department of Justice. He has conducted research, written, and lectured on national security, political violence, political crime, and policing for over a decade. His work has appeared in numerous academic journals (e.g., *Canadian Journal of Political Science, Justice Quarterly*, or *Comparative Politics*) and books, as well as in popular magazines in Canada and the United States. He is the editor of *Controlling State Crime* (Garland Publishing, 1995) and *Violence in Canada: Sociopolitical Perspectives* (Oxford University Press, 1995). In 1986, Ross was the lead expert witness for the Senate of Canada's Special Committee on Terrorism and Public Safety.

**Clifford Shearing** is a professor of criminology and sociology and Director of the Centre of Criminology at the University of Toronto, Canada. He is also Director of the Community Peace Foundation at the University of the Western Cape, South Africa. His theoretical and research interests lie in the area of governance.

**Louise I. Shelley** is a professor in the Department of Justice, Law and Society at The American University, Washington, D.C. She is the author of the forthcoming books *Policing Soviet Society* (Routledge) and the co-editor of *Social Changes, Crime and Police* (Harwood). She is currently studying post-Soviet organized crime. Professor Shelley is the author of numerous articles and book chapters and the recipient of Fulbright, Guggenheim, Kennan Institute, and NEH fellowships.

**Jim Smyth** studied at the Universities of Freiburg, Berlin, and Kiel. He has taught at the Universities of Bremen and Kiel and now teaches in Belfast, at The Queen's University. He has written a number of articles on counterinsurgency, terrorism, and related topics.

**William Stanley** is assistant professor of political science at the University of New Mexico, where he teaches international and Latin American politics. His research focuses on how domestic and international political forces interact with the institutional characteristics of military and police agencies to affect the frequency of human rights violations. His book *The Death of Moderation, the Death of Thousands: Elite Politics, State Violence and Civil War in El Salvador* is forthcoming from Temple University Press. He has published various articles on human rights, migration, and refugee affairs, and most recently on the role of the United Nations in post-conflict peace consolidation in Central America.

**Jon Vagg** lectures in criminology at Loughborough University, UK, having worked until 1994 at the University of Hong Kong. His previous books include *Accountability and Prisons* (co-edited with Mike Maguire and Rod Morgan, Tavistock, 1985), *Policing by the Public* (with Joanna Shapland, Routledge, 1988), *Crime and Justice in Hong Kong* (co-edited with Harold Traver, Oxford University Press, 1991), and *Prison Systems* (Oxford University Press, 1994). He has conducted research on issues as diverse as juvenile crime, community policing, and piracy and is currently writing a book on economic development, globalization, and crime.

**Neil C. Walker** is a senior lecturer in public law at the Faculty of Law, University of Edinburgh, where he has taught since 1986. He has published extensively in the areas of constitutional law and theory and in police studies. He is particularly interested in the organization and accountability of policing, and in the relationship between transnational policing and the changing international political order. He is the co-author of *Policing the European Union*, to be published by Oxford University Press in 1995.

# INDEX